# Story Starters

## Helping Children Write Like They've Never Written Before

# Story Starters

**Helping Children Write Like They've Never Written Before**

Karen Andreola

Charlotte Mason
Research and Supply
Company

My gratitude extends to my editors for their assistance.
James Stuart Bell, MA. University College Dublin
Mrs. Nancy Drazga, B.A. University of California, Berkeley



**STORY STARTERS: Helping Children Write Like They've Never Written Before**


Cover Design by Alpha Advertising
Interior Design by Pine Hill Graphics

Publisher's Cataloging-in-Publication Data
*(Provided by Cassidy Cataloguing Services, Inc.)*

Andreola, Karen.

Story starters : helping children write like they've never written before / Karen Andreola. — 1st ed. — Quarryville, PA : Charlotte Mason Research & Supply Co., 2006.

p. ; cm.

ISBN-13: 978-1-889209-04-3
ISBN-10: 1-889209-04-X
Audience: grades 4-12.
Includes index.

1. Creative writing—Programmed instruction. 2. Children—Writing—Programmed instruction. 3. Language arts—Programmed instruction. 4. Fiction—Authorship—Programmed instruction. 5. Fiction—Technique. 6. Religious fiction. I. Title.

PN143 .A53 2006
808.06/83—dc22 0603



**Printed in the United States of America.**

# Table of Contents

## *Section One*
## Notes for the Teacher


Preface . . . . . . . . . . 11
Exciting Writing . . . . . . . . . . 14
A Flexible Resource . . . . . . . . . . 19
Don't Take Creative Writing Too Seriously . . . . . . . . . . 22
Optional Teaching Tools . . . . . . . . . . 25
What Are the Symbols? . . . . . . . . . . 26
How to Use the Story Starters . . . . . . . . . . 27
Four Methods . . . . . . . . . . 29
A Word About Internal Motivation and Grading . . . . . . . . . . 34
What Is the Value of this Learning Activity? . . . . . . . . . . 37


## *Section Two*
## Story Starters


Introduction to the Story Starters . . . . . . . . . . 41

1 The Bookworm's Opportunity . . . . . . . . . . 43
2 The Night Visitor . . . . . . . . . . 47
3 The Unexpected Guest . . . . . . . . . . 53
4 The Runaway Motorcar . . . . . . . . . . 58
5 Saved from the Fog . . . . . . . . . . 62
6 Poor Polly . . . . . . . . . . 67
7 In the Twilight . . . . . . . . . . 70
8 Morning Wake-Up Call . . . . . . . . . . 73
9 The Brave Robin . . . . . . . . . . 77
10 Welcomed Birds . . . . . . . . . . 80
11 The Alligator . . . . . . . . . . 84
12 A California Flood . . . . . . . . . . 87
13 Perfect Weather for Cycling . . . . . . . . . . 92
14 Up, Up, and Away . . . . . . . . . . 95
15 Katie's Dilemma . . . . . . . . . . 100

16 The Toy Maker . . . . . . . . . . 104
17 A Friendly Horse to a Trickster . . . . . . . . . . 108
18 Jasper Saves the Baby . . . . . . . . . . 113
19 The Elephant's New Calf . . . . . . . . . . 116
20 Shipwreck . . . . . . . . . . 121
21 The Circus Clown's Son . . . . . . . . . . 124
22 Pamela's Hat . . . . . . . . . . 127
23 Worn Out . . . . . . . . . . 135
24 The Donkey's Deed . . . . . . . . . . 141
25 Mince Pies . . . . . . . . . . 148
26 Chad's Busy Day . . . . . . . . . . 156
27 Not Tired . . . . . . . . . . 163
28 The Rowboat . . . . . . . . . . 166
29 Sick Piggy . . . . . . . . . . 170
30 A Young Musician . . . . . . . . . . 173
31 The Surprise . . . . . . . . . . 177
32 Pocket Money . . . . . . . . . . 184
33 He Told the Truth . . . . . . . . . . 188
34 If at First You Don't . . . . . . . . . . 192
35 Miss Whitaker . . . . . . . . . . 197
36 Hunting for Rabbit . . . . . . . . . . 201
37 Whose Baby? . . . . . . . . . . 205
38 Mr. Madison's Classroom . . . . . . . . . . 209
39 Two Stepmothers . . . . . . . . . . 214
40 The Prowling Lion . . . . . . . . . . 218
41 A Bird Called Mischief . . . . . . . . . . 221
42 Marmalade . . . . . . . . . . 229
43 Father's Clock . . . . . . . . . . 236
44 Stopping a Bully . . . . . . . . . . 242
45 Making a Call . . . . . . . . . . 249
46 Marvelous Exertion . . . . . . . . . . 254
47 A Nasty Drawing . . . . . . . . . . 259
48 Ralph of Red Gables . . . . . . . . . . 264
49 Goodbye, Mr. Woodhouse . . . . . . . . . . 270
50 A Friend in Need . . . . . . . . . . 275
51 A Man-eating Tiger . . . . . . . . . . 280
52 Mr. Featherton and the Eagle . . . . . . . . . . 287
53 Lucy Fairchild . . . . . . . . . . 292
54 One Big, Happy Family . . . . . . . . . . 298
55 At the Railway Station . . . . . . . . . . 303

56 The Cabman's Old Horse .................... 308
57 Hazel Takes a Long Walk.................... 316
58 Vacation at the Seashore .................... 322
59 Coming to America.......................... 330
60 Amos—A Willing Worker...................... 334
61 Attending to the Wounded................... 340
62 Charged by a Rhinoceros .................... 346
63 The Good Prince and the Pirates............. 351
64 A Strange Present.......................... 358
65 Grandpa's Dog Pepper....................... 364
66 Toby and the Whale......................... 371
67 Deborah Misses Dad ........................ 377

## *Section Three*
## Hints for Polishing

Introduction to Hints for Polishing .................. 391
Sensory Language.................................. 392
Vivid Verbs ...................................... 397
Artful Adjectives.................................. 400
Advantageous Adverbs.............................. 402
Three Kinds of Narrators .......................... 404
Description of a Setting........................... 405
Character Description—Physical Appearance........... 406
Character Description—Personality.................. 407
A Lesson of Review for Additional Challenge.......... 409

## *Section Four*
## Just Pictures

Introduction to Just Pictures........................ 413
A Lesson on the Basic Elements of a Story ............ 414

## *Section Five*
## In Closing

Narration: Tapping into the Talking Resource .......... 445
Index of Literary Terms and Techniques ............... 453
Writing Resources .................................. 454
About Dean and Karen Andreola ...................... 456

# *Section One*

## Notes for the Teacher

# Preface

'd like my child to do more writing."

"My child needs a greater incentive to write."

"I have a difficult time getting two sentences out of him."

"My daughter loves to write and needs a wider range of opportunities."

"Writing seems too laborious a task for my son."

Perhaps one of the above comments mirrors your personal experience and that's why you've picked up this book. When parents meet me as one of the speakers at a homeschool conference, they often ask, "How do I get my child to write?"

"With narration," I reply. Then, I briefly explain the method of narration. I encourage home teachers to read aloud to their children, and then to request that the children tell, in their own words, what was just read to them. It's that simple. "At the heart of writing is the ability to tell—the ability to narrate," I share with them.

## *Narration from Books*

*"If we would believe it, composition is as natural as jumping and running to children who have been allowed due use of books."* Charlotte Mason

Books of quality will be the main source of a young child's composition. By putting what he* has read (or what has been read to him) in his own words, he is learning, from the authors of these books, how to use words. For instance, in his narration the child will naturally borrow an interesting "turn of phrase" from an author. Without even being conscious of it, the child learns from authors how to use words to describe setting, action, and what characters are feeling. He is developing writing skills (a talent for using words) as he practices narrating.

Wonderful arrays of good books are available from which a child can narrate.

---

*For continuity, throughout this book I use he/him in reference to any child.

## *Creative Narration*

With all of this reading and retelling going on, it isn't difficult to switch gears to make room for the occasional creative narration. By creative narration I mean creative *telling* rather than *re-telling*. While a child's "imagination muscles" do develop by narrating from books, these and other intellectual abilities also grow as they are used in a more playful way with creative narration.

## *What Happens Next?*

I have discovered the best way to prompt a child to narrate creatively. It is by giving him a story starter. Instead of expecting a child to compose "from scratch" by supplying him with only a topic, a task even the average adult finds daunting, we can kindle in him a keenness to write by using a story starter. An unfinished story is meant to draw him into a colorful situation. Some stories plunge him into a predicament that holds him in suspense. Upon the invitation, "What happens next?" the child then springs forth to enhance and embellish the story as much as he wants.

## *Writing with Feeling*

***Story Starters*** is based on a form of composition I call "Exciting Writing" because the story starters invite the child to write with feeling. Many of the story starters present an exciting or intense situation. Others are calmer, more open-ended, and the consequences are less momentous. Whichever ones you chose, ***Story Starters*** is about focusing on content. Let the first draft be as rough as necessary as the children express their ideas and impressions. They are encouraged to write with boldness, with zest, with gusto, and with far less restraint then they may be used to.

## *Stories of Virtue*

> *"A person's worldview almost always shows through in his creative output."* Francis Schaeffer

A host of biblical virtues are embodied in my stories. They are a mix of kind gestures and heroic deeds. Many characters willingly step out of their comfort zones to perform self-denying acts of bravery. It may be a small act of bravery, as found in "Making a Call," or a larger act, as suggested in "A Man-eating Tiger." Overall, the characters care about the welfare of others. In these stories, you will find correction and forgiveness, patience and gratitude, resourcefulness and responsibility, admiration and respect. You will discover friendship, love, and humor as well. Good stories show us what virtue looks like.

## *Worth a Thousand Words*

With *Story Starters* a student's imagination is also sparked by my collection of antique pictures. Much research and discrimination has gone into providing morally uplifting, exciting, or humorous illustrations that form the basis of my stories. If it is true that a good picture is worth a thousand words, then let the pictures be translated into the words of a child whose interest and imagination have been sparked by it.

The use of pictures and story starters together is designed to inspire the less confident writer in our media based, sight-oriented culture.

## *New Attitude*

*Story Starters* is my contribution to the art and discipline of writing for the home educated child, an aspect that I have found missing in standard writing courses. Its purpose is to empower your student to write at a new level of vibrancy that communicates the best of what is going on in his developing mind and emotions. May he discover that yes, he *can* write—and even like what he writes. It is my hope that Exciting Writing will foster a positive attitude toward writing in general and that this newfound confidence will carry over to other writing aspects of his schoolwork.

This book took root and grew from the many pleasures and rewards I have found in teaching my children at home. The article "Exciting Writing" explains how I came upon this form of composition that I put to the test with my own children.

The article "Narration: Tapping into the Talking Resource" explains further the beautiful simplicity and power of narration and how to use it in your homeschool.

# Exciting Writing

*Story Starters* has its roots in a form of composition I call "Exciting Writing." In researching the writings of nineteenth-century British educator, Miss Charlotte Mason, I borrowed old volumes of her magazine, *Parents' Review* from a British library. It was an article from the magazine by teacher Raymond Ward that introduced me to the idea of story starters. When I read of the success of Mr. Ward's scheme, I couldn't resist using it as a writing exercise with my own children. The experiment worked and I was quite pleased. The children composed directly from their imaginations. They wrote with descriptive phrases and vocabulary unlike anything they had written before.

## Writing with Feeling

What is Exciting Writing? In brief, the student is provided with a situation that involves conflict by way of a story starter and its accompanying picture. He sympathizes with the characters and, wrapped up in the emotion of the scene, calls on his developing skills of reason and imagination to continue the story. Emotions such as fear, joy, wonder, sadness, worry, or great relief create the spark to write more vividly. The student expresses himself spontaneously, leaving penmanship, spelling, grammar and punctuation for a later time.

An exciting story starter and picture create a vivid impression in the mind of the student. The story starter provides parameters and shape so that he can immediately visualize what the actors might do next. The student is free to write whatever he wants. He taps into any previous experience he has had with an emotion. It is a student's past personal and literary experiences that enable him to sympathize with the characters—to feel as they might in the situation depicted. He translates these emotions and concepts into words that are quite descriptive. In his article, Raymond Ward writes, "The deeper the emotion and the keener the feeling, the more readily will the child find words with which to express them; and this expression will be far more vivid, genuine, revealing and meaningful than the more conventional composition exercise." Standard exercises such as "What I Did on My Summer Vacation," "My Pet," "A Visit to Grandma's," "A Trip to the Zoo," all have their place, but an exciting story starter will better accomplish what Mr. Ward describes above. Even a student

who normally has a dull, rambling narrative will, with Exciting Writing, compose at least one notable phrase. Small though it may be, his one vivid description *is* a break through. It is something to rejoice in. The dormant writer in him has awoken and is emerging from his cocoon.

### *The Rough Draft*

I've always been a believer in the need to begin with a rough draft. At its conception, a piece of creative writing needn't be bound by formal style, because this can squelch budding enthusiasm. The birthing stage of writing should not be bound by all the rules of composition. Mr. Ward's article even advocates putting down an idea or an impression in a single phrase. The student keeps a list of what strikes him at the moment, or, he might begin each new idea, phrase, or sentence on a new line. Content is stressed over form. Sentence structure and connectors are secondary to this first creative stage. If the latter is not developed the former will be less effective. Students who are accustomed to Charlotte Mason's method of oral narration from books are apt to write in prose more naturally than others. When a situation of exciting conflict demanding resolution is presented to a child, his ideas develop faster, hence the suggestion of a list of phrases (rather than a paragraph).

For those students new at narrating and new to using these writing exercises, I suggest the home teacher take dictation.

### *Mr. Ward's Example*

Below is an example of Exciting Writing that Mr. Ward used in his classroom about half a century ago. He told his ten-and eleven-year-old students,

> *"I am confronted with a mad dog. See, there it is!" I called out urgently, and started backwards, pointing. "It's there, all right. Now—quickly write down what you feel about it."*
>
> *The children started. There was no pencil-biting, head-scratching, window-gazing, restless fiddling or doodling, but quiet intensive effort. There was not a sound in the class. One could almost hear the heavy breathing of the mad dog.*
>
> *Then I said, "Begin a new line. Write down what kind of dog it is. Say something about its eyes, its jaws, what it looks like. Remember to start a new line for each new idea."*

## My Experiment

Some years ago I adapted these ideas to my own elementary school age children. Instead of coaching them through it like Mr. Ward did, however, I stimulated their emotions with the following story starter:

*Dad was away on a business trip. Mom and little brother were in bed with the flu and their fever wasn't going down. An announcement came over the radio that rabies was on the rise. From her bed Mother asked her two young daughters to check the doors before all retired for the evening. They found the back sliding-glass door caked with ice—the latch couldn't lock. They tried opening it wide and slamming it shut to crack the ice. This activity attracted the attention of a rabid dog that some men were tracking in the dark. It was staring at them through the glass.*

I left them, pencils in hand, to continue with the story as I prepared lunch, because very soon we needed to run out to music lessons. They worked quietly and quickly at the kitchen table with a real sense of purpose. Just as Mr. Ward had noted, I also observed no dawdling, pencil biting, or other signs of restless fiddling. What they wrote wasn't long. Each wrote one paragraph that was brief but concentrated. The results were remarkable!

My nine-year-old daughter started out with, "The mad dog's huge face was contracted and of a hideous form. Poisonous saliva oozed from his mouth and dripped from his jowls." She then added a little comic relief: "I slowly edged away from the door. The dog's eyes followed my every move. I tripped over a large book—my math book. As I fell, the dog leaped…" In the story's climax she throws her hardcover math book—her least favorite schoolbook—at the dog.

I liked her younger sister's ending sentence very much: "The dog stopped, let out a long piercing cry, pawed the air and fell dead." Such words might describe a scene in *The Hound of the Baskervilles,* by Sir Arthur Conan Doyle, which we had listened to on cassette earlier in the year. The more imaginative reading a child does, the more images and words he will have in store to draw from in his efforts to create a story.

A week or two prior to the writing experiment described above, they had viewed the film *Old Yeller*. I should also confess that they were familiar with Louis Pasteur's experiences in finding a cure for rabies from listening to the dramatic *Your Story Hour* tapes. Thus they just happened to be primed when it came to wild dog stories.

So pleased was I with their creative narration (as I called it) that I made up some more story situations that posed a conflict, problem, or challenge that needed to be resolved. Some of my story starters were not as intense, though all contained emotions and situations to which a child could relate. My children felt sympathy for the characters automatically. I didn't have to tell them what to feel. They took to Exciting Writing so well that I decided to make the same kinds of story scenarios available to my fellow home educators by way of this book.

# A Flexible Resource

ost schoolbooks are designed so that the student does all the exercises in the order in which they appear. *Story Starters*, however, is different. It is a more flexible resource for the homeschool.

You needn't be overwhelmed by the book's big size. A student is **NOT** expected to do all the exercises. Rather, you and he are invited to choose from a panorama of stories. Skip back and forth among its pages to look for pictures and stories that appeal to you and your children. It is inevitable that some stories will be of better use to you than others. Therefore, I included a wide variety to strike your fancy.

This one book can be used with children of varying levels of writing ability. I designed it primarily for grade four through high school, but younger siblings can participate, too. Therefore, keep *Story Starters* on hand to use year-by-year, student-by-student.

*Story Starters* is flexible in yet another way. It can be used in layers. In more than several places I remind you that the purpose of the story starters is primarily to awaken the dormant writer in your child. He is encouraged to write freely with imagination and feeling, unencumbered by the usual restraints. If finishing the story is the only way this book is used, and it propels your student forward to write in ways he hasn't written before, I say, "splendid." Perhaps you will also decide to go even further and take advantage of the optional writing helps—i.e.; the other layers. The decision is yours. As with all teaching materials, it is best to make books our servants and not the other way round.

## Impetus for Writing

*Story Starters* is supplementary material for your English composition course. Although not a comprehensive writing course, it does incorporate some basic elements for good writing. If the various writing helps are referred to, the student will be introduced to hints and how-tos and a cross sampling of literary terms—incidentally, not incrementally.

Primarily meant to be an impetus for writing, *Story Starters* provides children young and old with plenty of opportunities to put thoughts into words and develop their powers of imagination. Odd and interesting illustrations stir up curiosity. Descriptive settings draw the child into the story further and create challenges that call for a resolution. All of these work together as a very buoyant jump-start to creative narrations.

Some of the pictures and stories are calm and endearing. Many more, however, are action-packed scenes designed especially to appeal to boys, who can be reluctant in getting out their words. Even though many of the story starters were chosen with boys in mind, both boys and girls can easily adapt the topics to their world. And it is my hope that they both will become keenly interested in a good number of them. My son and younger daughter had quite different favorites. Also, some themes sparked more fluent writing than others.

## A Notebook of Narrations

*Story Starters* is non-consumable. The student is invited to keep his narration in a notebook or as a document on a computer. Therefore, one book can be purchased for the whole family. Permission is granted, within one family, to photocopy pictures from the book so that your students can have a picture to accompany their story. Younger students may wish to use colored pencil on their pictures. The story starters themselves can also be photocopied if they are to accompany the student's polished writing in his portfolio.

### *Optional ways to incorporate story starters into your schedule:*

**Biweekly**

Write, "story starter" into your schedule to remind you to choose one biweekly.

**Monthly**

Assign one story starter a month to space out the assignments over a longer period (years). An occasional story starter will add spice and variety to any English composition course.

**A One-Semester Course**

If your student is especially keen on writing, you may certainly do a story starter as often as you like to accommodate his interest, pace, and developing skill. You may wish to use *Story Starters* as your regular writing course for one semester, working on one per week. This stronger focus on less formal writing may be one way to encourage a reluctant writer.

**A Group Setting**

Because our family has had positive experiences holding various group classes in our living room over our years of home teaching, I offer these suggestions—one formal, and one informal.

Start a creative writing group in your home. It need only be a few gatherings— possibly one afternoon a week for an hour and a half, for a limited time of four to six weeks. This may provide enough of an opportunity to get students more excited about writing. Using *Story Starters,* participants could choose a story to work on at home during the week. When the group meets together the children read their papers to the group. Expect some nervousness and giggles. Even in a small group there will probably be students of different ages, ability and experience. Therefore the leader (host or hostess) should keep the meetings light, of good humor, and non-competitive.

### A Game

My second suggestion is the game of Round Robin. As it is designed for two or more persons, it is suitable for a group or family setting. After the story starter is read aloud, the children take turns orally adding one or two sentences to the plot. As the plot thickens, you will hear the children chuckle. The last child, in turn, gives the story its final resolution. Passing a paper round the room so that each person write a line or two to what has already been written is another way to play Round Robin. When the writing has gone full circle, the story is read aloud. A teacher and one student can also play the game together.

If a "Just Picture" (Section Four) is used, rather than a story starter, those who participate will create the entire story.

# Don't Take Creative Writing Too Seriously

Although it may seem odd, I will remind you here and there in these Notes for the Teacher to "have a good time." Each story starter invites a certain aspect of "play" in the student's writing: it sometimes appeals to his sense of humor, and *always* appeals to his creativity. He can be more relaxed. What he writes is not being chiseled in stone. Anything he writes can be changed around and refitted. There is no one right answer. The important point is to allow the first draft be as rough as necessary.

The greatly admired author of stories J.R.R. Tolkien, said, "All who wander are not lost." I will reemphasis here that *Story Starters* encourages the student to write his first draft with more abandon than he might be used to, to write freely with enthusiastic effort, and to let his imagination *wander*, without concern for spelling, grammar, or other aspects of "good writing." All writers go over their writing again. The work of polishing up is done afterwards. The second or third drafts are more formal and not as fun. There is a certain amount of difficulty involved in writing so do let the first draft be as fun and free as possible.

Even if you, the teacher, find your student's narration to be weak, try to point out something you like about it. He can build from your comments. Encourage the student to feel free to play around with his writing. If he likes it, keep it; if not, enhance it or scrap it and tailor a new situation. Better yet, try a different story starter. Choices are plentiful—more than you will need. Your patience with any difficulty, such as writer's block, will demonstrate your confidence in him—confidence he may not have at the beginning.

If less writing (narrating) is accomplished in your first attempts, let this not worry you. Anxiety gives small things big shadows. Remember that a pleasant atmosphere is a tool of great advantage in the homeschool. Put all pickiness aside. And remember that patience accomplishes more than push—and far more than alarm or disapproval. Most children take time to warm up to writing. Allow them this time.

At the beginning my son would get discouraged with himself. Even though he had done years of narrating (retelling) from books, at age thirteen he found the newness of creative narration to be a challenge. I didn't expect too much from him at the start but let him warm up to the exercises without being too picky about the result. I had to remind myself that confidence and experience are slow-growing plants. We did not give up. Although it was awkward for him at first, we kept at it. I remember one day vividly. Nigel was in junior high and in his second semester of working on story starters. That day he hit upon one that sparked his interest amazingly. He chose a picture from a new set of pictures I had given him. It accompanied "Hunting for Rabbit," a story starter I had just written about the growling bear that had chased Uncle Gordon up a tree. For this new story he wrote oodles, using vocabulary that had me bowled over. Eureka! Keep patiently feeding and watering your slow-growing plant and he will, eventually, blossom.

## What About Style?

I wouldn't be too concerned about your child writing in any special or formal style within the exercises of *Story Starters*. Children who are accustomed to narrating their lessons from well-written books become stylists on their own. There are opportunities here for letter writing, writing in first and third person, getting into the heads of characters, using vivid verbs, artful adjectives, sensory language, etc. I call only a little attention to these aspects of writing, and trust the children to pick up on these naturally as the stories draw them into expressing themselves more and more vividly.

## Fiction or Fantasy

My story starters encourage realistic fiction. Whether or not to accept an element of fantasy in your student's stories is up to you. Some realistic fiction incorporates a certain amount of fantasy. Fantasy may contain elements of the supernatural, other possible worlds, or the future. The film, *It's a Wonderful Lif*e, a favorite of mine, is a good example of a realistic story that is embellished with an aspect of fantasy. In that film an angel was shown the events of the life of the main character so that he could intervene at a defining moment to help him see how his life had a positive effect on so many others. Science fiction is another example of intelligent writing that incorporates what *could* happen, based on technical or medical advances, or alien interference. Fairy tale elements such as mythical beings, may result from the student's past reading.

Here is one caution. If fantasy were allowed, I would dissuade nonsense. Any depiction of an absurd circumstance is getting too carried away.

## About the Pictures

The children's book illustrations in *Story Starters* were first published in the nineteenth century; hence my text was written in the spirit of the times. Therefore you will not find jet planes, plastic bags, Styrofoam, televisions, computers, or electric refrigerators in my stories, but if the student includes these modern artifacts as he finishes the stories, this is fine. The illustrations have a timeless quality.

The Victorians had high ideals, were sentimental, and were also believers in realism, which is reflected in their art and literature. Some of the Victorian pictures may represent situations too intense for young siblings or the very sensitive child. Please use them at your discretion.

You will find that a number of story starters are illustrated not by one picture but by a series of pictures. These are meant to give further aid to your budding writer.

# Optional Teaching Tools

## Writing Help

Many of the story starters include a section marked "Writing Help," which supplies leading questions to trigger the conception of ideas and give direction for developing and ending the story. Beginners may welcome its guidance. The questions are optional, however. I sometimes remind the student that answering all the questions is not necessary. He is invited to use one, any, or all of the questions if he likes—or none if he prefers. Because *Story Starters* encourages spontaneity, Writing Help can be ignored if your student is ready and willing to freely and spontaneously set the wheels of his creativity in motion.

## Additional Challenge

Writing Help can also be used to improve the student's rough draft "on second thought." For instance, where can he add more descriptive vocabulary or sensory language? Can he use a vivid verb in place of a general one? In short, he will be developing writing skills that will carry over to other forms of writing, including nonfiction. Writing is work, but the more he writes, the less daunting and more engaging he will find it to be.

If the Writing Help includes an "Additional Challenge," read through it to decide whether or not you would like him to give it a try. The student may not find it to be as difficult as you (or he) may suppose.

## Hints for Polishing

*Story Starters* touches upon just a few basic components of good story writing. If, after doing some exercises, your student is writing more fluently and is more comfortable about writing than he was before, you may read over the lessons in the section entitled "Hints for Polishing."

# What Are the Symbols?

I first marked every story with one of a set of symbols to indicate four levels of difficulty. Although the symbols were for the teacher, upon further consideration, I removed them, except for (B) beginner. I did not wish to hinder the student from trying out a picture that looked interesting or to prejudice his thinking.

My mother used to tell me, "Life is what you make of it." The same holds true with a story: a story is what you make of it. A child may choose a simple story that happens to have a (B) and "take off" with it, making it more complex. Or he may choose a potentially more complex story and keep it simple. Far be it from me to deter any creative directions by my system of subjective labeling.

## Just Two Marks

**(B)—Beginner.**

These stories have simple or bold conflict, simple action, and the outcomes are more predictable. In some cases the child will be describing what is taking place in the picture and little else.

I suggest younger students be *introduced* to the story starters marked with a (B). Of course, later, they need not stick to these exclusively. With some of the (B) stories there is greater challenge and encouragement to add detail or embellish in the Writing Help. Therefore, all (B) stories are not just for beginners.

**(I)—Intense.**

These stories are more intense. They are especially good for the reluctant writer and provide greater opportunity for Exciting Writing. I've written many of them with boys in mind, such as "A Man-eating Tiger," which was written with help from my husband Dean.

## Unmarked Stories

The unmarked stories are of varying levels of difficulty. They are more detailed, and involve greater interaction of characters as well as more complex characterizations. They have less predictable outcomes, and allow for a wider range of possibilities for plot direction than do the (B) stories. They are not quite as intense as those marked (I).

# How to Use the Story Starters

ere are the three basic steps to using a story starter. First, a picture is selected that grabs the student's interest. Second, the story starter is read. Third, the student tells or writes what comes next and finishes the story.

During the years that my children and I did story starters together we used four methods—variations on the basic three steps. The children, each at their own pace, progressed through them. Thus, it is by practical experience, home teaching different ages and abilities, that I come to make these notes for you. I recommend that a student begin with method one and progress through to the others. Of course, if you are already quite familiar with narration you may decide with what method you would like to begin. Along with "Picture Talk" I have outlined the four methods below. On the pages that follow I supply further instruction for each method.

## *Picture Talk*

Allowing young siblings to talk about a picture encourages them to be imaginative and more verbal. (A less intense picture is preferable.) Picture Talk prepares young children for writing.

Children in grades one through three may try a story starter once they have had practice narrating from books.

## *A Peek at the Methods*

### Oral Narration with Dictation

The teacher reads the story starter aloud. The student "tells" what happens next. The teacher takes dictation and reads it back to him.

**Oral Narration with Copywork**

After reading, telling and dictation, the teacher makes a model for the student to copy. He eventually does the exercises on sensory language in "Hints for Polishing."

**Written Narration—Rough Draft**

The teacher or student reads the story starter. The student writes a rough draft. He works with his teacher to polish and makes a second draft. The exercises in Hints for Polishing are recommended. He eventually tries a "Just Picture."

**Working Independently**

The student reads and writes on his own. The teacher may help with polishing. He does all the exercises in Hints for Polishing, goes on to Just Pictures and reads "A Lesson on the Basic Elements of a Story."

## *Before Embarking*

Read "Introduction to the Story Starters" silently to yourself. Read it aloud to your student with enthusiasm as a sort of pep talk the day he attempts his first story. Students working independently with method level four may read it to themselves but (since home teaching is relational) I think it would be a nice touch to read it to them.

# Four Methods

## Method One: ORAL NARRATION

Level one is a good place to begin for a young student—or a student of any grade—who is attempting creative narration for the first time. Start here, also, if your student has experienced discouragement with writing. Level one is the first step in getting the wheels turning and the juices flowing in a reluctant writer.

Oral narration, also known as oral composition, is "writing" in which the student does not actually write anything down. Robert Louis Stevenson, when a young boy, was frequently ill and had to spend much time in his bed recovering. To pass the time, his nanny would read aloud to him. Young Stevenson would also narrate his own little stories to his nanny while she took dictation. Could this have been his preparation for becoming a writer of stories when he was older? Undoubtedly.

These story starters are exercises in creating content. I suggest that the novice be permitted to flesh out the story orally, unencumbered by the process of putting pencil to paper. Some students may like to record their compositions on a tape recorder.

1. Select a picture that invokes curiosity. I most often let my students select one themselves. After they have done several stories, I eventually get my turn to choose one. (This provides more challenge, unless they have chosen the challenging ones first.) Stories marked with a (B) are for beginners of any age, but of course you are not confined to these.
2. Read aloud the story starter to your student with enthusiasm. Have a good time.
3. Let the student pause to think and sympathize with the characters.

These moments of contemplation are necessary. If a child responds instantly with "I can't think of anything" tell him that this is because he needs to pause to think. "Longer than a split second, if you please," I have said with a smile.

After some quiet, invite dialogue if necessary. Suggest that he run the scene in his head as if he were watching a film. Can he see the people or animals in the picture moving? What is happening? What are the people saying? Imagination takes work. Only by experience do the wheels of imagination turn more easily. In time he will be able to write with more spontaneity. "What else?" is what I've asked my students (with a ring of expectation in my voice) when I've wished them to tell me more. "Okay, good. What else?" I say again, continuing to give my full attention, and the narration unfolds.

Writing Help provides guided questions for those who want it.

4. Take dictation from his narration.

You will probably resort to scribbling, as I have, since a student can talk faster than you can write. Try not, however, to slow down your child too much while his creative juices are flowing. He will slow down just a bit if you require that he pause between phrases or sentences. To allow the student a more uninterrupted flow of words, I've developed a sort of shorthand over my years of hearing narrations. For instance, instead of spelling out the word "the" I just write a "t." "With" is a "w." I often leave out some vowels, like this: T hors rn w grt spd (The horse ran with great speed). After step four, I make a clean copy so that I can collect the narrations in a notebook. At the end of the semester I can encourage the student by showing him the notebook and saying, "Look at all the writing you have done!"

5. Read his narration back to him enthusiastically. We always enjoy this step.

Do not nit-pick at this beginning stage or be concerned with polishing. Little suggestions for improving his writing (or the story) as well as any light editing should be attempted only after the student has done a number of story starters. (See #4 in Method Two).

## *Having Trouble?*

If your reluctant writer is of a young age and is having trouble with story starters, discreetly postpone these lessons for a while. Continue reading aloud to your child, feeding his mind and heart with interesting and well-written books, requiring him to narrate. Try a story starter again after your child has become a bit more fluent with narration.

If your child is in junior high or older and having trouble, take heart. Patiently plod ahead. It may take more than several stories (and some months) for greater creativity to develop or for that certain story to ignite the right spark.

## Method Two:
## ORAL NARRATION WITH COPYWORK

1. Select a picture that grabs the student's interest. Read aloud the story starter enthusiastically. Have a good time.
2. Let him pause to think and sympathize. Refer to Writing Help if desired.
3. Take dictation from his narration.
4. Read his story back to him with enthusiasm. Have a good time with this, too.
   Point out something you like about it. Ask him if there is anything else he would like to add. The next day, suggest one or two ways he may improve his writing. For instance, suggest that he provide more detail, some sensory language, a bit more conversation, etc. "This is good. I like this, but *show* us the alligator by describing it more." (See note below.)
5. Assign copy-work from your model.

If you would like your child to write out his story make a model from your dictation using the same penmanship style you would like him to use. Require him to copy from your neat model. This provides him with all the proper spelling and punctuation. *The emphasis in this book is on content and on getting the student to narrate,* but he will also gain practice in spelling and punctuation simply by doing copy-work. Photocopy the picture and story starter from the book to accompany his paper, if you'd like.

A younger student's copy-work may take several sessions over a few days to complete.

You decide how many (or which) stories are to be copied or kept in a notebook.

Note: At some point have the child do the exercises on Sensory Language in the section "Hints for Polishing."

## Method Three:
## WRITTEN NARRATION—ROUGH DRAFT

1. You or the child selects a picture. Either you read the story starter aloud or the student reads it to himself.
2. He writes his creative narration in the form of a rough draft. If it is an intense situation, you may suggest that each new phrase or sentence begin on a new line, so that he can get his impressions down on paper faster. Phrasing, however, is not mandatory.
3. He is invited to use the Writing Help provided at the end of the story starter. He can polish with your help on the next day if you want to keep the lesson short. (Younger students give better attention to shorter lessons.) Or, polish after a suitable break.

Initial excitement may usher in the need for continuity. In this case, feel free to have a longer lesson to accommodate the desire to stay on a roll.

4. Make a model from his worked-over rough draft (we can call this a second draft), providing all the correct spelling and punctuation for him.
5. After doing a number of story starter exercises, at some point read over the section Hints for Polishing. Do the topics one day at a time. Explore with him ways to polish the content of the writing (perhaps adding vivid verbs, artful adjectives, sensory language, etc. for finer description.) These lessons, however, are of secondary importance.

### *Spelling & Punctuation*

If you notice that a commonly used word is misspelled in the rough draft and ask your student how to spell it, he will probably spell it out correctly for you. Errors in spelling are typical when a student is concentrating on content and the creative aspect of writing is at work. You can ask him to help you polish it by asking, "Isn't there a word here that needs to be capitalized?" "Quotation marks are needed where?" If he has been taught these things, he will probably correct his work without difficulty.

### *Rough, Rough Drafts*

I used the model copy-work method for some years with oral and written narration with my son because his rough drafts were very rough and because it eliminated the need for making red proofreader's marks all over his paper. I kept a list of his misspelled words for separate study. I did not point out *everything* that needed correction, but made note of it for separate study, also.

### *When No Model Is Needed*

I had a student whose rough drafts were not so rough. She produced a much cleaner copy. Therefore, she could then make a polished copy (a second draft) from her own rough draft. Some students may not need the help of a written model. During the polishing-up stage, she looked up for herself words in the dictionary or thesaurus.

### *Word Processing*

Older students who have learned to type enjoy editing their work on the computer. Reworking the story and making major content changes are more easily done on the computer. It amazes me that Charles Dickens wrote his extensive novels without a word processor!

### *Just Pictures*

If your student has completed a number of story starters and has become more proficient at expressing himself, he might like to try a "Just Picture." With Just Pictures he will be challenged to develop his own characters, describe the setting, and make up the entire story himself.

After writing a few of his own stories to these pictures your student may be ready for the additional challenge provided in "A Lesson on the Basic Elements of a Story, " which is written to the student.

## Method Four: WORKING INDEPENDENTLY

This level of writer may be an older student who has experience in both oral and written narration. Or perhaps this student is younger, but is innately keen on writing, and can work independently.

1. The student chooses a picture and reads the story starter to himself.
2. He writes a rough draft of his story.
3. He reads it aloud to you.
4. You provide encouraging comments for some light editing to help him polish. He writes a second or third draft. If you and he haven't already done so, read over the section Hints for Polishing. Do the topics one day at a time.
5. If the student has become proficient at expressing himself, suggest that he write a whole story with Just Pictures. In the introduction of Just Pictures is "A Lesson on the Basic Elements of a Story," which is written to the student and will provide additional challenge.

### *A note on polishing, for perfectionists only:*

Keep in mind that these story starters are predominately exercises in imaginative creativity and the kind of descriptive writing a student would not have the opportunity to use elsewhere. Save the larger "improvement" muscles for formal essay writing.

# A Word About Internal Motivation and Grading

## Satisfying Ideas

I wrote *Story Starters* to create a schoolbook from which children like to work. Yet it is a mistake to think that all lessons must be fun and easy. Rather, they should be interesting and satisfying, so that minds grow in knowledge. Children's growing bodies thrive on nutritious food. As Charlotte Mason said, "Ideas are to the mind what food is to the body" therefore, children's lessons ought to provide nutritious ideas. Ideas give us something to think about. Ideas are food for thought. An idea may be as small as a seed. Though quite small, it has just the right amount of life in it to develop and branch into a whole panoply of thought, as the mind makes its own associations. This process makes learning satisfying and enjoyable for children. To supply children with interesting ideas for writing was my aim in *Story Starters.*

## Grades

"What about grading?" some are sure to ask. Here is my suggestion. If your student is in eighth grade or lower, do not grade. Instead, give your student credit for his diligent effort. Write an evaluation of his progress if you desire.

## Interest—A Little Pearl of Great Value

In Charlotte Mason's practical philosophy, attentive interest in what the student is learning is promoted. Interest is a little pearl of great value. It creates a pleasant and valuable atmosphere in the homeschool. Unhappily, in the lives of many children, their progress is unceasingly measured and attention thus becomes focused on this continual measuring. What children are learning should be of more importance (and of more interest) than the grade on the report card. The fact that you are giving your child some personal attention with *Story* Starters—that you, also, take an interest in the work—is preferable to flattering praise, or tangible rewards such as happy face stickers, grades, M&Ms, etc. We wish to foster internal motivation in the student so that he sees that the activity of writing is satisfying in and of itself. We want him to have the experience that he is creating something that can be satisfying, especially when someone else appreciates it. External motivators have been proven to lessen interest in the learning activity.

## Awaken a Child's Curiosity

If the learning activity becomes a means to a reward, the attention is on the reward (or praise of progress—the grade) rather than the value of the activity. Children are trained in schools to learn something because it will be on the test (or count for the grade), not because it is good to know. This is why it is helpful to awaken children's curiosity with a question or two that draws interest. It is also helpful to tell children what it is about the learning activity that is of value. (I have done this for you below.)

## Grading: For High School Only

Some of you might be thinking, "This educational philosophy sounds all well and good, but my student is in high school and we must grade work that is to contribute to high school transcripts. Please suggest some way to evaluate a student's work that will facilitate necessary grading."

Here are two suggestions for grading the exercises in *Story Starters*.

1) If *Story Starters* is being used as supplementary material to an existing English course, consider it "extra credit," or consider giving the student more "points," which would enhance the student's overall grade for the subject.

2) If you are using this book as a one-semester course, here is a sample point system. 18 points is a C, 19 points is a B, 20 points is an A, 21 points is an A+
   - Give your student 18 points if he writes (free-flowing) at least a sizable paragraph typed or a whole page handwritten. His paragraph ought to reflect an affinity for the story starter plot and characters. Does his writing show that he is really getting "into" the story with at least a quiet element of enthusiasm?

     Remind your student to include what he learned in Hints for Polishing.
   - Give 1 point for at least one vivid verb.
     It could be added during the polishing stage. Some of the story starters provide vivid verb suggestions.

- Give 1 point for an artful adjective.
  This also could be added during a second or third draft.
- Give 1 point for sensory language.
  Has he described anything in the story by way of the five senses? If not, where can he add some description?

## A Warning

I ardently appeal to you not to reveal the above grading system to your high school student during his first attempts at creative writing. Let the student write, write, write, unencumbered—as is emphatically mentioned throughout this book. After he works on a good number of stories, let him later choose which ones he would like to improve upon to count toward a grade.

# What Is the Value of this Learning Activity?

## Imagination

irst, to add a student's creative narration to a story will exercise his muscles of imagination. Imagination grows with use. It is a necessary and pleasing mental capacity that works in conjunction with other capacities.

*The soul without imagination is what an observatory would be without a telescope.*
H.W. Beecher

## Narration

Story starters give the child an opportunity to tell. Much of the paper work given to children seems to be that of filling in blanks, choosing from multiple choice or true and false statements. The common worksheet enables ease of grading. It does not provide, however, the opportunity for the child to articulate his answers—to explain how or why. For a child to tell about something in his own words is to be exceedingly more verbal. Even to compose two sentences requires far more intelligence than to fill in a blank. The student is using more brainpower. His narrating is developing his verbal skills naturally and powerfully. Voila, he is writing.

## Reason

With story starters the student makes use of reason. He is invited to think in terms of cause and effect, and is required to use logic. While considering a natural and convincing consequence to actions taken in the story starter, he will be considering what will be likely to occur next—what will be a logical or reasonable outcome. In many of my stories, I provided the cause and the student provides the effect. He may decide however, to cleverly give the story an unlikely or surprise ending.

## Emotion

Ample opportunity is provided for your student to write in ways he may never have written before—to write with emotion, as explained in "Exciting Writing."

## Problem-Solving

In many of my stories there is tension and conflict. A problem is presented that begs to be solved. Solving the problem (that pulls on the emotions as well as the reason) will be creating a good story—a story that has conflict resolution.

## Vocabulary

Each story starter is a lesson in becoming more literate. The Writing Help section that follows most of the stories helps the student to be more literary-minded. He can use the hints, clues, and suggestions to help him create a good story. Guided by the occasional question, he is to fill out or polish his writing.

Some of the vocabulary in the story starters may be unfamiliar to students. I have placed an asterisk before them and put the definition at the bottom of the page. In most cases however, children will apply meaning to the word from the surrounding text. This is the natural way they develop their vocabulary.

Section Two
Story Starters

# Introduction to the Story Starters

Here is your opportunity to write freely; to write with zest, with gusto, and exuberance; to write with curiosity and imagination; to write with feeling and less restraint than you may be used to. Nobody else will write exactly like you. Your writing is your fingerprint. When you write freely, it is *your* thoughts and *your* past experience that will spring out from the pages of your story. Your love of running, riding, chasing, yelling, swimming, playing, eating, day-dreaming, building, singing, climbing, zooming, or snoozing will burst forth from your imagination to make your story your own. Let your imagination wander and you will write like you've never written before.

All I do is open the door with a story starter to help you. The rooms are set with people, birds, and animals that find themselves in situations that are sometimes intense, sometimes funny, sometimes calm, but always posing a challenge. *You* choose which rooms to enter. You offer the solutions. You make the characters speak. You rescue those in danger, comfort the sick, cheer the lonely, laugh with the ridiculous, tame the wild, do battle for good.

Pick out a picture that looks curious (or have your teacher do it). Your first story will help get you warmed up. Write all you want. It will not be picked apart. You see, I've instructed your teacher not to do so. He (or she) can offer advice. But I recommended that he or she help you polish your stories later on, not right away. Therefore, go ahead and write what comes to mind. Write with zest and energy. Dive in. Make a splash. With story starters there is no one right way of doing things.

All writers eventually go over their writing again. To make it better they write a second or third draft. But the first draft is *rough*. Let your first draft be as rough as you like, paying little attention to spelling, grammar, or punctuation. These can be straightened out later. If you are telling your story out loud, you are the most free to be spontaneous because your teacher writes it all down for you. Therefore, let the fires burn, the waters rush, the rhinoceroses charge, the bears growl, the horses gallop, the kittens purr, the ships sail, the rowers row, the babies coo, and the crows caw to their hearts' content. The story is the thing. And it's all yours.

# 1

## The Bookworm's Opportunity[B][I]

Emily loved to read, and on this particular afternoon she was curled up in a chair in the living room with her head buried in a book. Suddenly she was interrupted by her brother Clay.

"Come on, Em," he implored. "Bob and I are going downtown to meet Dad at the courthouse. We'll catch the end of his case and walk home with him through the park. How can you stay indoors on such a sunny day? Your face is always stuck in a book. You should get out once in a while."

Emily defended herself. "I was out yesterday. Besides, I like reading," she retorted with a grin.

"Bookworm," Clay mumbled in disgust as he left the room with Bob and briskly prepared to depart for the courthouse.

Emily detested name-calling, but she chose to overlook Clay's rudeness as she didn't want to have to explain herself. She wanted to complete her research for a certain Girl Scout badge, and then she planned to finish reading the last chapter of a most exciting novel. It was always hard to leave a book when she was so close to the end.

The room was suddenly quiet now that the boys had gone. “Finally, some peace,” Emily sighed. And in moments she was once again absorbed in her reading.

Half an hour later Mother came in with four-year-old Violet and asked Emily to watch her while she and Aunt Ethel worked in the kitchen. Emily looked up from her book just for a moment to say, “Yes, ma’am.”

"Thank you, dear. But how can you read in the dark?" She lit the kerosene lamp, and smiled down at her daughters. "Your father and the boys will be back soon," she added as she left the room and disappeared down the dark hall.

Violet had taken her little dolls out of her dollhouse and was playing with them and her blocks on the carpet for some time. Emily didn't notice that Violet had also set up some blocks on the table in a ring around the glowing lamp. When Clay and Bob bounded in Violet was standing at the table adding another layer of blocks to her ring. Startled by their noisy entrance, she looked up in surprise. As she did so, her arm knocked over the blocks and the kerosene lamp. Within just moments the rug caught on fire.

The picture shows an intense scene. Describe the commotion that arose and what took place afterwards. Give your story a happy ending.

## Writing Help

- Describe how quickly Emily worked and what she did. How did this spare poor Violet a burn that could have been more serious?
- Make your astonished characters speak.
- Describe the burning process with sensory language. What did the characters smell, taste, and feel?
- What did the boys do to help?
- Give your story closing remarks by the characters.
- Which Girl Scout badge might Emily have been working on, based on her knowledge of how to act during a fire emergency?

## Additional Challenge

### *Vivid Verbs*

Use some vivid verbs related to quick, emergency action. The vivid verbs below are some suggestions.

**Vivid Verbs:** startle, cry, call, fall, wave, hit, jump, spring, stamp, grab, pump, pour, throw, squelch, saturate, wrap, roll, carry, soothe, pat.

# 2

## The Night Visitor[B][I]

"Here's another one!" Walter called to Hilda. An earthworm dangled between two fingers as he held it out for Hilda, the greediest of all his young chickens. Whenever Walter came across an earthworm while digging in the garden, he offered it to Hilda, and she gobbled it up like a strand of spaghetti.

Hilda had been newly hatched in early spring with a brood of other peeping chicks. As they grew and their fuzzy yellow feathers began to be replaced by darker, more substantial ones, Walter let them out of their chicken run (fenced-in area) during the day to follow him around the garden or scratch in the yard for insects. They loved to scratch, but near nightfall he would call them back into their coop. They would come wobbling at high speed because they were always promptly rewarded with handfuls of cracked corn and sunflower seeds.

With all this attention, they grew rapidly, but Hilda outweighed them all. Dad told Walter that he believed that this was so because he hand-fed her earthworms. As a result of her size, she took her rightful place at the top of the pecking order.

When the vegetable garden was carefully planted, the chickens were kept in their run. They couldn't be allowed to scratch up the tender garden sprouts or Mother's flowers. But all summer Walter picked insect pests and slugs off the vegetables and threw them over the fence for the chickens. By August the chickens were plump and healthy. Hilda, especially, was a beauty.

"Why not enter Hilda in the county fair this September?" Dad suggested to Walter.

"Should I? Do you really think she'd have a chance at winning something?" Walter asked.

"Give it a try," was Dad's optimistic reply.

Finally, the day arrived for the judging. Walter was so excited. Never had he gotten dressed so quickly or so purposefully. He didn't even have difficulty with his tie! In Walter's day, people looked forward to the agricultural fair for weeks, and wore their Sunday best for the occasion.

"You look very smart," his sister Suzanne remarked with a smile. "And you tied your tie just right," she added. Walter derived comfort from his sister's compliments whenever she gave them, but today her kind words added greatly to his already high spirits.

All agreed that the 1905 Smithville County Fair was the best ever. Rows of horses, cows, sheep, goats, and pigs were admired. Inside the pavilion people crowded to see the many cages of small birds and animals. Moving along with the crowd, Walter and his family were enjoying the exhibits, but Walter was looking intently for one particular cage.

Suddenly his voice rang out. "Look! Here's Hilda, and she's won second prize!"

Dad and Suzanne were very glad for him.

"Well done, son," Dad said. "Now how about a piece of blueberry pie to celebrate?"

The crisp fall weather was soon followed by the icy winds of winter. In January the chickens couldn't scratch in their run because a foot of snow covered the ground. Walter shoveled snow into a mound to one side of the run and put some straw down for them, but they were still inactive in such cold weather. They huddled together much of the time, especially when the wind picked up. One evening, two of the chickens were left out in the run. It was so overcast that when Walter secured the

chicken coop door for the night he failed to see two little dark shapes huddled together in the straw, in the far corner where the mound of snow blocked the cold breezes.

Walter's feet dragged as he made his way to bed. He had spent all afternoon skating with his sister and a friend, had eaten a good dinner, and, after completing his evening chores, was very much ready for bed. As he slowly climbed the stairs to his bedroom, he heard a cackle and a screech. He stopped on the stair, *flabbergasted. Then a whole chorus of cackles and screeches burst forth, and Walter's feet were instantly revitalized. He ran lickety-split down the stairs.

Let your imagination run with the story to keep it moving. Were there any loud exclamations? What were Walter's first dreadful thoughts?

## Writing Help

- What did Walter think to himself as soon as he saw the fox?
- Which other chicken was left out of the coop? There were two, remember?
- A good writer sympathizes with his characters. If you were Walter, what would you feel? Depending on how you wrote your story, Walter might be very upset at first, but later relieved.
- What does Dad say to Walter? How does Walter explain the incident to Suzanne when he enters the house?
- Did the fox return?

## Additional Challenge

### *Vivid Verbs*

Go back over your story and see where you can replace weak verbs with vivid verbs to describe the action. A few verbs are suggested here, but of course you can think up your own.

---

*To be "flabbergasted" means to be surprised or astonished.

**Vivid Verbs:** hurry, dash, yell, holler, chase, race, pursue, throw, hurl, kick, tumble, plunge.

Here is a different set: quit, abandon, droop, hang, mosey, pat.

### *Cause and Effect*

I've given you a cause and effect: the dark night caused the chickens to be overlooked. Therefore (the effect) they were left out. But judging by the picture, there is another cause in the story. The fox is hungry and perhaps has hungry cubs waiting at home. As you write your story, you will be describing this cause and its effect.

### *Moral*

Stories also have lessons. You may have heard the phrase, "the moral of the story." What could Walter learn from this situation that would be of value to him later?

### *Suspense*

Suspense is the term used to describe the anticipation the reader feels while waiting to find out what happens next in the story. To suspend means to hang. What will the reader find around the bend in the road? You've provided clues and your reader watches and waits for what will happen next.

As Walter walks through the snow toward the chicken coop, he will be worrying about what he will find. His mind is on Hilda, his prize chicken. Was it she that was stolen away? Even a little suspense makes your story more interesting or exciting.

# 3

## The Unexpected Guest

Reggie and Jeff and I are good friends. Reggie, however, is a boaster. Jeff and I try to be gracious to Reggie, but lately we have found ourselves having to put up with more and more of his boasting.

The day of the lodge supper, we were walking along the road discussing the matter. Jeff sighed, and said, with some *vexation in his tone, "You know, Baxter, there's sure to be more boasting tonight. Reggie has already told me twice this week how he got three bulls-eyes the last time he went to the archery range with his uncle."

"Yes, and all I've heard this week is how great a hunter his uncle is, how many geese he shot last fall, and how many deer he has already shot this fall," I responded. "It's really getting wearisome." I expressed my irritation by kicking at some pebbles in the road.

---

*The words "annoyance" or "irritation" are used today in place of "vexation" which was used more in Victorian times. I thought "vexation" went well with this older style of story and would give you a new word to learn.

We walked along in silence for a while, each lost in his own thoughts.

"Baxter," mused Jeff finally, his smile becoming increasingly wider as an idea took hold of his imagination, "I think we're going to have some fun tonight."

I was just thinking how strangely positive Jeff was being about the whole thing, but that was as far as I got, because he then turned to me, eyes alight with mischief, and said fervently, "I have a plan! I'll need your help, though." Vigorously he pulled my arm, urging me to pick up my pace. "Come on Baxter!" he said excitedly. "We've got to catch the trolley and go downtown to the costume shop. There's no time to lose!"

"What's this all about?" I asked, puzzled. "There's an odd gleam in your eye."

He pushed me on. "I'll tell you along the way. Come on!"

Take up the story up from here. Where did the boys go? How did they prepare for the evening at the lodge? Describe the incident at the lodge.

Hint: Do you see the black shoe the "bear" is wearing in the picture?

## Writing Help

- Which young man is Jeff in the picture, which is Baxter, and which is Reggie?
- How does Reggie react to the events?
- Are Jeff and Baxter honest with him about their reason for the joke?

### *Exploring Possibilities*

What are the dangers of something going wrong? One possibility would be that one of the boys picks up a baseball bat in defense. Another is that the waiter who is serving the food might run out and report the bear's presence to the cook.

## Additional Challenge

Use vivid verbs and exclamations of surprise, laughter, or fright to make your characters come alive.

Use First Person Narrator with this story—that is, continue writing with "I" or "we" to finish telling the story from Baxter's point of view. (You may wish to refer to "Three Kinds of Narrators" in Hints for Polishing to read a description of the different points of view.)

## A Tip for Good Writing

### *Relating to a Past Experience*

Do you like costumes? Have you ever worn one? Recalling certain past experiences will greatly help you perk up your writing. Experiences not only give you ideas of what to write about, but they influence how descriptively you write, because you know what it is like to be in a similar situation.

### *A Scary Costume*

When I was a ten-year-old girl I attended the slumber party of a girl who lived in a spacious old colonial house. We were sitting in her family room eating popcorn when all of a sudden a gorilla wobbled into the room. We all screamed. He grunted and scratched and began chasing us around the room, so we screamed again. We ran into another room that had a pool table and were chased round and round the pool table. We ran into the dining room and were chased around that table, too, all the while alternating laughing and giggling with waves of screaming as he lunged at us or got close. The thick (and convincing) gorilla costume must have been hot. We watched as the girl's dad, at last, took off the headpiece and gave us a huge grin. He had successfully stirred us up and brought fun to the party. Yes, we had been a little frightened, even though we knew all along that it was just a costume.

The mixed reactions and feelings of the boys at the lodge would probably play out differently than a girls' slumber party, but you can understand how one experience can relate to another.

# 4

# The Runaway Motorcar[(I)]

Grandpa had just arrived for a visit. The minute his car had pulled up in front of our house, we had stopped everything we were doing and had rushed down the walk to greet him and to help him carry his bags into the house. Shortly thereafter, he was comfortably seated on the screened porch with a glass of iced tea, surrounded by all of us and receiving our complete attention. We knew it couldn't be easy living alone without Grandma, and we were all very glad he had come to stay for awhile.

Rubbing his white beard and frowning with his bushy eyebrows, he picked up the book that lay on a side table, and asked, "What's this? Hmm, *The Wind in the Willows*, by Kenneth Grahame. I read this book when I was a boy. Actually my father read it aloud to me. He was a very busy village doctor, but he always read to me in the evenings, no matter how tired he was." He paused as he added, "Even up to the time I was this tall." As he said this, he reached out his arm and placed a hand over Philip's head. "Your grandmother read it to your mother, too."

At the mention of Grandma, a tiny tear formed in the corner of one of his eyes, but with the back of his other hand he whiped it away instantly. “Who’s reading it?” He didn’t give us a second to answer, and we glanced at each other excitedly, realizing he was in a talkative mood.

"That Toad character was quite a fellow. He sure loved motorcars. It's too bad he was addicted to speed and let every ride he took get out of control. Rattie was my favorite—a more sensible creature." He chuckled, which made his eyes squint. He was enjoying our company immensely, and we his. When his eyes reopened, his whole face had taken on a far-away look. "Did I ever tell you about the *two* Toads in a motorcar?"

"No," we managed to get in. Grandpa launched into a story about the days of his youth; about the time his father had bought an old motorcar to drive on his rounds. Even though it had been an older model, it had nevertheless been one of the first cars in town. One day, Grandpa related, he was returning from the market with the groceries his mother had asked him to get, and he had spotted his father's car parked across the street in front of the house of one of his patients. At the same time, he had noticed that two boys were looking it over in a suspicious manner. Suddenly, it was as if a scene from *The Wind in the Willows* had come alive. But instead of one Toad, there were two!

Continue Grandpa's story, describing the boys' *escapade. I invite you to write freely with zest and gusto. Follow where your imagination leads.

## Writing Help

- What did the two boys whisper to each other before they entered the car?
- How easy was the old car to handle? In what way did the boys get carried away?

---

*An "escapade" is a playful or reckless adventure.

- Where did the boys and the car end up?
- Tell about how their thrills turned into a misadventure.
- What were the consequences or results of their escapade? Did they get in trouble?
- What did the Grandpa's listeners think of the whole adventure?

## *Anthropomorphism*

*The Wind in the Willows,* by Kenneth Grahame (1859-1932), is an odd sort of novel. Mr. Toad, Ratty, Mole, and Badger are characterized as bachelors that live in the British countryside. These four main characters are animals that have been given human characteristics. There is a long word for this: anthropomorphism. *Thomas the Tank Engine* is another example of anthropomorphism, because the author gives human attributes to a train engine. Anyway, most of our friends and acquaintances agree that *The Wind in the Willows* is funny, well written, and chock-full of interesting and challenging vocabulary words. A few others found it not to their taste. To our family, however, the personalities of impetuous Mr. Toad; dependable, well-mannered Ratty; kindly, sympathetic Mole; and unwaveringly sturdy Badger are unforgettable, even lovable.

# 5

# Saved from the Fog

*Perhaps this exercise shouldn't be called a story starter because I have supplied the end of the story. You will supply what happened earlier—how Jane was saved. Anyway, it is meant to start you writing. Have you ever gone ice-skating?*

"I don't remember much," said Jane. She was sitting in her father's lap, warming her feet by the fire, and at the table next to them her mother was pouring some hot chocolate. On a plate were English muffins—crisp, brown and buttered, with a generous dollop of bright red strawberry preserves in the center of each—just the way she liked them.

"I can't remember, really," she repeated.

Donald and Roy, who were half kneeling, half lying on the rug beside her, begged, "But Jane, tell us what you *do* remember."

"Well, while you boys were skating and running your races, I went with the girls. They said it would be such fun to go as far as the other end of the pond. We decided to split up to look for winterberries

growing on the shore. I wanted to find as many as they did, so I skated and skated, and never thought…till all at once I saw that the fog had come; and I looked back and couldn't see the girls. Then I couldn't see the shore either, and it was getting dark, and all I remember after that was that it was *so* cold. I called out the girls' names, but no one answered. I kept thinking they would come any minute, but they didn't. Then I felt so cold I didn't want to call anymore."

"You gave us an awful fright, I can assure you," said Dad.

"I'm sorry," Jane said honestly.

Her dad continued, describing the moment he and her mother had discovered she was missing. "We were sitting around the bonfire, talking with friends, when Mother saw in the corner of her eye that the girls had returned and were taking off their skates near the fire. She heard them all giggling in their stocking feet as they looked for their shoes and she assumed you were among the gigglers. But when they walked off to get their hot cups of chocolate, she happened to glance down at the one pair of shoes left and recognized them as yours. Alarmed, she immediately came hurrying over to me.

"'Where's Jane?' was all she said. Instantly I began making inquiries. When no one gave me the answer I wanted to hear, I dashed over to your brothers and rallied the help of the men."

Continue Dad's tale of the rescue. Did the characters experience any difficulties in their search because of the fog, the approaching darkness, or slippery ice? How did the characters overcome any of these difficulties? Did they follow an organized plan? Did they have to get more help?

## Writing Help

How do you think Jane felt when she was alone on the ice? How did her parents feel or act during the search? Explain the energy put into the search. How difficult is it to remain calm when you feel very nervous and frantic? What steps were taken to find Jane and to bring her home? Can you hear the search party calling for her? Who found her? Were the girls she was with of any help at all?

## Additional Challenge

### *Flashback*

As you write Dad's description of Jane's rescue, you will be adding to the "flashback" of this story, because our story begins with the scene of Jane resting at home surrounded by her family. You can picture her there telling her story. Then Dad begins telling his. In a flashback, the author, sometimes by way of a character, interrupts the story by telling about an earlier incident. In the story starter, "The Runaway Motorcar," Grandpa's reminiscing is a sort of flashback, too.

### *Relating an Experience*

Have you ever searched for a brother, sister, or a pet that was lost? Any experience you might have had of searching for something (or someone) dear to you that was lost can help you sympathize with the characters in your story.

I lost my three-year-old son on a crowded beach at the seashore one hot summer afternoon. It felt dreadful. I said a prayer as I ran to alert the life-guard. Then I began running up the beach while his dad headed in the opposite direction. As I ran, my eyes frantically scanned every person under every umbrella. To my great relief, after running only about fifty yards (and it isn't easy running in loose sand), I found him. He had wandered off aimlessly.

# 6

# Poor Polly(B)

*Do you notice something not right about this picture? If you are thinking "snow," you are correct. Parrots are tropical birds and live in places where it does not ever get cold enough to snow. But Polly is a pet and lives with a family in Michigan near the Great Lakes where it does snow. Here is how she came to experience her first chilly snowfall.*

It was early afternoon, and Mother was dusting and giving a bit of airing to the library, where the children had their morning homeschool lessons. With her long-handled dust mop, she polished the oak floor under and around all the furniture. "Where does all this dust come from?" she said wonderingly. Opening the window, she stuck the mop out and shook it vigorously, letting the breeze carry the dust away.

By accident, Polly's cage door had been left unfastened at feeding time, but Mother hadn't noticed. Polly pushed it ajar and flew happily through the open library window to the top of a maple tree. Immediately Mother gasped and started calling, "Children, come at

once! I'm in the library! Amy, Alfred, Mark, hurry!" She didn't want to leave the library because she didn't want to take her eyes off Polly.

The children sensed the urgency in their mother's voice and came running from the kitchen, where they had been washing up after lunch.

"Polly's gone! She's gone out the window!" Mother exclaimed, standing motionless in the same spot, still shocked.

The children's eyes went from the empty cage to the window.

"How do we get her back?" Amy asked, with a tremor in her voice.

Alfred, who had been, of late, reading about King Alfred in his history book, felt a kind of knightly urge to save the day. "I think I know what to do," he announced with an air of decision. He spun on his heels and in a flash was running down the hall to get something he needed from his fishing gear.

Tell the rest of the story. Describe what is taking place in your imagination so that those who read your story can see and hear and feel what you do.

## Writing Help

What was Alfred looking for? How did he put himself in command and rally his brother and sister to help? Describe the sequence of events that occurred to get Polly back to her cage. Do any neighbors get into the act? When their dad comes home, hours later, in what state does he find his family? Was dinner ready on time?

# 7

# In the Twilight

Sylvia was having a disheartening day. It was such a hot summer day in Savannah, Georgia, that her feet were dragging as she went about her chores. Even so she helped her mother hang the wash in the hot sun and helped her can vegetables in the hot kitchen. The canning of tomatoes and pickles took long hot hours. Helping with the wash was often even harder, because Mother became a "washer woman" whenever the money began to run out. Every day, with Sylvia's help, she washed, dried, and ironed whatever laundry the neighbors brought by. Mother always tried to make Father's pay last until he returned from his voyage on the vast ocean, but it was often difficult to make ends meet. June had been especially difficult, as baby Joey had been born while Father was still away and Mother had had to pay the midwife. In these last few months, she had had to rely on Sylvia and her twin brother Teddy more than she would have liked.

The air was stagnant and heavy with humidity. The baby cried throughout the day. And Mother missed Father, who had been a sailor on a merchant ship far out at sea for what seemed very long months. All

of these things wore away at their smiles. As the day was nearing its close, Mother was putting the baby off to sleep for the night and settling in for a much needed early repose herself. Sylvia had curled up in the window seat to read. It was her favorite spot in the house.

Finally it came—a soothing cool evening breeze off the ocean. Ahh. It was just as much a relief as was the peace and quiet. It evaporated the perspiration from her heated brow. For Sylvia, this refreshment seemed to give her a new perspective on her day. Teddy found her in the window seat, still enjoying the cooling breeze. He had come home late, after having worked all day for old Mrs. Moffat. Throughout the heat of the day he had weeded and watered her large vegetable garden, walked her dog, and continued painting her fence. Now he could enjoy the cool breeze as well. Together the twins stared sleepily out of the window as twilight fell. Then something on the horizon caught their eyes. They both spotted it at the same time. Could it really be what they hoped it to be?

Make the picture come alive. What did the children see and what did they do next?

## Writing Help

- Supply an exclamation from one or both of the characters: what did they say in their excitement? They should be tired after a day of work in the heat of the summer, but their excitement gives them new energy.
- The girl in the picture could be praying. What do you think is her great need that she is begging God to answer? What if her need is being met in some way as she is in the process of praying? If so, can you describe how God might have answered her prayer?

## Additional Challenge

What kind of relationship do Sylvia and Teddy enjoy as twins? Can they understand each other almost instinctively? Do they feel the same way about things?

# 8

## Morning Wake-Up Call[(B)]

Getting Rosie up in the morning was the hardest work. Ever since the baby had been born, six-year-old Rosie had taken to staying in bed while Mother attended to the baby in the next room. Brother Lionel had an idea. "I know how to get her up, Mom," he said one morning.

"Rosie, it's time to get up!" he called.

"In a minute," she answered.

But Lionel knew that his dawdling sister would be lying in her bed for more than a few minutes. A big smile spread across his face as he energetically ran down the stairs to the kitchen, remembering the basket of crabs he had caught the day before. He liked crabbing in the Chesapeake Bay, down at the docks after homeschool lessons were through. He liked being out of the house and in the warm September sun. The salty sea air smelled deliciously of seaweed. The fact that his mother always appreciated what he caught, and fried up the best Maryland crab cakes, was an added bonus.

Lionel was in high spirits. He worked quickly and quietly, all the while suppressing his urge to laugh. From the dining room he collected candle stubs.

Continue the action of the story as if you were in the next room watching all that takes place. Explain step by step how Lionel got Rosie out of bed. You are free to use the picture of Lionel's cat, too, to add to the action.

## Writing Help

What was Rosie's reaction? Make your characters act and speak—or, should I say, shriek. Do you think Lionel's stunt helped Rosie break her slothful habit of staying in bed?

## Additional Challenge

Tell the story from any point of view you would like. "Point of view" determines the perspective from which the story is told. Changing the point of view, therefore, can radically change the perspective of the same story. How would the story about Lionel and Rosie be told differently if it were told from Lionel's point of view, or from his mother's point of view? We tend to justify our actions. How would his mother view Lionel's method of getting his sister out of bed? To eat a creature because of hunger is one thing, but to tamper with it and possibly harm it is another matter. How would Lionel view any correction on the part of his mother?

You could even tell the story from the cat's point of view. What would the cat think Lionel was trying to do? How would the cat and the crabs act toward each other?

Refer to "Three Kinds of Narrators."

# 9

## The Brave Robin[I]

Recently our Aunt Philippa traveled all the way from London, England, by ship, to visit us. It is her first stay in America. These April days are cool and moist and remind her of her home. Yesterday afternoon we took a leisurely stroll along our road. A hillside of bright yellow daffodils nodded to us in the breeze. The meadows around our house are covered with what seems to be dozens of newly-arrived robins, which hop back and forth across the grass waiting for the right moment to pull up an earthworm.

Watching the robins, Aunt Philippa commented, "Everything in America seems to be so much bigger than in England! Your streets are wider; your houses are farther apart from each other and have such large back gardens—so much grass. Your cars are bigger; even your robins are bigger."

"You have those cute round robins back at home, don't you?" my mother responded. "I've seen them pictured on the Christmas cards you've sent."

"Oh yes, they're lovely little robins, and they are also tough and fearless."

"What makes you say that?"

"They will defend their territory against other birds and they will defend their nests quite viciously, I can assure you."

Aunt Philippa then went on to tell us a true story about a pair of robins that had a nest of eggs in the low branches of the apple tree by her barn. Over the course of a week, she said, from her kitchen window she witnessed a series of unusual incidents. One of these incidents surprised her. Aunt Philippa said she couldn't believe what she was seeing.

What did Aunt Philippa observe? Was the robin trying to protect something? If so, was it successful?

## Writing Help

- Aunt Philippa recorded her observations of the robin's behavior in her nature journal. What if you had read her journal entries describing the incidents she had watched from her window? Tell a story about what she observed, keeping a sequence of events in mind. What events lead up to what is taking place in the picture?
- What a writer reads or experiences feeds his creativity. You are welcome to read about birds and robins in an encyclopedia or observe the ones that live in your neighborhood.

# 10

## Welcomed Birds

A man named Maxfield was shipwrecked near a lonely island in the Atlantic Ocean. He managed to get ashore with his damaged boat, but when he realized that all of the edible provisions had been lost, with the exception of a few potatoes, he despaired for his life. Chewing on some leathery, slimy seaweed relieved the gnawing pain of his empty stomach only briefly. He would have starved, had not some penguins arrived on the island. The penguins laid many eggs, and Mr. Maxfield welcomed the supply with joy and gratitude. Every meal was a breakfast of a very large egg.

Mr. Maxfield would have been bored if it hadn't been for the penguins. He watched them for hours upon hours and, to pass the time, made mental notes of all their peculiarities. But of course he longed for the hour of his rescue. Eventually, after many weeks, the thought of eating yet another egg disgusted him. He began dreaming of the kind of meals he once had enjoyed.

Imagine Maxfield's circumstances and describe them in detail. Tell about the exciting day of his rescue. How did Maxfield react to seeing a ship on the horizon?

## Writing Help

What food would you crave if you could eat nothing but eggs for weeks? What meals do you think Maxfield was dreaming about?

On the cover of *Story Starters* you can see a picture of Robinson Crusoe. It depicts the scene in which he finds in the sand the footprints of another human being. Mr. Crusoe was excited because he had been stranded alone on the island for so long. The footprint startled him. Have you ever read this classic story? Crusoe was stranded on an island for years. The length of time Mr. Maxfield spent on his lonely island was much shorter—only several weeks but his island was in a colder part of the world. Imagine what it might be like to be alone on such an island.

Use sensory language. What does Maxfield see, smell, hear, feel, and taste? Do you know what a small chicken coop smells like? Multiply this by many birds and imagine how strong the odor would be.

Upon attempting this story starter, my son became interested in reading about penguins in our encyclopedia. He found a surprising amount of information on them. Factual information found in an encyclopedia, or a film, could help round out your story.

What was Maxfield thinking about during his time on the island? Did he pray, as Robinson Crusoe did? Did he think out loud and talk to the penguins in order to hear the sound of a human voice? Did he construct anything? How did he keep himself warm at night?

Can you imagine his excitement on the day of his rescue? Perhaps you would like to write your story from Maxfield's point of view, as he relates the tale of his adventures to his rescuers.

## Additional Challenge

### *Hyperbole*

The literary term "hyperbole" is defined as an exaggeration or overstatement made to emphasize a point.

One example of a hyperbole that you might be familiar with is:

*"I'm so hungry I could eat a horse."*

Other examples:

*He is carrying the weight of the world on his shoulders.*

*A dad asked his son, who was busily digging in the sandbox, "Are you digging a hole to China?"*

*Her constant nail biting is driving me crazy.*

*One confident man told his friend, "If I'm wrong, I'll eat my hat."*

In our story, Maxfield might distort and exaggerate things because of his hunger, fatigue, or loneliness. Can you think of something he might say, based on what he might be feeling?

# 11

## The Alligator[B][I]

Years ago, when my father was young, he went to South America on business. While there, he planned to visit a missionary who had spoken at his church some months earlier. He had been fascinated with this man's account of the natives. Therefore, when his business meetings were over, he ventured out on horseback to the area where he had been told the missionary lived. As he was riding along a shore, something shiny lying among the grasses caught his eye. With his riding crop still in his hand, he leapt from his horse and ran down to see what it was.

As he got nearer, a huge alligator suddenly sprang at him. "It was the largest one I ever saw!" said Father. He had only his riding crop with which to defend himself. Swiftly he removed his coat and wrapped it around the crop just in time to thrust it into the alligator's gaping mouth, yelling for help as he did so. Again and again the creature sprang at him. Father's strength was almost gone, but he kept calling out for help while pushing back with his meager means of self-defense.

How did Father free himself? Did anyone else enter the scene? Follow your own free flow of writing about what you imagine is happening in this picture and what will come of it. Then refer to Writing Help if you would like some suggestions of how to fill out (or polish) your story with more description.

## Writing Help

Describe the alligator by *showing* with words what he looks, smells, or sounds like. Describe the struggle that took place. Tell about the surroundings. Also, describe the various emotions Father experienced over the course of time, especially at the end of the struggle. What role might any added characters play in the story?

## Additional Challenge

### *Vivid Verbs*

When there is strenuous or exciting action in a good story, you will find vivid verbs. (Refer to the lesson "Vivid Verbs.") Can you pick out any vivid verbs in the story starter? Go back over what you have written and insert vivid verbs in place of any less descriptive ones you may have used. If you would like some ideas, here are a few suggestions below.

**Vivid Verbs:** shove, propel, plunge, stumble, ram, slip, sink, brace, exert, plummet, strike, recoil, stagger, boost.

Hint: If a person is able to hold an alligator's snout closed, he is less likely to be bitten. An alligator has a weak muscle for opening its mouth, but very strong ones for closing it.

# 12

## A California Flood(I)

One day my neighbor, Mr. Robbins, and I set out in the wagon in the direction of the forest, which was in the foothills some miles distant. We were going to look for old wood for fuel. The dirt road through the plains was muddy, because it had been raining hard for days. Once we had crossed the plains, however, the going was fine. The mountains before us were dazzling white with snow. As we were nearing our destination, we met a man who said that rising swells of water were coming along the *slough, flooding everything. We hesitated for a moment, but as we were in need of fuel, we ventured on, supposing that the man was exaggerating.

Within moments the horses, sensing danger, became nervous. Mr. Robbins stopped the wagon and held the reins tight. Then we saw it! The water was plunging down the river in a vast wave. We yelled at the horses, urging them to go at full gallop. And they *did go*! The water in the first ditch was not flowing at any great speed, so we crossed that easily, and

---

*A "slough" is a wide shallow ditch; an overflow of the river.

made another mad gallop for the next. Here the water was overflowing on both sides, carrying stumps of trees and debris along with it. At first the horses refused to cross this wide ditch, but after some encouragement they boldly plunged in.

The horses swam and scrambled in a manner that made me fear that they would break their legs. We got across, although we were carried a long way downstream. Then we made another mad gallop across the flat plain towards home, the water following us nearly all the way. Mr. Robbins was greatly concerned for his wife and children because their ranch is near a brook. Mine is on higher ground a little farther away. I said a prayer for them and us as we were being roughly jostled about in the wagon. Floating debris and branches hit the sides of the wagon with such bangs that I thought we would never get it home in one piece. The sky got darker. Would it rain again?

What did the two men find upon returning home? Using the pictures describe the continuing action.

## Writing Help

Who was brave? Helpers need to be brave as well as those who are being helped. There is no dialogue in this story starter, but you may add characters and conversation to your part of the story.

Mr. Robbins' friend, one of the two men in the wagon, is telling the story as a first-person narrative. You may continue to tell it from his point of view, or from the point of view of any character you choose.

## Additional Challenge

### *Theme*

The literary term "theme" means the general idea, principle, or insight about life that a writer wishes to express. As you finish the story,

especially as you give it a conclusion, you'll be developing the theme. Is the focus on bravery, self-sacrifice, God's care in our lives, or teamwork? Think about defining and developing your theme.

# 13

# Perfect Weather for Cycling

October in Ireland was unusually warm and dry that year—perfect weather for cycling. During the early weeks of October, Eddie McLaughlin frequently rode his bicycle over to Brendan O'Riley's cottage on the edge of town. Just beyond Brendan's street was the countryside, which was Eddie's favorite destination. Every time he asked Brendan to join him, he was turned down. Eddie knew Brendan had a good bicycle, because he rode it to school and back every day. But he never rode it after school.

When he talked to his mother about it, she couldn't think why the boys were such good friends in the classroom but after school were not able to get together. Neither boy had a brother and Eddie's mother believed they would have benefited from each other's company. However, Eddie decided to stop asking Brendan to accompany him on his trips out to the country. He didn't want to be a bother.

One evening Eddie mentioned his disappointment to his father. "Do you think it's because they're Catholic and we're Protestant?" he asked.

"I don't think so, son. At least, I hope not." At Dad's suggestion, they prayed about the matter. Meanwhile, as Mom was tucking Eddie's little sister into bed, she was giving the mystery more thought.

Later, Mom and Dad were sitting downstairs having their nightly cup of milky coffee together. "I think I saw Brendan's mother working in the bakery yesterday afternoon," she said to Dad. "She wasn't waiting on customers. She was working in the back. When the swinging doors were open for a moment, I caught a glimpse of her. I didn't recognize her at first, because she was wearing a *charwoman's clothes and she was covered with flour from head to toe. But the more I think of it, the more I'm guessing it was Mrs. O'Riley. She must start the clean-up shift as soon as Brendan is home from school and available to watch his little sister." She sipped her coffee and continued, "She should be about the same age as our Lizzie."

"As a fisherman, I expect Mr. O'Riley is at sea for weeks at a time. It mustn't be easy for her." Even before he could reach the end of his sentence, Mom's eyes brightened.

"I have an idea!" she said enthusiastically. "I'll drop by to see Mrs. O'Riley in the morning. I hope she accepts my offer."

"Jolly good," said Dad. "And what offer is that?"

Mom attempts to solve a problem in this story starter. Your part of the story will be carrying that out. Add more conversation in the story if you'd like. Does everything go smoothly? Does Eddie ever go cycling with Brendan? How does it all work out?

## Additional Challenge

Would you like to go cycling with a friend across the countryside and still be home in time for supper? What would you see in Ireland if you cycled there?

*A "charwoman" is a cleaning lady. The little word "char" inside charwoman means chore.

# 14

## Up, Up, and Away

Jacques' mother had grown accustomed to Jacques' daring attempts at ballooning. He was always trying new experiments. Jacques was the young successful chemist in town who spent all of his spare time at his hobby—building balloons and flying in them. Sadly, Jacques' father had died of influenza during the winter, and Jacques had noticed a change in his mother. She had begun to worry. And she often told him that he should settle down and marry. Jacques waved it off. He knew his mother was lonely now that Papa was gone.

"Oh Jacques, must you go out ballooning today? Wednesday you didn't come home until after dark. Each time you fly, you go higher and farther away. What if you land in the streets of Paris, or are blown out to sea?" Her eyes grew large as the thought suddenly presented itself. "And you're not a very good swimmer."

"Mama, it isn't like you to worry. What's come over you?" But he silently answered his own question. His mother was afraid of losing him, too.

Actually Mama had a secret. She had invited a lovely young lady to supper. It was to be a surprise. The young lady was Sylvia, the nurse that had so tenderly attended Jacques' dad when he was so ill. She knew

Jacques probably thought of Sylvia as being "nice," but she also knew that his mind ran in a rut—on all the possibilities of perfecting his skills as a balloonist. She had been hoping to give him a new interest. Now she would have to postpone her birthday surprise, and the thought of walking all the way to the hospital to tell Sylvia the change of plans perturbed her.

"But Jacques, it's your birthday! I'm cooking your favorite dish of roast stuffed goose with orange sauce. You didn't tell me you'd be flying again so soon."

"Sorry, Mama. I thought you knew. I shouldn't have assumed. But you *did* know the balloon race is coming up and I need all the practice I can get. Why not save the goose to celebrate my winning the race?" He was a jolly boaster, wiggling his eyebrows as he poked fun. When this didn't bring a big smile to her face as he expected, he was a bit *chagrined. Mama instead sat down calmly. She was taking a few moments to swallow her disappointment. When she spoke, Jacques thought she sounded more like her old cheerful self.

"You're right, of course. You need to be ready for the race. I'll cook the goose tomorrow and we can celebrate your birthday then, if you like."

"And you'll promise not to worry?" Jacques urged.

"I can't promise, but I'll try," she spoke truthfully. "Here, take this bread and cheese just in case."

"In case of what?" he asked, for he had just eaten.

"Just in case, that's all," she said, not really knowing the answer.

"Thank you, Mama. You're sweet." He graciously accepted the bundle she held out to him, kissed her good-bye on the cheek, and was

---

*To be a bit "chagrined" is to be slightly uneasy, disappointed, or humiliated.

off. Remembering one last thing, he turned around to say, "Oh, I'm taking Jip with me this time." Jip was their obedient dog.

"Why?" she called after him.

He called back, "He likes flying. Today he's going to be my opponent. We're racing."

Finally he got her to smile. She threw her tea towel in his direction—a gesture that let him know she thought he was *bonkers.

Using both pictures, tell about Jacques' adventurous day. Then tell what else happened that week and how the balloon race went.

## Writing Help

This story will give you plenty of opportunity to use sensory language. Go back over your story and add a description what any of the characters could have watched, heard, smelled, touched, or tasted.

What do your characters say? Adding conversation lets your readers learn more about your characters.

*If someone is "bonkers" he is not in his right mind. It is slang for "crazy."

# 15

## Katie's Dilemma[B]

Katie's dad works in an office downtown, but his hobby is keeping an orchard of cherry trees behind their house. He faithfully keeps his trees pruned, fed, weeded and watered. Katie and her dad often walk up and down the rows of the orchard together. These walks are particularly splendid in the spring when the bows are thick with bright blossoms. This is how Daddy likes to unwind from the tense cares and concerns of the office, and it allows him to spend some time outdoors with his Katie.

One bright warm morning during the hot month of June, Katie was helping her mom pick cherries. She didn't mind working in the strong rays of the sun, because she was allowed to eat the delicious ripe cherries as she picked. "Daddy probably wishes he were here with us," Katie thought out loud.

"Yes," Mother agreed, removing her straw hat momentarily to fan herself with it. "Rather than be in his office on a beautiful day as today," she added. "But he picked bushelsful last evening. Now it's our turn," she reassured Katie with a smile.

After about an hour and a half of picking, Katie and her mom went inside to have some lunch. Immediately following, Mother set about to prepare for the guests that were expected for supper. Some of Dad's business associates and their wives were coming. While Mother attended to the details required of the evening's four-course meal in the big kitchen, Katie tidied up the house. She dusted, polished, and swept. Then she very willingly helped set the dining room table with the fruit-patterned dishes and crystal glasses from the china cabinet. Mother inspected Katie's work and was pleased. "The table looks lovely," she said. Their afternoon's preparations were nearly finished. After Mother fluffed up the pillows in the parlor she climbed the stairs a little heavily. Laying out Katie's best dress on her bed, she announced, "I'm going to get off my feet for a bit." Giving her some instructions that included one last detail, she retreated into her bedroom for an anticipated repose (nap). After her own quiet time Katie was to dress and then, at six o'clock, set out a basket of Dad's freshly-picked cherries in the parlor—just before the guests arrived.

The time had come. Katie, in her prettiest dress, carried the cherries in from the cool pantry, to the parlor. "How pretty the dark red cherries look," she thought. "Daddy will be so proud of these," she said aloud. Katie decided the cherries would look nicest displayed on the polished table, but then conscientiously noted that the table should have a doily on it so that the basket would not scratch it in any way. Very carefully she placed the cherries down on a chair while she searched the china cabinet for an extra doily. Just then she heard voices. The sound of laughing and talking came from the front hall. She was caught by surprise. "They're here!" she realized.

Poor Katie! Describe how the accident took place. Have you ever accidentally stained anything nice? If you have, you will be able to sympathize with Katie; that is, you will know how she feels. Good writers sympathize with the people in their own lives, and consequently with the characters they write about.

## Writing Help

- Do the guests arrive at the very same moment as the accident? Or does Katie, run upstairs, take off the dress and try to clean it herself? Is she in tears? What does Mother say when she discovers Katie and her dilemma? What is Dad's response? Did Katie care more about her dress, the parlor chair, or the cherries, or all three?
- What creative kind words could the guests speak that would make her feel better?
- How was Katie learning to be a hostess? What encouragement did she receive for all her efforts to serve?
- How did the rest of the evening go? Did the guests get a tour of the orchard?

# 16

## The Toy Maker

When Winslow was very young, he enjoyed playing with the wooden toys his father secretly made for him each Christmastime. What so fascinated him was that the little figures of people, animals, and buildings could be taken apart and fitted back together. As Winslow got older he became more interested in how his toys were made than in playing with them, and he shared his curiosity with his father. His father was happy to spend some of his free time with his son in the workshop behind their house. Thus Winslow was taught how to work with various tools. He first learned the skills of sawing, measuring, carving, and painting by constructing larger toys. Gradually, over the course of a year or so, Winslow developed enough ease and *dexterity in the use of his tools that his father began to instruct him in the making of smaller toys with more delicate pieces.

One night at eleven o'clock, Winslow's mother got up to close a drafty window and noticed that Winslow's light was still on in his room.

*If you have what the word "dexterity" describes, you have skill in your hands.

After investigating, she woke her husband. "Where's Winslow? His lamp is lit in his bedroom but he isn't there."

"Could he be in the workshop at this late hour?" responded Father. "I'll go have a look."

"I'll go, too. He knows he has schoolwork to do in the morning. What's this all about?" Mother was *miffed.

They walked onto the back garden in their slippers and robes without taking a lamp, as the moon, though hazy, was full and softly luminous. A gentle, almost undetectable drizzle of rain moistened their cheeks as they crossed the lawn in the cool night air. A moment later they were standing in the open doorway of the workshop, motionless and speechless, their eyes fixed upon their son. He didn't notice them. His eyes were fixed as well—on the tiny toys he was painting.

At last, Father broke the silence. "Well done, son! These toys are capital!"

Winslow turned in surprise. "Oh, I didn't know you were there."

Mother stepped over to the worktable and gingerly picked up one toy that wasn't yet painted, examining it closely. "They're lovely, Winslow. And what a large batch you've made!"

Father was still amazed and rather impressed at his son's capabilities and raised a discerning brow. "There's real talent here."

"Thanks Mom and Dad." Winslow smiled widely.

Then Father, as was his duty, referred to the hour. "You must not have realized how late it's gotten. You really should clean up now and get to bed."

"Yes, sir. Sorry, sir. You see, a few weeks ago I got an idea of how I could make some money."

Continue the story, introducing the shopkeeper and other characters. What does the shopkeeper think of Winslow's toys? If he does put the

---

*To say Mother was "miffed" is to say she was not pleased (and perhaps a little cross) at the situation.

toys in his shop, does anyone buy them, or do they not sell well? Have you ever made anything that you wanted to sell?

## Additional Challenge

### *Conflict*

Other than Winslow staying up past his bedtime, there is very little conflict in this story starter, which leaves room for you to add conflict. Perhaps Winslow makes a habit of staying up *very* late (even past midnight). Though warned by his parents not to, he is in the workshop much longer than is good for him. Would his studies or household chores suffer because he is giving so much energy to toy making? Perhaps he learns a lesson of moderation.

For added story development, provide a business history of Winslow's toy-making venture. Does he make the money on his toys that he had envisioned making? Do they sell well or do they remain in the toyshop untouched?

### *Artful Adjectives*

I invite you to go back over your story and give more description to something in your story by using adjectives. Refer to lesson "Artful Adjectives."

In my story starter I described the moon and the rain with adjectives. I wrote that "the moon, though *hazy*, was *softly luminous*" because I wanted you to see the moon I saw in my imagination. I wanted you to feel the rain my characters were feeling in the story and so I described it with adjectives. I wrote that it was, "a *gentle, almost undetectable drizzle* of rain.

# 17

## A Friendly Horse to a Trickster

One day as I was leaving my field, one of my horses galloped up and repeatedly nudged my arm. "Hold on, Snowdrift. What's come over you?" Snowdrift had never before acted in such a manner and I didn't know what to do. Finally I realized that Snowdrift was trying to pull me in the direction he wished me to go. Once he realized I was paying attention to him, he turned and trotted off towards the pasture that was on a neighboring farm. Moments later he trotted up to me again. He was very excited and seemed by his actions to wish me to follow him. "Yes, I'm coming," I reassured him.

When I reached the pasture, somewhat bewildered and out of breath, I saw Houdini, my neighbor's horse. The poor horse had had an accident on the bridge that spanned the stream that ran through the meadow. At that moment I recalled how the horse came to be called by his *new* name, the name of that world-famous escape artist, Harry Houdini. The horse had been spotted in places where his master had been surprised to find him. Evidently, his ability to slip his head out of his halter was finally spied out, as well as his ability to withdraw the bolt

of the stable door. Because it was also observed that after enjoying himself in the open air for a time, he would return to the stable and bolt the door behind him, nothing was done to prevent this horse-escape-artist from performing his tricks when he wanted. Houdini's master found the tricks a funny joke. They gave him something to brag about.

As I approached the poor animal, I thought that perhaps something *should* have been done, because now he was in a dangerous predicament, one that Houdini, this time, could not get out of by himself. My own horse Snowdrift was pacing back and forth and stomping the ground in an agitated manner.

Look at the picture. Describe Houdini's predicament. What steps were taken to rescue poor Houdini?

## Writing Help

- Horses are beautiful animals. I put horses in my story starters because I know some of you like them, too. Horses can become very frightened and panicked. Was Houdini hurt? What happened to his legs when he struggled? How could his struggling cause more difficulty?
- Does your story have a happy ending? When Snowdrift's master takes care of the situation, how does the horse react?
- Would you like to have a horse like Snowdrift? How might Snowdrift be rewarded?
- Continue to tell the story any way you like or like I did; from the point of view of Snowdrift's master.

## Additional Challenge

### *Conflict Resolution*

Every good story has conflict. In this story-starter, nature caused the conflict. The weather, over time, rotted some of the boards of the wooden bridge and made it dangerous. Conflict resolution is a fancy term for how the conflict is made right. How is the problem dealt with? How do the characters struggle to do what is right or make things better? As you finish this story, you will be providing conflict resolution. Add characters, if you like, to help the main character. On the other hand, perhaps your added characters will make things even more difficult by having conflicting opinions about how to solve the problem.

Snowdrift's master suggested another conflict. He thought that perhaps Houdini's master should have done something to prevent his horse from getting out whenever he wanted.

# 18

## Jasper Saves the Baby[B][I]

*Note to Teacher: Although I specify that the baby is unharmed in the title and the questions, this picture and story may be too intense or too scary for the very young child.*

One lovely spring day, Mother set the baby in its little wicker cradle on the screen porch for some fresh air. She hummed a lullaby as she rocked the baby to sleep. Near her feet, Jasper, their faithful dog, was napping, too. After awhile she opened the porch door and stepped out into yard to see whether the sheets on the clothes-line were dry. They were not. Returning to the porch, she smiled as she saw that the baby was still asleep, even though the porch door had squeaked as it closed behind her. "I guess something should be done about that rusty spring," she thought halfheartedly.

Walking into the kitchen, only a few yards away from the baby, Mother checked on the soup simmering on the stove and started to mix some biscuit dough. Her husband, Seth, who worked nearby, would be home for lunch very soon. A breeze was picking up and she heard the

porch door squeak and bang as it always did when it was windy or when anyone went in or out. "That must be Seth," she thought to herself sensibly. But as she stood on the threshold of the porch, expecting to greet him, her eyes, instead, where met with a horrible sight. A mangy, desperate-looking dog had slunk onto the porch. She was frozen in shock, both hands covering her mouth to repress a scream.

Describe Jasper springing into action. How does he save the baby?

## Writing Help

- What frightening sounds do you hear? What does Mother do?
- Does Seth, the baby's dad, enter the scene? What does he do?
- How relieved is Mother that her baby is unharmed? Was Jasper unharmed or does he need attention? What becomes of the mangy dog?

# 19

# The Elephant's New Calf[B]

*Do you like elephants? I do. That is why I am happy to include a story about an elephant in this book. The first part of the story is rumored to be true.*

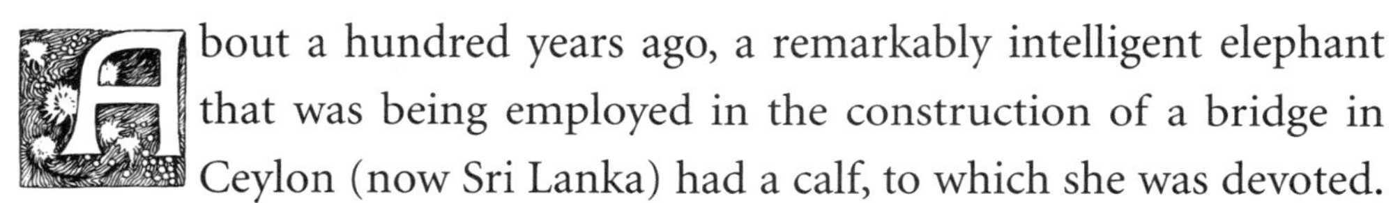

About a hundred years ago, a remarkably intelligent elephant that was being employed in the construction of a bridge in Ceylon (now Sri Lanka) had a calf, to which she was devoted. (A baby elephant is called a calf.) The calf became sick and died. The mother became inconsolable. Formerly the gentlest of creatures, she grew irritable. Her irritability made her dangerous, and her owner was forced to chain her up. One day, with the strength in her powerful body, she broke the chain that confined her and escaped into the forest. Nothing was seen of her until one night, about ten days after her escape, the man who had been in charge of her went out to fish at a pond in the jungle some distance from the camp. As he and his attendant were returning early in the morning, the attendant silently nudged him, and

they saw, in the dim, gray light, an elephant with a calf making their way towards the camp.

The two men hid behind the trees so they could watch without being seen, and when the elephants had passed, they agreed that the

elder one was their old friend, the inconsolable mother. When they reached the camp they found that the runaway had returned, and had gone from person to person, touching each one with her trunk, as if exhibiting her adopted child, which she had evidently begged, borrowed, or stolen from somewhere in the jungle. Her good temper and usual docility were at once restored, and her owner was very thankful for the vacation that had enabled her to procure a new baby elephant.

Tame and trained elephants were needed for a construction site closer to the city. Being warned that the baby elephant was not, under any circumstances, to be separated from its new mother, the two were transported together by train to the work site. During the trip the calf had somehow gashed its head, probably on a sharp piece of railing.

The cut was beginning to swell and ooze with infection, and so a veterinary surgeon was called. He came prepared to dress and care for the wound. The calf let him come near, but as soon as the surgeon reached out to touch its head, it drew away. The surgeon tried over and over again, with no success. He stood motionless, medicine in hand, wondering what to do next, when suddenly; the mother elephant lifted her trunk up and trumpeted a high-pitched wail. Obviously she was becoming irritated, so the surgeon thought he had better give up, sleep on what to do, and come back the next day, hopefully with a new idea. Yet it wasn't the surgeon that irritated the mother elephant. She was irritated and impatient with her baby.

What did the mother elephant do when the vet arrived the next morning? Describe the reaction of the onlookers? What was the surgeon thinking?

## Additional Challenge

For story development, think up other episodes involving the same Asian elephant characters. You will find pictures and information on both Sri Lanka and elephants in the encyclopedia that will help you imagine your setting. Perhaps you would like to write a story about the African elephant. The African elephant has larger ears and in fact is larger all over. The African elephant is more difficult to tame than the Asian elephant.

# 20

## Shipwreck (I)

Many ships had been coming from Ireland bringing destitute families and orphans who were fleeing the potato famine. Often the ships were ill equipped and unfit for the journey, but their passengers' empty stomachs caused them to take risks they wouldn't ordinarily have ever thought of taking.

One day Grace and her father were riding along the hillside by the rocky shore near their home. One glance at the ship amid the foamy waves below alerted them to the disaster brewing.

"Let's go!" her father yelled out. "We must help them!" Without a moment's hesitation, Grace's father dashed ahead on his noble steed. Grace, an excellent rider, followed her father down the slope of the pebbly cliff to the shore. She had little time to think about the danger that lay ahead. As she entered the cold, rough water, however, she asked God for courage. Numerous passengers called for help. She didn't know which way to turn.

"Grace, help the children!" her father yelled above the roar of the waves. "And don't go in too deep!"

Take over the story from here. Make the characters come alive.

## Writing Help

You don't need to answer all of the questions here. Choose only the ones that bring the best ideas to mind.

How are the passengers helpful to each other? How frightened and weak are some? What role did the horse play? What difficulties could have arisen? Could Grace and her father manage the rescue themselves, or did Father send Grace to ride off to get help?

What happened to the ship and its passengers, the captain, the families, the sailors, and the children? I invite you to write your story either from Grace's point of view or from that of a passenger (perhaps one of the children).

How do the good people of the little white church in the seaside town care for the survivors? Are the survivors thankful to God, and to Grace and her father, and to the townspeople? How would you describe their gratitude?

Were there relatives who were expecting the passengers and praying for their safe arrival? Does Grace make a friend? Create characters that are passengers from the wrecked ship.

# 21

## The Circus Clown's Son[B]

It was another busy day under the big tent. Bubbles the clown was doing his best to make the children in the bleachers roar with laughter. He juggled china plates that sometimes fell to the ground with a crash. He imitated the circus animals. He turned clumsy somersaults and demonstrated tricks with paper flowers. He usually liked performing for the crowd, but today he couldn't stop thinking about his son Mark, who lay in bed, sick with a fever. He finished his act by pulling a live wiggling fish from his trousers and ran from the ring, anxious to reach his son's side.

Back in his trailer he knelt down beside Mark and felt his head. The fever hadn't left him. Just then Mark awoke, and his dad got him to swallow some water, imploring him to try some pieces of candy apple.

Suddenly there was a knock at the door. Bubbles opened it and before him stood a boy, neatly dressed. The boy had a pleasant and polite way about him and complimented Bubbles on his very funny

routines. He explained to the clown his reason for coming. His father, the local town doctor, wished to hire Bubbles to entertain a group of children at the hospital before the circus left town the following morning.

The boy looked around at the dark trailer with its tattered rug and *scarcity of furnishings. With a start he noticed Bubbles' son lying pale and still in a small bed behind the door. He wondered to himself, "What could possibly be the matter?"

What does the clown decide to do? What happens next?

## Writing Help

I left out conversation in this story starter, but you can be the one to break the silence. Make the characters speak. If the clown gives a performance to the sick children in the hospital, will there be a kind deed done toward him in return? Who does the kind deed? What happens to his son, Mark?

## Additional Challenge

*Sympathy*

A good author cares about his characters, and this makes his readers care, too. Sympathizing with the characters in a story starter enables you to write your part of the story as if you really care about what happens to them. Such characters seem to come "off the page," because they seem more real. Can you sympathize with what the clown might feel at this moment?

---

*The word "scarcity" tells that there was very little furniture in the room. "Meager" is another word to describe the opposite of plentiful.

# 22

# Pamela's Hat

Pamela lived with her parents and four brothers in a brick row house in the city of Philadelphia. There was no grass in front of her house as its front steps touched the sidewalk that was only a few feet from the cobblestone street. Spaces had been left at regular intervals in the sidewalk and in each space a small tree had been planted. A fancy wrought iron fence encircled each tree. Flower boxes adorned the windows. The people who lived in these houses were pleasant, quiet, orderly, respectable people who worked diligently at their professions. They went out regularly and came home punctually. Pamela's father played violin in an orchestra and also bought and sold string instruments. The instruments were displayed in the front parlor, where customers were served "by appointment only." Over the front door hung a wooden sign carved in the shape of a violin with the words "Marton's Strings" painted in gold letters.

Pamela loved the part of the city in which she lived. She knew all the neighbors on the block and had many friends at the girls' finishing

school that she attended. She could get anywhere easily by foot or by streetcar, which made window-shopping convenient. Hats were her favorite item. In those days a lady would not think of leaving the house without her hat and gloves. It was considered disgraceful.

Because Pamela was so dependable about completing her chores as well as waiting on customers in her father's shop, her mother, knowing how much she loved hats, encouraged her to buy a new one. Pamela happily browsed the shops for months. Finally she spotted one that she said would "positively make" her summer and made her purchase.

One sunny Saturday on the brink of summer, she was getting ready to visit the Philadelphia Zoo with her brother Robert and two other friends. It was a very special occasion, because she was planning to wear her brand new hat.

"What do you think of my new bonnet, Robert?" Pamela asked, gazing at her reflection in the front hall mirror and making tiny adjustments to the position of her hat on her head.

Tactfully he replied, "If *you* like it, that's all that matters."

"Oh, I shouldn't have asked you," Pamela responded in a bit of a huff. "Come on, or we'll be late meeting the others."

Robert turned to his mother, who stood in the doorway, to see them off, and asked in a low tone, "Mother, how can you let Pam go out in that ridiculous hat?" He pretended to be disgusted, but he was smiling.

"It's not so bad, Robert. A young woman likes to feel pretty and to have pretty things."

"She's pretty enough without that hat."

"Why don't you tell her?" she cheerfully suggested. At that, Robert shrugged his shoulders and turned to go.

The pair met Pamela's friend Deirdre and Robert's college chum Sinclair at the corner grocery where they were to catch a streetcar. "I've been so looking forward to today, haven't you, Pammy?" Deirdre asked.

"Yes! It *was* my idea, remember?" Just then the trolley pulled up to where they were standing. As Pamela stepped to climb on to the car, her foot slipped on the edge of a crumbling piece of curb.

"Oh, dear!" she cried. "The heel of my shoe has come off!"

"Don't worry. Joe's shoe repair shop is just across the street," said Robert.

Joe's shop was deep and narrow, and somewhat cave-like, as the main source of light came from the front window. But Joe's cheerful smile made the shop seem bright, and he was willing to put his other customers' shoes aside to work on a "good lady's" shoe. "Because it is an emergency," he said. The musky scent of leather and shoe polish hung heavy in the air as they waited. After a bit of hammering the shoe was finished. Then Joe knelt before Pamela and buckled the shoe on her foot as if it were Cinderella's glass slipper. Robert, very grateful, gave Joe a firm handshake and some coins.

With smiles of relief they all walked back out into the bright sunshine and crossed the street to wait for the next streetcar. Suddenly, a newspaper boy on a bicycle flew by, riding through the center of the muddy puddle in the street right in front of Pamela. The muddy water splashed up and made a brown stain at the hem of her dress.

"Oh, what a shame," Deirdre said sympathetically.

Pamela was beginning to feel a little upset, but she responded gaily, "Never mind. It can easily be washed out. Here's the trolley."

Evidently, after two weeks of gray skies and drizzly rain, a lot of other people had also decided to spend this sunny Saturday out of doors. A crowd had gathered at the entrance to the zoo, which only made the outing all the merrier for Pamela, who loved a bit of society. They stood waiting in line and chatting, shaded by a row of lovely chestnut trees. The wait was a pleasant one, until it was interrupted by a woman plowing through the crowd, pushing a baby carriage. The baby was screaming. As the carriage squeezed past them, they were wedged against a metal fence.

"Really! What manners!" Sinclair commented.

"Never mind," Pamela responded, "the line is moving." But when she stepped forward to go, she found that the back of her dress was caught on the fence.

"Don't pull it," commanded Robert at once. "Here, let me unhook it for you." At that very instant, as he was working to free the material, a squirrel scrambled down the branch of a tree, and using Robert's arm as its last path to the ground, boldly begged handouts from the crowd. Robert jerked his arm in surprise and the dress tore. A piece of it clung to the fence.

Robert expressed his surprise, "What on earth!"

"Where'd *he* come from?" Sinclair asked rhetorically.

"It's torn!" Pamela whimpered, as she twisted round to inspect the damage. She thought to herself that such a tear would not be able to be mended properly.

"Never mind," said Deirdre, who guessed what she was thinking. "We can hold the tear together with a pin. I know I have one in here somewhere," she added, as she fished in her handbag. At last the pin was found, but it was a small consolation to Pamela. Not wanting to spoil the day for those with her, however, she tried to make light of it. "First my heel, then my dress. What more could possibly go wrong?" she said lightly, hands in the air.

No one, of course, answered. Sinclair politely turned their thoughts back to the purpose of their excursion. "We've got to see the lions first."

"Yes, we must," Robert echoed. The two escorts each lifted an elbow for the ladies and the walk began. It took them clear away to the far side of the zoo. Much of the walk was in the sunshine, and when the lemonade stand came into view, Pamela realized how thirsty she had become.

"I'm buying," said Sinclair cheerfully. Refreshing iced drinks were handed all around, and then Sinclair said, pointing to a sign, "The African animals are just up ahead. Let's go this way." Sipping their lemonades, they continued their stroll.

Suddenly Sinclair noticed that a sugar-loving wasp had perched itself on the brim of Pamela's cup. "Pamela, don't move," he commanded her. "I'll get rid of it." Waving his hand over the cup proved unsuccessful, so he attempted to take the cup away, but in the process he knocked the cup and spilled the lemonade down the front of Pamela's dress. Sinclair was sincerely sorry. Deirdre, covering her mouth, held back a gasp. Too stunned for words, tears filled Pamela's eyes.

Robert speedily supplied a clean handkerchief and ushered them forward to a fork in the path. He suggested letting the girls have some time to themselves for a while. "Look over there. There's a water fountain, girls. That might help. We'll meet you in about twenty minutes at the um…the giraffes, okay? You can't miss those things."

Pamela only nodded and gave her brother a weak smile. She felt *buffeted by the mishaps of the day. Some time alone with Deirdre, however, to chat as ladies do, while her dress dried, helped Pamela slowly to unwind. When Deirdre commented on her friend's hat, asking if it was new, Pamela replied, "I was wondering when you'd notice. Do you like it?"

"I love it," Deirdre said honestly. Then she added, "You know, I don't think we've seen a single animal at this zoo yet today."

Pamela lifted her eyebrows, and then laughed. "How silly. You're right. Shall we go?"

And off they walked toward the giraffes, happy friends in the sunshine.

---

*To be "buffeted" is to be struck repeatedly.

Tell what happened next at the zoo next and the remainder of the day.

## Writing Help

- Employ a little conversation in your story. Consider Pamela's feelings. She had worked hard for this hat and the day hadn't been going well for her from the start. What is the cause and effect—the action and reaction of the characters?
- What was Robert's response? You know a little about his character from his early responses. What action does he take?
- Describe their surroundings at the zoo.

### *Foreshadowing*

Foreshadowing is a literary term that means the use of hints or clues about events that occur later in the story. Pamela's question (What more can possible go wrong?) is one foreshadowing that I wrote into the story. There is another. Do you remember the brief conversation Robert had with his mother before he left the house? Go back and read it again. How can you use this clue for your ending? In other words, upon Mother's suggestion, what might Robert admit to his sister to make her feel better? How does Deirdre react?

## Additional Challenge

### *Artful Adjectives*

Adjectives will help describe the objects (nouns) in your story. At the beginning of the story, when I described the setting—the street in Philadelphia where Pamela lived—I wrote that the *small* trees were each protected by a *fancy wrought iron* fence. If I had written "fence" without its adjectives (*fancy wrought iron*), you might have pictured it as a *white picket* fence.

I might have written that above the front door there was a sign with the words "Marton's Strings." But don't you have a better picture in your imagination of that sign because I've written that the sign was *wooden,* that it was carved in the shape of a violin, and that the letters on the sign were painted in *gold*? These details create in my reader's imagination a better picture of the street where Pamela lived.

Where can you add one or two artful adjectives to your story? You can go back after you've written your first draft and polish it up with adjectives.

# 23

## Worn Out

Mom was going away to visit her sister, who was about to have a baby. She would be away for at least a week and was taking two-year-old Christy with her. Dad was to be left "holding the fort" as he called it. His list of chores would get longer, as he would be doing so many of the things that Mom usually did, as well as his own day's work.

"Are you sure you can cope?" Mom asked Dad after she had told him, again, of all that needed doing.

"No, not *absolutely* sure," Dad confessed, "but I will do my best. I keep the gristmill running, don't I?" Dad was a miller, and ground grain for the whole community. He continued, "Allister and I want you to see your sister. Don't we, Allister? And we know she will be glad for all your help after the new baby arrives."

Mom turned to Allister. "There is a lot to do and you will be kept very busy. Remember all the outside and inside chores we talked about?"

"Yes, Mom."

"Remember to bring in the eggs from the coop every day and keep the chickens fed and watered."

"Yes, Mom."

"And water the vegetable garden, too, if it doesn't rain."

"Yes, Mom."

And keep your clothes on their pegs and not on the floor."

"Yes, Mom. I'll be very good, Mom."

Uncle Oswald was waiting in the wagon. His horse was pawing the ground in impatience. Therefore, Dad insisted that his wife go straightaway. He picked up Christy and leading his wife firmly by the arm, he steered her out to the wagon. "Go. We've gone over the list enough times. If you don't get in this wagon this instant, your sister will have her baby without you." Once she was finally seated in the wagon he set Christy on her lap and gave them each a kiss.

"I shall miss you," she said, and waved again and again as the wagon carried her down the road.

That evening, after finishing his work in the mill next door, Dad began cooking supper. Allister watched. "Did you feed the chickens, son?" Dad asked, as he flipped a pancake and added more fat to the pan.

"Yes, Dad. Whatcha making?"

"I've got some bacon, a nice stack of pancakes here, and with the peas you picked and shelled, we'll have a nice supper."

Allister watched his Dad pour some milk over the peas. "Pancakes and creamed peas?"

"Yes; and it's very wholesome nourishment, too. You may set the table now."

As the two were eating their meal—Allister trying to keep his pancakes separated from his peas—a knock was heard at the kitchen door, and then it was opened.

"Come in John. What's the latest?"

"I'm looking for my goats. Two broke free of their pen this afternoon. Have you seen 'em?"

"Have we seen any goats out this way, Allister?"

"No, *I* haven't."

"We'll keep a lookout though, John." Dad assured his neighbor.

"Thanks. Sorry I barged in on your supper."

"Will you join us?" Dad put in politely.

Their neighbor frowned at the plates of food as if he had bad eyesight, scratched his head, and said, "No thanks, I best get looking for my goats." Then he couldn't help smiling. "Where's the missus?"

"She's off visiting her sister."

"That figures." He threw his head back and laughed as he closed the door after himself.

Allister's hands were immersed in soapy dishwater. Dad told him conscientiously, "When you're finished with the dishes, don't forget to sweep the floor."

"I won't Dad. I usually do it every night anyway."

"Oh, right. Did you remember to bring in the eggs?"

"I didn't do that yet." Egg collecting was the morning chore he had forgotten, but Allister kept quiet on *that* point.

"I'll do it son. You're busy."

"Thanks, Dad."

How Dad loved evenings in early summer! After a day of clear blue sky, the coolness of the air and the shade of the lingering shadows, made by a sun more slow to set, were so refreshing. He placed the eggs he collected in the basket and walked around the edge of the vegetable garden. Suddenly he burst out, "What on earth?" A wooden fence surrounded the garden, but the gate was open and Dad could see the ravages made on certain rows. Upon closer inspection, much of the lettuce was gone. The peas were still clinging to their trellises, but some of the bush beans had been eaten down to their stems and the carrot tops were definitely cropped. Only the peas, onions, and tomatoes had been left entirely untouched. "John's goats!" Dad thought to himself.

Perturbed, he fastened the gate and with great haste returned to the house and made his announcement to Allister.

"Sorry Dad, I must've left the gate open after I picked the peas."

"Okay, fine. I'm sure you know not to do *that* again."

"Yes," Allister confirmed. "Were there any eggs?" he added, seeing that his Dad was empty-handed.

Dad remembered that he had set down his basket of eggs in the garden when he had made his inspection. "Never mind that. I'm going to look for the goats. Are you finished with the dishes yet?"

"No, but should I let this greasy frying pan soak?"

"Yes. Fine, let's go."

They found the goats lounging under a large shade tree, half-hidden in the tall grass looking very content, their stomachs full. It was no surprise that they didn't budge when a rope was first tied around their necks. It was no easy chore getting them to walk all the way back to neighbor John's. "As stubborn as mules," Dad blurted out, and he treated them accordingly.

Similar mishaps occurred daily throughout the week while Mom was away. Although they could be congratulated for doing their best, in their spare time, the men-folk were not able to keep things running as smoothly as Mom was. At the end of a long week, they were worn out.

Continue the story. Look at the picture of Dad and Allister. Why did I title this story starter "Worn Out"? Write Mom's return into the story. What other mishaps or awkward situations occurred while Mom was away? Did she catch them by surprise when she returned?

## Writing Help

All the hundreds of little daily chores a mother does for her family can be undervalued, or seen as unimportant, because they may *look* easy to do. Over time a mother learns how to "keep up" by doing two or three things at once out of necessity. When Mom is absent the family may appreciate how indispensable she is.

- What were some other chores that they attempted?
- What sorts of things did they miss, or do without, because Mom was away?
- What did she notice about the state of things when she arrived?
- Were they happy to see Mom?

## Additional Challenge

This story starter is full of conversation. Put conversation in your story if you haven't done so already. Notice how the conversation I wrote carries the action. What did you learn about the characters from their conversation?

# 24

## The Donkey's Deed[B]

Roland was a ten-year-old boy who lived on a farm some miles outside a small town in the 1920s. He was a country boy, and country boys had their own donkeys for getting around. Some of the boys in town, however, had acquired bicycles. During the summer only one or two townsmen had purchased bicycles, but by late autumn it was apparent that bicycles were "all the rage." Men, women, and children were seen riding bicycles in town at all hours of the day.

Near the end of autumn Roland noticed that when he came to town on Dingle, his donkey, and encountered the boys in the town on their bicycles, they waved to him as always, but then turned to their buddies and snickered. What was a donkey compared to the speed and convenience of a bicycle? One day, as he was leaving the post office and getting ready to ride Dingle home, he overheard one boy say to another, "Only country bumpkins ride donkeys." Roland was beginning to feel left out.

Back at home, when he related these incidents to his mother, she would say, "It will be a long time before we can save up enough money

for such a thing as a bicycle, Roland. You'll have to be content with what you have, for now. You do like Dingle, don't you?"

"Of course I do, Mom," Roland replied.

"Can you be patient?" she asked gently.

"I'll try."

Though the winter was mild, Roland rode to town only once in awhile. His mother wondered whether he intentionally stayed away so he wouldn't come into contact with the town boys. Mostly Roland studied his homeschool lessons at the kitchen table near the warmth of the cook stove. Once in awhile his friend Ned would ride over to see him. Ned, a country boy like Roland, also had his own donkey. It was a great comfort to Roland to have a friend who, like himself, was also waiting, working, and saving for a bicycle.

Spring came early and it was wet. The rain turned the dirt roads leading to town to *glutinous mud. The country people used their pack animals to bring their wares into town to sell. One Saturday morning, Roland's mother gave him an errand. "Please take these eggs into town for me," she instructed. "The grocer is expecting them. And here's list of things I need. You can use the egg money to buy them." Then she added brightly, "We've a lot more eggs to sell since your help with the chickens."

"Thanks, Mom."

"'Work hard and work smart,' your father always says," she added.

"Yes, Mom."

In town only a few people were out and about. Roland handed the eggs to the grocer and commented on how quiet it was. The grocer told him, "Folks can't get around much when the roads are this muddy."

---

*"Glutinous" is an adjective. Gluten is an elastic protein substance that forms in bread dough when it is kneaded and helps hold the bread together so it won't be crumbly when you slice it. Glutinous mud, therefore, is particularly glue-like and sticky.

"Can't they walk?"

"Sure they can, but they're spoiled, aren't they?"

"Spoiled?"

"They're used to their bicycles and bicycles don't do well in mud, do they?"

"I hadn't thought of that," said Roland.

"That donkey of yours, he can get through *any* weather, can't he?"

His comment brought a big smile to Roland's face. It made the grocer glad to know he had encouraged a boy he knew had been mocked. He handed Roland the money for the eggs and Roland bought the items on his mother's list. He was glad to be starting home with an extra handful of pocket change in the bargain.

Along the way home, he passed Ned, who was also on an errand for his mother. "Come over to my house tomorrow, Ned, and we'll play chess," he said.

"Right–o," Ned replied, then asked, "Did I tell you that I'm getting a bicycle soon?"

"No."

"Dad's taking me to the bicycle shop in Westfield. They have a few used bicycles, not as shiny as new ones, but real swell."

"That's good," Roland said happily. "Well, I'll see you tomorrow."

"Right-o," Ned said.

Roland was glad for him. On second thought, however, he couldn't help concluding that he would soon be the only boy around who did not own a bicycle. Again he felt left out.

Dad met him in the barn on his return. "What's on your mind, son?" he asked, noting Roland's subdued expression. Roland told him Ned's good news. Dad's remedy for keeping his son from self-pity was to respond with his favorite saying, "Work hard and work smart," which reminded Roland of the bonus money from the sale of the eggs. He dug it out of pocket to show it to his father, his good spirits returning. The two walked side by side to the house, where Mother had supper ready for them.

It was a family custom for Dad to read aloud a portion of the Bible every evening. In preparation for Easter, which was fast approaching, this evening Dad continued his reading from the New Testament. When he read the part about Jesus' triumphant entry into Jerusalem, Roland quietly pondered, "Jesus is a king who rode on a donkey."

As he was taught to do, Roland mixed wishes with work. Day after day, although he dreamed of a bicycle, he looked after Dingle devotedly. Perhaps this was one reason his beast of burden always seemed eager to serve. Very soon Roland was to be assisted by Dingle in a very special way. It happened this way:

One of Roland's morning chores was to walk down to the horse pasture and let the horses into the far field. He did this routinely at nine o'clock every morning without fail. Roland didn't have a dog, so he took his walks with Dingle. When Dingle heard the back door shut and saw Roland approaching, he was ready and eager to be Roland's companion. He followed Roland around the farm, but he especially seemed to like the walk they took together out to the far field at nine o'clock to let out the horses. When Dingle and Roland returned, Dingle was always penned, and Roland slipped out of his muddy boots and sat at the kitchen table working on his homeschool lessons. This morning, however, the day Ned was supposed to visit, Roland did not get out of bed. His head hurt and he had the chills. His mother found that he had a fever.

Dingle was agitated. He was accustomed to taking his morning walk with Roland. Even without hearing the signal of the kitchen door shut Dingle was ready. He paced back and forth in his pen, expecting to accompany Roland. But Roland didn't come.

What was Dingle's deed? Dingle's deed is a story within our story. Tell whether Roland ever buys a bicycle.

## Writing Help

- Animals are creatures of habit. With this fact in mind, what did Dingle accomplish without Roland? What were the reactions when Dingle was spied out?
- What story was Ned told when he came by to play chess?
- Write about Roland's experience with a new bicycle. We appreciate things more when we have to wait and work for them. Can you remember learning how to ride a bicycle?

# 25

## Mince Pies[B]

Wesley and Walter were delivery boys. They delivered packages from the shops in town to the homes in the surrounding villages, and sometimes even further out into the countryside. As today was the day before Christmas, the wagon this pair of brothers was pulling was extra full of packages. By the time they had handed the last packages to the family that had been anticipating them, it was dark. Their noses were red with cold. Some snow was already on the ground, and as they headed home, foot-sore and weary, more snow began to fall—the light fluffy kind that indicated that the night air was really as cold as it felt.

Wesley had only one thing on his mind now. "Pick up the pace, Walter. Mom is making Christmas Eve supper and I'm hungry."

"Mmm, can't wait," replied Walter, pulling their wagon with renewed vigor.

As they reached the outskirts of their village, they came upon an odd scene. A horse-drawn cart lay on its side. The horses were free but close by and dragging their reins.

"What's happened here?" exclaimed Wesley. Holding up his lantern, he examined the inside of the cart. It was half filled with old wooden trunks, wicker hampers, and some packages. Other hampers and packages were strewn about the ground surrounding the cart. "What a mess! I don't see the driver, do you?" Wesley asked.

"I wonder where he's gone," Walter replied.

"I don't know. It's strange," spoke Wesley, his eyes narrowing in thoughtful consideration.

He was soon distracted when Walter exclaimed, "Mmm, something smells good! I think it's in this hamper." Walter opened it. "Hey, mince pies!"

"Really?" Wesley responded cautiously.

"Yeah, and I'm hungry. Hear that growl? That's my stomach."

"Walter, we'd better not. This hamper isn't ours."

"If we don't eat these pies, they'll only freeze and go rotten," Walter rationalized.

"I guess you're right," Wesley responded, giving in to the temptation.

Ignoring the address label attached to the wicker hamper, the boys dived into the mince pies with great relish. Suddenly they heard a deep moan. Startled, they stopped chewing, their mouths still full of mince pie. The moan turned into a kind of desperate raspy cry, followed by mumbled and repeated words that they couldn't understand. Both boys swallowed, then held their breaths while they listened. Finally Wesley said bravely, but very quietly, "It's coming from over there, from under that trunk and pile of packages. It must be the driver."

What happened next? Add to the story by explaining further events of the boys' Christmas Eve. You are invited to use the whole set of pictures. Still, there will be more pictures in your head as you *animate* the characters, that is, make them move and speak, as you like.

Imagine. Let your mind wander. The greatly admired author of stories, J.R.R. Tolkien said, "All who wander are not lost."

## Writing Help

You need not answer all of these questions. Only use the ones that give you the best ideas for your story.

- What did the boys try to do first? Were they successful?
- What would you do if you were in their circumstances?

- Did the boys go for help? How long did it take to find help? (A bit of difficulty in searching for help would create suspense.)
- Who did they meet up with? How were those they met with otherwise occupied? How do people busy themselves on Christmas Eve?
- What was the condition of the driver and what was the cause of the accident?
- Did the boy's family wonder where they were or go out looking for them?
- Did it continue to snow or stop snowing?
- How late were the boys for Christmas Eve supper?
- What became of the undelivered hamper? Were they embarrassed? Did they recognize the name and address on the label of the package?

### *Sensory Language*

What does snow feel like on the ankles when you walk through it with shoes instead of boots? What else could the boys see, feel, hear, smell or taste, in the story?

## Additional Challenge

What lesson did the brothers learn about respecting the property of others? Do we sometimes make excuses for using the property of others? Were apologies given? What work might the boys offer to do to pay back the owner of the pies?

# 26

## Chad's Busy Day

Chad had a younger friend named Billy. Not only was Billy the youngest of a group of boys who were pals but also he was small for his age. Chad and his friends were happy Billy liked to "pal around" with them, but Billy always felt the need to keep up. His pals were not just older and bigger, but Billy thought them smarter and more experienced. It didn't matter to Chad or the older boys that Billy was younger, but it mattered to Billy.

One Saturday morning Chad had agreed to cycle with Billy. When Chad got to Billy's house, Billy said, "My cat, Lucky, is missing. He's been lost for days. Do you want to help me look for him?"

"Sure. What does Lucky look like?" Chad asked.

Billy described his cat and they both kept their eyes out for him as they rode. The day was dry and sunny, perfect for cycling outside of town on the long dirt roads. Thinking he needed to prove to Chad how brave and *proficient he was at cycling, Billy wouldn't slow

---

*If you are "proficient" at something you are quite good at it; highly skilled.

down when they came to the hill. "Hey, Billy, not so fast!" Chad called out, but Billy was already far ahead. A moment later his front tire struck a stone. He skidded, lost his balance, and fell just beside a brick wall.

"Thank God he didn't crash *into* the wall," thought Chad as he knelt down beside Billy, who was lying on the ground. "Billy, how do you feel? Are you all right?" Chad asked, with shakiness in his voice. He patted Billy's back, but Billy didn't answer. "He must've hit his head. Do I leave him here to go for help?" Chad was beginning to panic.

Then he heard the clomping of horse's hooves and looked up. Nervously he waved down the man in the cart, who turned out to be Farmer Abbot. He recognized Chad and stopped.

Mr. Abbot got out to see what was the matter. He said calmly, "Billy seems to be unconscious. We'd better get him over to Doc Patterson's." They placed Billy securely in the back of Mr. Abbot's cart between some sacks of flour, and then loaded on the boys' bicycles.

They were greatly relieved to find the doctor in his office. Billy opened his clear blue eyes and said, "My arm hurts, and my knee. That's all." His thin lips quivered, but he didn't show any tears. Chad rode over to Billy's house to tell Billy's mother what had happened. When she heard the news, her eyes widened with concern. Not long afterwards Doc Patterson arrived in his motorcar with Billy, and Billy's mother greatly relieved, helped the doctor bring Billy into the house.

"Chad, will you please take this loaf of bread I just baked to Farmer Abbot? I'm so thankful for his kindness and also for yours, Chad. This other loaf is for you."

"Yes, ma'am. Thank you, ma'am. Goodbye, Billy. Hope you feel better soon," Chad said. Hopping on his bicycle, he headed out to Abbot's Hollow several miles down the road and repaid the neighbor as instructed.

Halfway home he stopped. The fragrance of freshly baked bread could be resisted no longer. He sat in some tall grass, tore off a hefty hunk of bread with his teeth and chewed a mouthful with great contentment. A thought occurred to him as he chewed, "Billy's bike probably

needs fixing. I'll ride out to tell the fellows about it. They'll know what needs to be done to it, and would go out and get it, too."

So Chad cycled into town to see his pals.

It had been a full morning for Chad. He had cycled with Billy, gone to Doc's, cycled back out to Billy's, cycled out to Abbot's Hollow, and then cycled all the way into town to see his pals. But the day was about to get busier still. He suddenly remembered that he had promised his mother he would run some errands for her. He cycled home, only to head out again. By this time his legs were beginning to get tired. Soon, however, he would not be thinking about his tired legs. While he was on Main Street filling up his bicycle basket with the items on his mother's list, he noticed that a crowd had gathered outside the church. Everyone was gazing up at the roof of the church. There, clinging for dear life to a protruding carving near the top of a tall steeple was a black cat!

"How did it get there?" said one person to another.

The next question was, "How will it get down?"

The terrified cat was looking down on the people, mewing as though appealing for help. Once it slipped, and exclamations of pity came from the crowd. But the cat's claws caught on another projection, and so for the moment it was safe.

A thought suddenly occurred to Chad. "This might be the cat of Billy's that he said was lost! It looks like what he described to me. But would it have strayed *this* far?"

Using the third picture, finish this story.

## Writing Help

- What idea did Chad come up with to try to save the cat?
- How nervous do you think he felt? How long did it take to save the cat? How many tries did it take?
- Was it Billy's cat, Lucky, after all? You decide. This is your part of the story and you can make it turn out how you would like.

Remember, however, to include what the reactions of certain characters will be to whether it is or isn't Billy's cat.

- Did any of the boys decide to tell Billy that his age didn't matter to them, and that he didn't need to prove anything to them?
- How glad was Billy to have the boys as "true" friends?
- What did Billy's grateful parents do for the boys?

## Additional Challenge

How did Billy resolve his desire to show off in front of the older boys as a result of his fall?

# 27

## Not Tired[B]

Dear Mother,

Thank you for your note. I am so glad that you and Dad are feeling better and will be up to traveling to Maine this month to visit us.

Let me tell you what happened today with your first grandchild. Baby Darla is crawling now. She crawls around as if she is looking for all sorts of things to put in her mouth because that is what she *does* when she finds anything—even something as small as a piece of fuzz from the fringe of the bottom of the sofa. I sat on the rug with her, hoping to interest her in some toys, but she wouldn't sit still for long. Then she crawled around the kitchen floor and found a stray bottle cap. I retrieved it just as she was putting it between her lips. I had to take away her teddy bear, because all she would do was suck on one of the paws until it was wet and soggy, or try to pull off its eyes.

In the early afternoon I held her, fed her, and rocked her to sleep. It was a beautiful spring day, and I thought some fresh air would do her good. I lay her, still sleeping soundly, in her pillowy basket. Since the air

was deliciously warm with a light breeze, I decided to hang the washing on the line, intermittently keeping an eye on her. She must have awakened when my back was turned because when I turned around, I gasped at what I saw!

You know that Darla likes putting things in her mouth. Therefore, using the picture of Darla attracted to the chick, as a clue, finish the letter.

# 28

## The Rowboat

School was out for the summer. Taylor had been invited to stay with Roy for the first week of the summer holidays.

The two friends were standing on the dock in front of Roy's parents' summer cottage. "Roy, I'm not really a water sports person, and I never learned to swim very well. I haven't ever had a reason for getting in a rowboat. I'm from the city, remember? How often do you take this thing out, anyway?"

"All the time—every summer holiday," lied Roy. "Get in," he directed his guest with a wide grin. To be civil, Taylor did what his host urged him to do, but sat in the boat unimpressed. Roy took the oars and began rowing out to the middle of the pond. He rowed steadily and rhythmically without talking.

When they neared the center of the pond, Taylor surveyed his surroundings. His eyes followed the *iridescent dragonflies hovering over

---

*If something has "iridescent" qualities it produces an array of rainbow-like colors. "Iridescent" is the artful adjective I chose to describe the noun, dragonfly.

the sparkling water. He noticed the honeysuckle fragrance of the water lilies and the low rhythmic croaking of the frogs. To be in the midst of all this nature was new to him. Except for having to swat the occasional mosquito on his neck, he was finding this rowboat business to be surprisingly pleasant. But he was too proud to admit it. Roy, on the other hand, thinking his friend was bored, and wanting to show off, decided to add a little excitement to the excursion. He stood up, placed one foot at each end of his seat, balancing himself carefully. Then without warning he rocked the boat back and forth sideways by alternately bending his knees.

"I'm making waves," Roy announced.

"I'm getting seasick. Stop it!" Taylor complained irritably.

"Would you like to see bigger waves?" Roy responded.

"No!"

"Watch this!"

Describe what happened next.

## Writing Help

Continue the conversation between these two boys in the water. How clever is the dog? How did the rest of the morning turn out? Were there apologies given? Were they able to find anything to do later that they both enjoyed? What did they find that they had in common?

## Additional Challenge

There is a problem in this story. The boys weren't quite honest with each other. Each also didn't hear what the other said. A problem in a story is called "conflict." You can solve the problem in your ending. You will then be providing "conflict resolution."

Was there any adult who helped them communicate better? How will each boy represent what happened?

Taylor was proud and somewhat defensive. Perhaps he felt uncomfortable (or on edge) at first in his new surroundings.

Honesty allows people to trust one other. Show how trust can actually be deepened through this adventure.

# 29

## Sick Piggy(B)

*Do you like pigs? Today pot-bellied pigs are sometimes kept as pets. If you have enjoyed a tale or two by that famous veterinarian James Herriot, or are familiar with* Charlotte's Web, *or if you like animals, and especially if you raise animals yourself, you may want to try your hand at finishing this story.*

ad, my pig isn't getting better," lamented Warren.

"I think you should call the vet, son," said his dad.

"Me, call Mr. Thompson?"

"Yes, the pig belongs to you, and you are old enough to take responsibility for its health," Dad said encouragingly.

Warren was not accustomed to calling grown-ups on the telephone, especially one as esteemed in the village as Mr. Thompson. But he didn't hesitate to ask his dad what he should say, and then he got up his nerve and made the call. His pig needed him.

What happens next?

## Writing Help

- What questions did the vet ask Warren over the telephone? When the vet arrived, what did he instruct Warren to do first? Did they have any difficulty administering the medicine? When an animal (or a person) feels sick, they are often lethargic, making it docile and easy to manage. When one feels better, one usually becomes livelier. With this in mind, how cooperative was the pig over the next few days, once it started feeling better?

- Was this the same pig that would later be used in a greased pig contest? Would it ever be entered into the country fair for a prize? Was it ever to be sold?

# 30

## A Young Musician

*Before the days of radio, phonographs, or electronic recordings, most music that people heard was either what they played themselves, or what was played at church and at community gatherings.*

"Hans, are you in the attic again?" his mother called up the narrow steps. "I've been looking everywhere for you."

"Yes, Mother. I started reading up here, because it's so nice and quiet," Hans answered, as he promptly made his way down the winding back staircase. "Have you seen the view of the town from up here?"

"Yes, I have. It's very nice, son," she said abstractedly, because something more pressing was occupying her mind. She held out a piece of paper. "A message was delivered here for your father, and I need you to deliver it to him straightaway."

"Of course, Mother." Hans tucked the folded paper securely into the inside pocket of his jacket, slipped on his best boots at the door, and waved goodbye. Hans hated hurrying, but his father was a doctor and

Hans was used to urgency. People came to the house at all hours of the night when a loved one was very ill, or when there had been an accident. Hans spent several hours a week assisting his father at his surgery after school hours. His parents expected that he would study to be a doctor, too. But Hans was uncertain whether he really wanted the kind of life his father had, and he wondered whether he could be as sincerely full of mercy as his father was.

He made rapid steps and delivered the message speedily, but did not stay until his father finished. He walked home in a more leisurely manner, ambling towards home through the back cobblestone streets of his little Austrian town. His stomach was growling and, unable to wait for supper, he stopped at the bakery just before it closed and bought a penny bun. Biting into it with delight, he let the crumbs from its crispy crust fall where they would.

As he continued to stroll along, he suddenly heard the faint but clear notes of music coming from the second story window of a house just ahead. Hans loved music. What a curious tune, he thought. It was new to him. Stopping in front of the house, he wondered who lived in it. Wishing to keep the sweet melody in his head, he hummed it as he walked the rest of the way home. He feared the tune in his head would soon slip from memory if he could not duplicate the notes. There were no musical instruments in his household, but his resourceful mind struck on an idea.

What did Hans think to do? Describe step by step how Hans went about setting up his music making.

## Writing Help

When my son added to this story, he wrote, *"He heard the church bells ring and duplicated their melody."*

- What strange noises could be heard coming from the attic? Did they startle or frighten anyone? Who first discovered his setup?
- Use conversation in your story.

- What took place over the next days and weeks? What did his father think of Hans' preoccupation with music?

## Additional Challenge

Write an extended story about Hans. Here are some ideas. The questions are numerous but you need only use what sparks your creative leanings.

Why might his father be opposed to his music making? If he would rather Hans focus on his studies elsewhere, this would add conflict to the story that would then beg to be resolved.

Would his father ever decide to purchase Hans a musical instrument? If so, how often did he practice his instrument? How quickly did he progress? What instruments did he learn to master? What help did he receive? Was there anyone in particular that especially encouraged him?

What role might the church across the street play in his musical future? What did the community think of Hans' playing? Did he become an accomplished composer in Austria? Or did he continue to *play* beautiful music but decide to redirect his attentions to becoming a doctor rather than a composer after all? What event may have brought about this turning point?

Do you like classical music? Who were some of the great musicians in Europe several centuries ago?

# 31

## The Surprise

Joan's mother had a cold. She was lethargic and dreamy. Nine-year-old Joan noticed that her mother moved more slowly around the house and often lounged on the sofa in loose comfortable clothing. What Joan didn't know was that her mother was expecting a baby in a few short weeks. Not many generations ago, parents didn't talk with their children about such things has "having babies." Therefore, the arrival of a new baby was often a complete surprise.

That night, when everyone was in bed and the house was quiet, Joan heard her mother cough. She could hear her parents talking in low tones. Every now and then, another cough came from her mother. That's when a question popped into her mind, one that she had never before entertained. Lying in the dark, staring through her window at the moon, Joan worried and fretted. "What if Mommy dies?" she thought. "It would be so dreadful. Oh, I don't want Mommy to die!" Joan buried her head in her pillow and sobbed herself to sleep.

In the morning the sun was shining brightly and Joan was able to tuck her fears away. When she came down to the kitchen for breakfast, her big brother Douglas was already at the table.

Mother greeted her pleasantly. "Good morning, Joanie," she said. "Here's your toast and marmalade." Putting the plate of toast and the jar of marmalade on the table, she smiled at her daughter as she sat down beside her.

"Mommy?" Joan asked, a note of uncertainty in her voice.

"Yes, Joanie?"

"Mommy, you need to take better care of yourself." This pronouncement was made with such seriousness Joan sounded for a moment very grown up.

Mother's smile widened. "I shall, darling. I shall." She discreetly dabbed her nose with her lacy handkerchief and, after a brief pause, looked very purposefully at both Joan and Douglas. Then she asked, "Would you two like to visit your Aunt Peggy and Uncle Bob and see your cousins again? You always like our visits in the country. And the fair will be next week."

"Yes, please," the children chorused politely.

"This time, however, your father and I will need to stay here," she gently disclosed.

Joan was about to ask why when Douglas blurted out, "Yes, Mommy, you aren't well for traveling and visiting, and you need your rest." This time it was he who sounded grown up.

"I quite agree with him, Mommy," Joan chimed in, a touch of worry returning to her voice.

"Then it's settled. We shall pack your bags and you'll be ready to travel to the country tomorrow. You're old enough to travel by train yourself and Uncle Bob will meet you at the station when you arrive."

"I like trains," Douglas responded.

As the day progressed, Joan forgot all about the dark thoughts she had had in the night. Mother was in good spirits and an interesting trip was before her. She loved the country and Shepherd's Wood, the little village where Aunt Peggy lived, had always appealed to her.

Romping about the countryside of Shepherd's Wood with cousins provided an opportunity to explore and experience interesting things. The children found new uses for their arms, legs, and backs. Joan and Douglas climbed trees, ran through the meadows, fished for minnows in the brook, rode ponies, picked strawberries, helped clean the barn, and won goldfish at the fair. After three weeks it was time to leave for home.

Meeting the children at the station around the corner from their house was their neighbor Mr. Brown.

"Where's Dad?" Douglas asked.

"Yes, where's Dad?" Joan echoed. A wave of anxiety surged through Joan. She was quiet as she climbed into Mr. Brown's big car. Neither she nor Douglas asked the question that was on their minds. They looked at each other in puzzled silence as the car approached their home.

Mr. Brown parked the car in front of their large brick Victorian house. While he opened the trunk to take out their suitcases, the children ran up the stone steps to the granite doorstep. The heavy oak door was unlocked. Opening it, they stepped inside, but no one was there to greet them. The house was so oddly quiet that the clomp-clomp of their footsteps on the polished floor seemed to echo against the high ceilings. Mr. Brown came in with some of the suitcases and set them down in the silent hall. Douglas returned with him to the car to get the other suitcases, and Joan was left alone in the central hall, bewildered at the stillness and apparent emptiness of their house.

Then it hit her. Her old fear resurfaced. A chill ran through her and left her weak. Plopping down at the bottom of the staircase, she burst into tears.

Douglas was coming in with the last load of suitcases. "Joanie, whatever is the matter?" he asked, sitting down beside her.

"Mommy's dead. I know it."

"Dead?" Douglas was dumbfounded. But before he could say another word, Dad appeared at the top of the stairs. Quickly advancing halfway down the stairs, he exclaimed, "Children, you're home! Wonderful! You've been away so long!" He was more jovial than they had ever seen him. "Come up, children," he insisted with mounting excitement.

They were startled, and momentarily stuck to the bottom stair, looking up at their father. Mr. Brown patted them on the shoulder nudging them to go on up. Again Dad called to his children—this time with greater impatience. "Children, your mother and I have something to show you? It's a surprise. Come!" He turned and went back upstairs, anticipating that they would follow him at once.

"Let's go," Douglas urged his sister, as he shot up the stairs. Joan sprang into action, too. At the top of the stairs, her dad gave her a bear hug. "In there," he pointed.

Using the second picture provided, finish the scene. How does the day turn out? Write with zest. Keep going. Then, if you want more ideas, go back and use any of questions in the Writing Help below to polish or fill out your story. I think, though, that you will find that you will have already answered some of the questions.

## Writing Help

- What else did Dad say to them? Did he see Joan's wet eyes? This is your story, and you can make the characters do and say what you like. How might Douglas rally his sister into action? Did Joan's confusion change to something else?
- Are the children curious? What questions might they ask?
- Where is Mommy? Does Joan ever get her fears "off her chest" and share them with her mother? Mothers are usually very sympathetic toward the feelings of their children. What conversation takes place between Mommy and Joan? What does it feel like to

have a sense of relief? Have you ever said, "I'm so glad that's not true," or "I'm so glad that's over with"?

- Had Mommy's cold gone away? Does she let Joan hold the baby? Have you ever held a baby? Is the baby a boy or girl?
- What does Douglas think of it all? Is he surprised, too?

You can add to the happy mood of the story even more by bringing cheerful visitors to the house with gifts and lots more chatter.

# 32

## Pocket Money

*This story starter will mostly interest the American history buff. It could be used as a creative writing project in conjunction with studying the years of our nation's founding.*

Dear Cousin Owen,

How are things at the *College of New Jersey? We haven't heard from you since Christmas holiday. You must be nearly finished with your studies.

We had a long gray winter. Ethan and I took advantage of the weekends. We split wooden shingles in the barn. We made stacks of them and have calluses on our hands to prove it. Our schoolmaster has taught us that some of the best things about this great country of America are freedom to own land and to buy and sell, and low taxes. Father is wholly in agreement with him and is quite pleased with all of our shingles. Mother didn't mind our work as long as our chores were done and we kept up with our Latin.

---

*later renamed Princeton University

Early this spring, since we had a short mud season, we were able to load up Father's wagon and sell all our shingles in Boston. As you know, the city is not far from us—it is only a two-hour walk. Today we plan to go there and anticipate spending our pocket money with great satisfaction. Last evening Mother looked a little worried at our after-school plans, but Father reminded her that the lion's share of the money we made is carefully saved toward our Harvard tuition. But perhaps we should try for the College of New Jersey? Our schoolmaster told us that as many as one-sixth of the members of the Constitutional Convention studied at your school, so it must be good.

I will finish this letter when we return from our shopping trip. I will tell you all about what we did in the city.

Finish this letter to the boys' older cousin by describing their spending spree in the city. Include the sights and sounds (and smells and tastes) of their experience. Give an early American name to the writer of the letter.

## Writing Help

Can you tell that I wrote this story starter to take place in the late eighteenth century? Your description of Boston and its wares therefore will need to be a somewhat historical one. I got the idea about spitting shingles from the picture book *The Oxcart Man,* by Donald Hall, which I read aloud each autumn to my children when they were young. This book and others like it (available in your local library) may give you some ideas. You probably already have some knowledge of early American history, but a bit of research from a history book would enable you to provide more details in your story.

Was their pocket money spent for pleasure or for something else? Did they meet any opposition in the city?

Comment: In *The Oxcart Man*, not much money was exchanged. Lots of the transactions were trades. What kinds of money were used then, and how common was it for young boys to have money?

## Additional Challenge

Did the boys join their cousin at the College of New Jersey? What did they choose as careers and what contributions did they make to the society in which they lived? How did living in such a young nation affect them?

# 33

## He Told the Truth

*This is not a story starter, but a story conclusion. I wanted to give you the opportunity to write a creative beginning (and middle) of a story.*

And so Michael walked to the village school that morning, happy that his innocence had been proven and that the truth was known to and accepted by all his classmates. One by one, they had come up to him and said they were sorry for believing him to be guilty when all along he had been innocent. The charges that had been heaped up against him (with circumstances set up against him) by the new boy in the school had been all lies told out of pure jealousy and wicked intent. But Michael did not hold a grudge. What had been most difficult for him had been the way Teacher had peculiarly sided with the new boy, and had seemed to take pleasure in accusing Michael as well. He tried not to hold a grudge against Teacher, although this wasn't easy. He was glad Teacher had been dismissed and anticipated meeting the new teacher of their school. He was relieved that things were now looking a little better.

Did this ending get you asking any questions? You are probably wondering what charges were placed against Michael, and how the new boy contrived to make it seem as if Michael were in the wrong. To accuse someone wrongly, especially with wicked intent, is worse than gossip. It is called "slander." It certainly is bearing false witness, or lying.

Make a beginning of the story that shows how Michael perseveres through his difficult time. You will be putting a problem into your story and then solving it. Remember, this is what is called conflict and conflict resolution. This story may take you more than one sitting to complete. Don't let that discourage you. Most of the short stories I wrote for this book took more than a day to write. I went back to add, adjust, and improve them after I had "slept on them." You can do that, too. Be creative and see what your imagination comes up with before you refer to the Writing Help. You can use the picture of the policeman who seizes "the new boy" at last. He is the *culpable one, not Michael.

## Writing Help

### *Exploring Possibilities*

Perhaps:

*-The new boy is assigned a seat next to Michael.*

*-The new boy's pride is hurt because Michael will not join him in certain bad, devious activities.*

*-The new boy starts whispers of untruths by gossip.*

*-False evidence of some kind is planted in Michael's desk.*

- Was anything stolen or destroyed or defaced?
- How long did this go on before the new boy was, at last, found out? The evidence must have seemed quite incriminating for Michael's classmates to believe *him* to be the devious one.
- Who came to Michael's rescue?
- What was Michael's parents' advice to him during this trial?

---

*To be "culpable" means to be deserving blame.

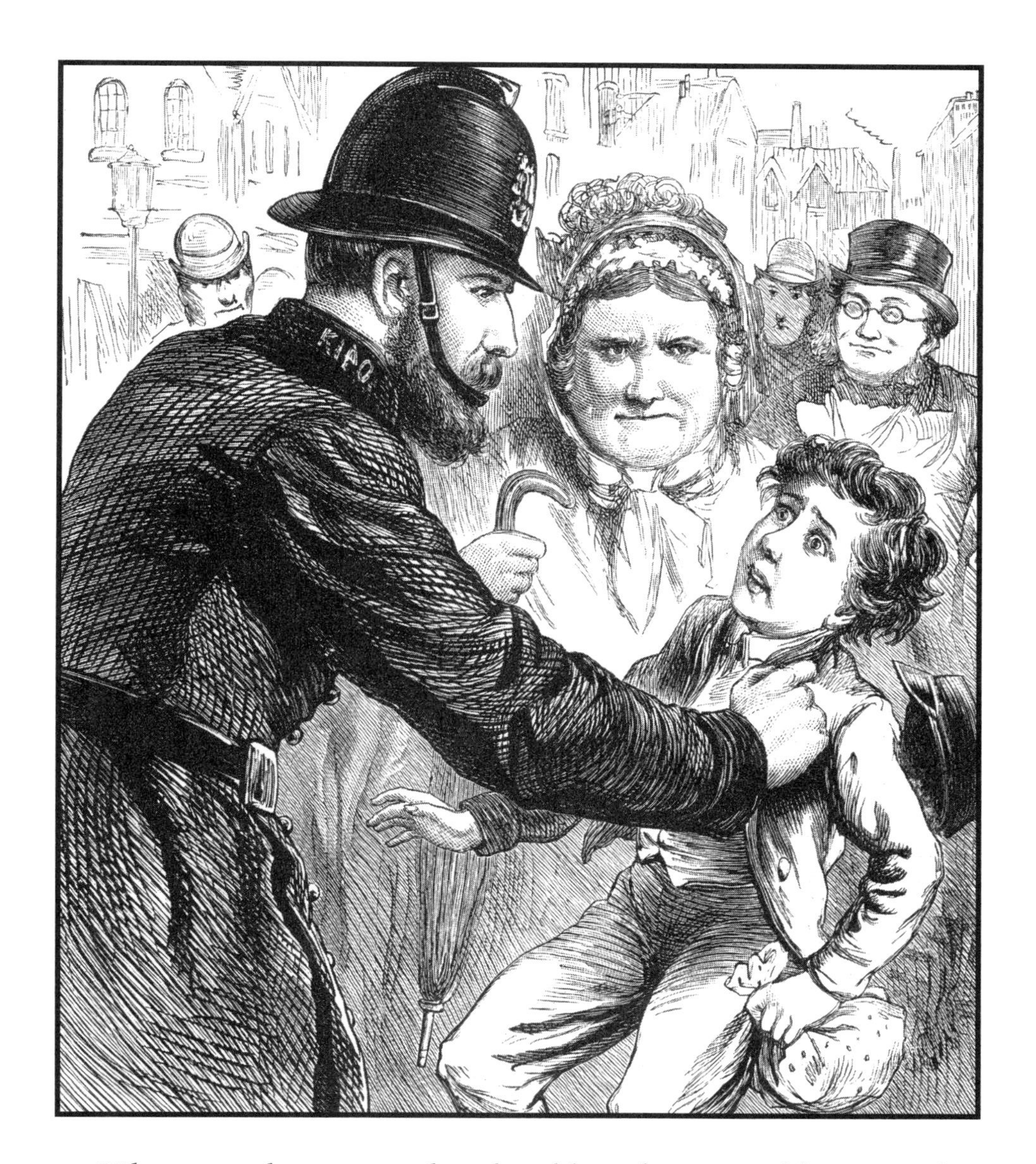

- What were the reasons that the old teacher was told to go? Why might he not like Michael, even though Michael was a very good student?

Read my story ending again or whenever you need to refresh your memory.

# 34

## If at First You Don't[B]

My father spends many hours a week at his print shop printing books, advertisements, and pamphlets. He likes his work, but he also looks forward to some rest and a change of scenery. Fishing was recommended to him by one of his business associates. I was happy he asked me to go down to the stream with him. He seemed to take such pleasure carrying his tackle and heading out early Saturday morning while the dew was still on the grass. I carried our lunch and had bright prospects as the morning emerged. He whistled while he set up his gear. When the hook was dangling properly, he *amicably agreed to satisfy my wishes and teach me how to whistle as clearly as he does.

"Jiminy Cricket, I think I've caught something!" he blurted out excitedly. We were both surprised to think he could hook a fish so quickly. We had assumed fishing was a pastime that involved lots of relaxation and waiting.

---

*If you do something in a very friendly, warm, and attentive way you do it "amicably." This "ly" word is an adverb.

He had caught what looked like a very fine trout, and was carefully drawing it in, with no eyes for anything but his prize. Just then I saw a flash of something that seemed to drop out of the sky, and heard a plunge in the water. There was a great splash and struggle in the stream for a second or two. Before I could recover from my surprise, I watched my father grab hold of a rock to throw at what looked like a fish hawk. But the rock missed, and we watched the hawk sail off with my father's trout. His fine rod was yanked from his hands, and it trailed in the air behind the hawk and fish like the tail of a kite.

What an abrupt ending to a much anticipated morning's outing! At first, my father appeared greatly offended by the bird's shocking greed and thievery. Yet he must have followed an inner resolution to be light-hearted. He let out a loud, "Shiver me timbers!" Then he threw back his head and laughed. "Ha! Think of the story I'll have to tell to the fellows at the print shop. This will lighten up their work a bit."

We had an early lunch by the stream and walked home in good spirits.

The following Saturday we set out again. This time it was my father's idea to take Chipper with us. He is an affectionate dog, but he can become overexcited. He keeps his senses on the alert, except when he is asleep by the fire. "Chipper will keep those clever fish-hawks from intruding upon our fishing," Dad asserted.

Finish the story by first describing the adventures of father, son, and Chipper on this particular Saturday, and then narrating their adventures on a few other Saturdays to come.

## Writing Help

- Does Father ever catch any fish that he can bring home to Mother?
- What "whale of a fish" story could be told by the Father each week?
- How might the father describe his adventures in the local newspaper he prints?

## Additional Challenge

Tell the story from the father's point of view.

# 35

## Miss Whitaker

I'd like to tell you about my big sister's friend, Miss Whitaker. She is our newest neighbor. She moved here this year. She has a beautiful singing voice. I know because I sit near her at church. I think she should sing solo.

Every once in a while my sister invites Miss Whitaker to tea. The first time she came, I showed her the watercolor paintings I had made of the flowers in the park. She liked them all, especially the tulips. "They're marvelous, Clara!" she told me. What is even more wonderful is that she has painted the same kinds of flowers herself.

I also found out that she likes animals as much as I do—dogs, horses, and birds especially. When she met my dog, Sheba, she said, "Oh, what a beautiful creature! And such a nice disposition, too." I was very happy to hear this, because I had spent hours training her. When I showed Miss Whitaker Sheba's newborn puppies, she spent nearly the whole visit sitting with one puppy or another asleep on her lap. That was two months ago.

We hadn't seen her for some time, because over the Christmas holidays she went by train to visit her relatives. Today, she surprised us by paying us a call unexpectedly. A minute after she came through the door she was sitting with us in the parlor chatting gaily, her face glowing with happiness. Sheba was excited about seeing her again and politely held out a paw. Miss Whitaker shook it appreciatively and just after she did Sheba trotted away as if being summoned by someone in another part of the house. Anyway, Miss Whitaker said she had something to announce to us, and my sister and I gave her our closest attention. As she took off her gloves, I noticed she was wearing a beautiful ring. It was sparkling just like her eyes. Then Sheba came prancing in. I couldn't believe what I saw. I was speechless.

Explain what happened next, and then tell the rest of the story.

## Writing Help

- Was Sheba carrying in her mouth a gift for Miss Whitaker?
- Who did Miss Whitaker meet during her trip? How did she spend her time?
- What exciting news did Miss Whitaker eventually announce?
- Look at the dashing horseman outlined in the painting above the sofa. Could Miss Whitaker have gone on a fox hunt? Would she have to be a good rider to take part in a hunt during her trip?
- Will she and her family be moving again?
- Did she say she had missed the puppies? What might she ask of Clara (who is telling the story) that would make Clara pleased?
- If Miss Whitaker did have to move away, would she ever invite her friends to visit her?

## Additional Challenge

Can you tell how much the young writer, Clara, admires and looks up to Miss Whitaker? Continue writing from Clara's point of view with this same attitude of admiration and perhaps you will point out more of Miss Whitaker's positive qualities.

# 36

## Hunting for Rabbit[(B)(I)]

Uncle Gordon was hunting for squirrels and rabbits. He had been traipsing through the woods and briers for hours, but had come upon nothing. "I best take a break. I could do with some food," he thought to himself. He unwrapped the lunch Aunt Tess had prepared for him and ate it while he sat back in the dappled sunlight. "It's rather peaceful-like here," he mused. He leaned back further and gazed up at the sky through the leafy boughs of the trees, then closed his eyes for a short nap. But his nap *wasn't* short. When he awoke, twilight was approaching. "Oh well, this is a much better time of day for hunting rabbit, anyway."

He set off toward home, stopping now and then to detect any critters—as he called them—that might be scampering beneath the bushes. "Ah, I hear some leaves rustling in that direction," he thought. Kneeling on one knee, he aimed at what appeared to be something small and furry at the base of a great big blackberry bush. "If I miss, I can always take home

---

*By choosing to use the word "traipsing" I was hoping to give Uncle Gordon's walk an aimless carefree attitude.

some blackberries," he thought, as he aimed his gun. Bang! "Did I get 'em?" he wondered. He came closer to his prey. But what he saw gave him the fright of his life. The "small, furry something" was the hind paw of a bear!

Continue the action, using the picture of Uncle Gordon and the bear to help you.

## Writing Help

### *Exploring Possibilities*

Perhaps:

-*The bear's foot was bloody and the bear in a dangerous rage.*

-*The shot missed the bear. It was only the loud noise of the shot that awakened the bear's anger.*

-*In the tree Uncle Gordon climbed was a bee's nest on a higher branch. Why and how could he use it to provide a distraction?*

-*The bear had cubs that came out of the blackberry bush to find their mother. This could contribute to further distraction.*

- It would soon be dark. How would this fact also provide tension or further suspense to the story? What might be Uncle Gordon's prayer to God during this distressing time?
- Did he come home with any wild food?

There are many possible endings to this story. A happy ending for Gordon, his wife, and the bear, would be what I would write, but this is your story, and you are free to make it turn out the way you please.

## Additional Challenge

### *Artful Adjectives*

I described the bush in the story as a *big blackberry* bush. Why might I mention this detail? Bears eat blackberries and in the wild the bushes grow rather big, making it easy for an animal to hide behind them.

Do you find the bear in the picture to be impressive? Describe it for your readers with adjectives, as well as showing us what it is like by its actions. You may use adjectives to describe its size, its teeth, its tongue, its fur, its claws, its facial expressions, the noise it makes, or even its disposition.

# 37

## Whose Baby?[I]

It was a sunny afternoon, and Amanda was singing a happy melody as she walked to the end of the gravel drive to where the lilies grew. Mother had gone to the train station to greet Aunt Nancy, her sister. Amanda was planning a special welcome for her aunt. She had decided to make an arrangement of lilies, daisies, and buttercups and put it in the spare bedroom where Aunt Nancy would be staying. She needed to get started because her mother and aunt were due to arrive back from the station in an hour.

Beforehand, Mother had shared with the family the importance of being especially kind to Aunt Nancy at this time, because she was grieving. Her little girl had died of that dreadful disease, polio. She had been the only child Aunt Nancy and Uncle Charles had had in their ten years of marriage.

Father, Amanda, and her five brothers and sisters completed their indoor and outdoor chores in good time so that they could be refreshed and ready for the arrival of their company. Mother hoped it would be a comfort to her sister to spend a week with the family at this very sad time.

Amanda had only picked a few stems of wildflowers when *"whoosh," two birds sped passed her in a rush and a whirl. A bigger bird, probably a hawk, was chasing a little bird. How fast they flew! Amanda spun around to follow their flight, but the birds were out of her sight within seconds. "Where'd they go?" she wondered. Before she turned her attention back to her flower-picking, she spotted something odd. Half-hidden by some tall grass was a yellow blanket.

"What's this blanket doing here?" Amanda wondered, as she went over to have a look. Inside the blanket she found the surprise of her life.

What does Amanda do next? Let your own creative juices flow as you write your part of the story. You are invited to use the Writing Help only if you want ideas.

## Writing Help

- Amanda's facial expression looks concerned to me. Was there a note inside the blanket? If so, what did it say? Did Amanda have any fears or hesitations? In what condition was the abandoned baby found?
- How would Father react? What would Mother find when she returned home? How did the family go about making inquiries about the baby? Do they ever find the baby's mother?
- What you know about Aunt Nancy might give you ideas for conversation and possibly even a happy ending. Stories are often a mingling of sadness and joy as life is.

---

*What does the word, "whoosh," mean? See my description of Onomatopoeia below.

### *Onomatopoeia*

Isn't this a fancy word? I put an example of "onomatopoeia" into my story starter. It is the word *whoosh*. Onomatopoeia is the use of a word that imitates the sounds associated with the objects or actions to which they refer. You may have fun including onomatopoeia in your story. I've written some examples for you:

*Splat, the egg fell to the floor. Felicity reached for a cloth to wipe it up, but crunch, it was too late. Kelly had stepped on it.*

*The teakettle hissed at me and I knew the water was finally boiling.*

*Obadiah's stone landed in the pond with a kerplunk.*

*At the Christmas recital the drummer boy played pa-rum-pa-pum-pum on his drum.*

*Her horse's neighing woke me with a start in the middle of the night.*

## Additional Challenge

This picture reminds me of the story *Silas Marner*, by George Eliot. Silas is an embittered miser whose stash of gold is stolen. But his heart changes as he takes care of a little girl he finds abandoned in the snow near his home. Do you know this classic story?

# 38

## Mr. Madison's Classroom

I'm Brian, the boy sitting at the far right of the picture in the front row. I'd like to tell you about my teacher, Mr. Madison. He is the best teacher I've ever had. He always starts each day with an interesting tidbit of news. He somehow makes what we learn in science relate to our everyday life. Inventions and discoveries all have a story behind them, he says. We review our history names and dates every Friday by way of a relay race of sorts—except that in this race we walk, not run, around the edge of the classroom. One Friday we got a little carried away, and we had to forfeit reviewing by relay the following Friday. He didn't get angry with any of us. He just told us how it would have to be. Then he gave us a second chance and we have been as good as gold at relays ever since. History is my favorite subject, anyway. Mr. Madison has a way of using different voices when he reads that always makes us smile. He talks about people in history as if he had met them himself.

There is one boy, however, who doesn't appreciate Mr. Madison. His name is Benedict. He makes fun of Teacher during recess. I don't

like him much. He likes to put pebbles in his sling and gives a deep chuckle when his shots come dangerously close to hitting one of us.

One day a pigeon flew through the open window. Mr. Madison gave it some bread crumbs from his lunch and let us watch it. It flew to the windowsill, but didn't fly out right away. It stayed and cooed for a while. The next day it returned. Mr. Madison gave it crumbs again and it stayed even longer. Teacher said that if we gave our spelling as much attention as we gave the pigeon and used neat penmanship, he would let the pigeon stay as long as it liked whenever it visited the classroom. If the pigeon proved to be too much of a distraction, he'd shoo it away. We all cooperated, because we all hoped the pigeon could stay.

For two weeks the pigeon visited us for crumbs. We started bringing extra bread to class so we could take turns feeding it. We named it Harry, because we were reading about King Henry VIII in history class. Then one day, though we set crumbs out on Teacher's desk, Harry didn't come. When Teacher asked "Where's Harry today, boys?" I couldn't help overhear Benedict's low snickering behind me. Maybe it was the rain, we thought at first. But I secretly wondered if Benedict had had anything to do with Harry's disappearance.

When Harry didn't come the second or the third day in a row, I decided I would set about looking for him at recess. I thought I remembered his markings well enough to distinguish him from other pigeons. "Where do you think *you're* going, Brian?" called out Benedict in a nasty tone. He took out his sling and shot a pebble in my direction. It only hit the back of my shoe, but it sure was annoying.

What happened to the pigeon? Do you think the pigeon lady (feeding the birds) would be able to help Brian as he plays detective? What part does Benedict have in your story?

## Writing Help

- The pigeon might not be male. Harry could be a female. What do female birds do?

- Sometimes in stories (as in life) things get worse before they get better. Think through possibilities and then tell how it could have all worked out.
- Did Mr. Madison ever lead the boys out of the schoolroom for any outdoor learning experiences?
- Look at the picture of the lady who is feeding pigeons. Did the boys discover her, the teacher, or the whole class, during one of their outings? What did they think of her? Did they learn anything from her?
- Did Brian have any talks with his parents concerning the matter?

## Additional Challenge

Why did the boys (at least most of them) like Mr. Madison? What science project might he have an opportunity to teach? Remember that he has a way of making science relate to everyday life. How might Mr. Madison get involved in correcting Benedict or teaching him a lesson in character?

# 39

## Two Stepmothers[B]

"Mom, how could you do such a thing?" Betsy asked, frowning.

"Aren't you taking this too seriously?" her mother responded.

"But Mom, that duck had eggs it was brooding."

"You know our neighbor Mr. Radcliff has been sick. Well, he's feeling a lot better and when I was visiting the other day, he mentioned a favorite dish of his, and I piped up that I'd be happy to make it for him."

"Are you saying that Mr. Radcliff has eaten my favorite duck?"

"I didn't know she was your favorite, dear. I'm sorry. But I placed all of her eggs under our old hen and she's been brooding them quite faithfully."

Betsy and her mother opened the door to the coop. It was dark and quiet, as all the chickens were out scratching the ground, except for one white hen that quietly whined when she saw them peering in at her.

"She thinks they're hers!" cried Betsy. "I'm going to get her some cornbread from the kitchen. What a good mother she is."

"All right, dear," said Betsy's mother with a smile. She was relieved that it was all working out.

Less than a month later Betsy came bounding into the kitchen to report to her mother that the eggs were hatching.

Use the scenes in the pictures as you continue telling this story. What part do the animals play in the upbringing of the ducklings?

## Writing Help

- How does the hen take care of her little ones?
- Is there a rooster that helps guard the ducklings from predators?
- Look at the picture of the cat that sleeps in the barn. How does this circumstance contribute to the story? Is the dog that is looking on jealous or protective? Why would the mother hen across from the dog give up her territory?
- Why might Dad return to the kitchen with a puzzled look on his face when only a few moments before he had left for the barn for morning chores?
- What might a visiting neighbor say when she happens to see ducklings following behind a hen?

# 40

## The Prowling Lion[B][I]

The lion is the symbol of strength in England. We find it pictured on family crests, or carved in stone and placed on either side of the entrance to manor houses. John Bunyan, in *Pilgrim's Progress,* makes reference to a pair of lions standing on guard in an estate, though his lions were alive. C.S. Lewis created a character in his *Chronicles of Narnia,* who takes the form of a terrifying but majestic and good lion. His name is Aslan.

There is a certain nobility associated with the lion. It has been called the king of beasts. Perhaps it is because in its bold character it differs from the slinking habits of tigers and leopards. Although the lion is fond of forest retreats, it frequently exposes itself. It is easy to spot it on the grassy plains. This fearless exposure or carelessness of concealment renders its destruction comparatively easy. Because of this habit, the number of lions in the world has greatly diminished. In India and other parts of Asia they have become very scarce. In Africa they were hunted and destroyed from the time of the Roman Emperors, when hundreds at a time were killed in the arena for sport

during a Roman holiday. In the nineteenth century, the lion had but little chance against the rifle's bullets.

A thrilling story was told of a traveler's adventure with a lion in South Africa, which illustrates the recklessness with which the king of beasts exposes himself to danger and destruction. In crossing a wide plain, the traveler saw at a short distance behind him a lion slowly following. When the man quickened his pace, the lion did likewise, and it was evident to the traveler that the lion was only awaiting an opportunity to spring upon him.

In much fear, the anxious man hurried on until he reached a high cliff, below which was a deep ravine. "I must keep my wits about me," he thought. "I mustn't panic." He crept down the side of the cliff into a crevice in the rock, where he hoped he would be concealed. He tried to quiet himself with prayer. Regaining composure, he then pressed himself to use his wits.

What witty idea came to him? Finish describing the action in this intense situation.

## Writing Help

- What was the look on the lion's face? What did he sound like as he approached? Describe his appearance. Could he smell the man's fear? Did the man have any kind of protection?
- What was his plan with the suit of clothes? What might be his prayer to God at that stressful moment?
- What happened to the lion? Did the man have a story to tell when he finally arrived at his destination, disheveled and wet with perspiration?

# 41

## A Bird Called Mischief

Grandma and Grandpa live in the most charming cottage. Grandma named it Rose Cottage the first year she and Grandpa moved into it. Grandpa, known to the villagers as Dr. Kendal, is the well-loved veterinarian for the region. He is fond of animals and loves his job. Grandma is fond of birds and flowers. As a result of her faithful tending, her garden stays in bloom for much of the year. As long as the ground isn't frozen or there isn't snow on the ground, Grandma digs and weeds in the beds. A stone wall wraps the back garden in seclusion and traps the sun's warmth. Birds find it a safe haven. There are bees and butterflies in profusion. All the singing, buzzing, and fluttering of these creatures are a comfort and joy to Grandma.

A shiny black crow has been visiting her garden for quite a few years. He has gotten bolder and bolder over time. An incredibly curious bird, the crow can often be spotted nearby on a high branch, keeping watch over the garden.

In the morning Grandma gardens. In the afternoon she sews. Because the bright sun makes it easier to see the tiny stitches that are

WJWebb

needed for mending and the doing of other needlework, Grandma brings this work outdoors. She sits in her cushioned wicker chair under a favorite tree or in a shady place on the patio.

The crow sometimes seems to be keeping especial watch over Grandma. Although careful to keep a certain distance between them, he sometimes paces the middle of the lawn with a *proprietary air, quite *conspicuously, and even paces the *periphery of the patio where Grandma sits. When she is at the sink washing dishes, she often views him through the kitchen window. Since she and Grandpa eat supper outdoors all summer, perhaps the crow, like other birds, anticipates the proverbial crumb under the table.

Early one afternoon, one of Grandma's friends paid her a visit. "We are so happy that you are willing to embroider some flower buds on the sleeves of these bridesmaids' dresses. It's going to make them extra special!"

"I'm glad you asked me to do it. I like to make a little money of my own. And I already know what I'm going to spend it on."

"Oh, what's that?"

"Every summer I visit the museum gardens at Chelsea, and this year I'm going to buy some snow drop bulbs. I haven't gotten any before because they are so expensive."

"Lovely," her friend said. "We'll need the dresses back in a week's time. Do you think you can have them finished by then?"

"I'm sure I shall," Grandma assured her.

---

*A proprietor is the owner of a business or a property. The adjective "proprietary" describes the bird's attitude (or air) as if it said, "I own the place."

*To be "conspicuous" is to be very noticeable.

*The "periphery" of an area is the outermost edge within a boundary or the area just beyond it.

The two ladies shared a pot of tea and chatted more about flowers. After her friend had departed, Grandma got to work straightaway. It was a perfect warm, sunny day for sewing outside. But after answering one of the many telephone calls that came to the house for Grandpa, she returned to her embroidery to find her needle missing.

"Perhaps it's fallen into a crack in the stone patio," she thought. She felt around for it, but was unsuccessful. Searching through her sewing box, she found a spare embroidery needle.

The following day was also sunny, another perfect day for working outdoors. The sky was deep blue with not a rain cloud in sight. The crow was appreciating the day, too, sitting atop a high branch, lord of all he surveyed. Grandma was making good progress and was already working on the sleeves of the second dress when, as usual, she had to get up to answer the telephone. Leaving the dress and her wire-rimmed glasses on the patio table, she went inside. The call was from a dairy farmer who reported that one of his milking cows had fallen sick.

"Dr. Kendal gave me his *itinerary for today. If you call Mrs. Brown, you might reach him there," she told him.

When Grandma was once more in her chair, dress on her lap, needle in hand, she found to her dismay that her silver thimble was missing. "It's vanished," she said out loud, much perturbed. She got up and went inside to look for her porcelain one. Once inside, she decided she could use a bit of lunch.

She ate in the shade. The crow was slowly pacing the lawn near the birdbath, with the usual appraising look in his eye as if he were sizing up the place. Finally, he hopped onto the birdbath to take a few sips.

"You're too big a bird to be standing on my birdbath. I suppose what you really want is a crust from my sandwich. Here you go." She tossed the crust as far as she could and took her plate inside. She washed up at the kitchen sink, watching through the window as the crow flew away with something in his mouth. "He does love his treats," she smiled.

"Now I can finally get back to my embroidery," she sighed. Moments later she burst forth, "This is the last straw!" Her wire-rimmed glasses had disappeared! Grandma was beginning to get suspicious of the crow when she saw that the sandwich crusts were on the lawn untouched. "That wasn't a crust in your mouth," she called out. "You took my glasses!" Thinking back on other things that had gone missing, she said, "So you're the one to blame for all this mischief. How will I get these sleeves done in time without my glasses?"

---

*An "itinerary" is a scheduled route of a journey. Grandpa often drove from farm to farm.

What happens next? Bring in some characters to help Grandma. I collected some pictures for you to choose from. You may use any of them to explain what else is going on in Mischief's (the bird's) life and Grandma's.

## Writing Help

- How does Grandma find and retrieve her things?
- Who might she get to help her?

It would be funny if, within an hour, lots of people, for different reasons, come to her door, one after another, including Grandpa. It's always funny when lots of people try to help at once and they get in each other's way. However, you write your story the way you want.

# 42

## MARMALADE[B]

Quite an exciting thing happened a week ago. Susan's orange and white cat, Marmalade, had kittens. Both Susan, eight years old, and Olivia, four, have been captivated by the warm, soft, cuddly creatures ever since. Their weak imploring meows are so charming. Susan spends hours looking after them. She makes sure Marmalade eats and drinks and she often makes trips to the basket to check on the kittens while they sleep. She tries to guard them from young Olivia, who continually wants to hold them. When the kittens are asleep, Olivia is not allowed to pick them up, but when they are awake, she is allowed to hold them carefully.

Repeatedly finding Olivia at the cat-basket petting the kittens, Susan finally realized that Olivia must have figured out that petting them wakes them up. Once they are awake, Olivia knows she is allowed to hold them. Then she happily picks them up and carries them all around the house, much to Susan's dismay.

"Olivia," Susan spoke sternly to her sister, "Mother told us that kittens are fragile." Susan, however, still found Olivia carrying around a

kitten so often it was beginning to exasperate her. She tried to make Olivia understand. "We are to let them sleep and only pick them up when they wake up on their own. They're just babies, and they need to sleep a lot," she explained further.

Olivia sensed the concern in her big sister's voice and tried to obey.

When the kittens do wake up they are hungry. The girls like to watch them drink milk from Marmalade. Then it is bath time. This is when Marmalade licks her kittens clean and they purr contentedly. It is then that Susan tells Olivia it is okay to hold them. She is a dedicated supervisor.

One morning Mother set Susan at the kitchen table to copy some verses into a copybook and then carried some laundry down to the basement. Marmalade was contently crunching food at her bowl. "Come on, Susie; let's go play with the kittens," whined Olivia.

"No, it isn't time. I have to do my lesson."

Olivia left. Susan found it difficult to concentrate. She got up and went to the closet under the stairs to check on the kittens and saw Olivia sitting there. She was being very good, actually. She wasn't petting them. She was just sitting next to them. Susan came up with an idea. She wanted to be sure to keep Olivia busy while she copied her verses.

She led Olivia into the living room and set her up with Susan's most special of toys—her little wicker baby carriage, a knitted lace blanket, and her porcelain doll. It was a toy usually kept on a high shelf, a toy Olivia was normally never allowed to play with. Olivia's eyes were widely fixed upon her sister's as she listened to Susan explain just how carefully to play with this toy. Susan knew it was risky, but at least it kept Olivia from gravitating toward the sleepy kittens. When she returned to her writing, Marmalade had left her bowl and Susan assumed she had gone back to her kittens. She didn't know what was taking place in the living room.

What happened to Susan's special toys? If you prefer to write spontaneously (at least at first), start your creative narrating without reading the Writing Help. You can always refer to the Writing Help afterwards.

## Writing Help

What feelings is Susan experiencing? Bring Mother into the story. Other characters can be brought into the story as well. Perhaps someone came along and replaced the broken carriage and doll with something else—what might that be? How could Susan explain to Olivia that accidents do happen and ease her mind, despite her own feelings of disappointment?

Go on to tell more tales about Marmalade, using the picture in which she is swimming the flooded creek. How did she end up here? Cats usually try to avoid water. How determined was she to return to her kittens? What were the boatmen doing?

You might want to talk more about the kittens in your story. Do the kittens have different personalities when they play at home? What kind of antics are they up to? What if a large dog or fox entered the yard—or the house!

# 43

## Father's Clock

Father glanced at his pocket watch. Boldly, and with an unmistakable tone of excitement in his voice, he announced to the party in his living room that, very soon, the nineteenth century would end and the twentieth century would begin. Mother, in her beautiful blue velvet dress, was gracefully ladling small portions of red punch into glasses for their guests—the members of the music society. She was secretly embarrassed that there was less money to buy the exotic ingredients that made up her famous fruit punch. She wished she hadn't had to be so sparing, and wondered if anyone was noticing. Her table was set with no fancy snacks this year, and fewer friends had been invited. She smiled and tried to be jolly, though she really felt awkward. What a disappointment it was to her that the majority of the clocks in her husband's shop had not sold that year—even at Christmastime.

Father whispered something soberly into the ear of the elegant old gentleman standing beside him. As soon as his instructions had been received with a nod and a smile, Father disappeared. He had not forgotten his promise to his sons. His large strides carried him to the boys' bedroom in a flash. Gently placing a hand on the shoulder of Fritz, his eldest son, he said in a low but excited voice, "Boys, boys, wake up. It's time!" Fritz woke fairly quickly, and the noise of his own excitement helped to wake his two brothers, Ernest and Guston.

"Gussy, Gussy, it's time!" Fritz said, shaking his youngest brother's shoulder vigorously. Guston woke up wanting a cup of water.

The boys usually needed reminding by Mother to put on their slippers and robes in winter, but since Father's mind was occupied by one object—an object that was waiting for them downstairs—their bare feet went unremarked.

The murmuring conversation and tinkling glasses of the party grew fainter as the boys followed their father, creeping noiselessly in their bare feet down the narrow back stairs to Father's shop below. Father was proprietor of a clock shop on a very fine street in Holland. He sold new and antique clocks, and repaired both clocks and watches.

A very special clock had arrived this December. Father had hoped that it would be sold by Christmas Eve, but he had still kept the clock a secret from the boys. During the month of December, a busier month than most, one when more customers than usual bustled in and out of all the shops along the street, the boys obeyed their father's wishes to stay out of his shop. But the clock had not been purchased by anyone. Father loved clocks and, in a way, he was glad that this clock hadn't sold before the New Year.

Earlier that evening Father had placed the clock on a mahogany display table in the center of the shop and had covered it with a clean muslin cloth. Now he carefully removed the cloth, and turned to the boys. "Well, what do you think of my surprise?" he asked the boys.

The bright moonlight of the clear night sky shone through the tall shop window. The combination of shadow and light caused the hundreds

of details of the meticulously carved clock to stand out dramatically. For a moment there was silence, as all eyes feasted on the finely crafted work of art. Then Guston said, "It's beautiful, Papa."

"Yes, but it is more than beautiful, Gussy," Father responded. "Because this is a special year, this clock will bring in the New Year with a celebration all its own—a celebration of hope for the future. We thank God for His all-sufficient grace that allowed us the accomplishments of the past century."

The hands on the clock came together precisely at midnight. Though it was a rather large clock, it wasn't a loud one, as might be expected. Twelve deep-sounding but delicately muffled bongs struck the time. Then, above the face of the clock, little double doors opened wide to let out a procession of finely carved miniature people. They were dressed in brightly colored folk costumes. Inside the clock, hidden from view, a metal cylinder with tiny raised metal dots was turning—the workings of a music box. The dots plucked a metal row of teeth that produced their clear notes in perfect time.

The melody was one by Beethoven. Mother was an accomplished pianist, and the boys recognized it as a melody they had heard her play. They had never heard it performed quite like this, however. The miniature dolls slowly circled around the balcony—the ladies twisting to and fro and swirling their fringed skirts. The men opened and closed their arms, clanging tiny cymbals. One little man held a miniature key in his outstretched arms.

Everyone was still standing in absolute silence, dumb with amazement, when a cough from behind knocked them out of their trance and they turned to see who was there. The "elegant old gentleman," a distinguished member of the music society, stood in the shadows. He had been watching the clock's performance as well.

"Bravo! Magnificent clock! Delightful! Never seen anything like it in my life!" exclaimed the gentleman with obvious admiration for the marvel before him. "Forgive me for intruding. May I have a word with you when you rejoin the party?" he asked Father.

"Certainly. Happy to," Father answered. Disappearing into the shadows, the man proceeded up the stairs to the merry assembly above.

Father's attention switched to his boys. "Well, what did you think of it, my lads?"

"It's wonderful," they chorused. Father was greatly pleased at the success of his surprise.

Father was about to herd the boys upstairs when it occurred to him to give the clock a good winding. He put down his candle and, reaching around to the back of the clock to wind it, he suddenly exclaimed, "What's this?" His fingers had found a little partly-opened drawer. Inside was a scroll of paper. As he lifted the paper gingerly between two fingers, something slipped out of it and landed with a clink onto the floor.

"It's a key!" Fritz announced in an excited whisper. "It's like the tiny one held by one of the dolls."

Puzzled, Father picked up the key and placed it on the table. In the light of the candle he smoothed out the paper. Fritz made a second announcement: "It's a map!" Ernest and Guston crowded in. On the reverse side of the map was a letter written in pencil.

"The drawer must have been timed to open just at the turning of the New Year," Father thought to himself. "How very intriguing!"

What happened next?

## Writing Help

- What is the main conflict (problem) of the story? Has another conflict arisen?
- What is the elegant man interested in doing?
- Do Father and the boys keep the key and map a secret? What do you imagine the map is like? What does the letter tell them?
- What conversation will take place between Father and the man?
- What will Mother think of all that is happening?
- What did Mother say when she discovered her boys with cold arms and feet, no robes or slippers? (This is a small matter but small matters can put some humor into a story).
- Who will embark on an adventure? What takes place on the adventure? What do they find? How does the key fit into your story?

# 44

## Stopping a Bully

Hello, Garrett," said Sean cheerfully. Sean had come to visit his sick friend, who was in bed with bronchitis. "Are you feeling any better? My mother asked me to give you this orange as a get-well gift. I hope you enjoy it."

Garrett smiled widely. "Thank you Sean. I love oranges. We rarely have them, except at Christmas. This is a real treat!" Sean's father had died when he was little, and his mother worked very hard to make ends meet.

"You're welcome," responded Sean. "We're all missing you at school. There's no one in class who can come up with the right answer when the rest of us are stumped." Then Sean paused. His *countenance turned serious. "I have something else on my mind Garrett, and I need to talk to you," he ventured.

"Talk away," said Garrett good-naturedly. "I've got lots of time on my hands just now."

---

*The "countenance" of a person is his face, especially his facial expression.

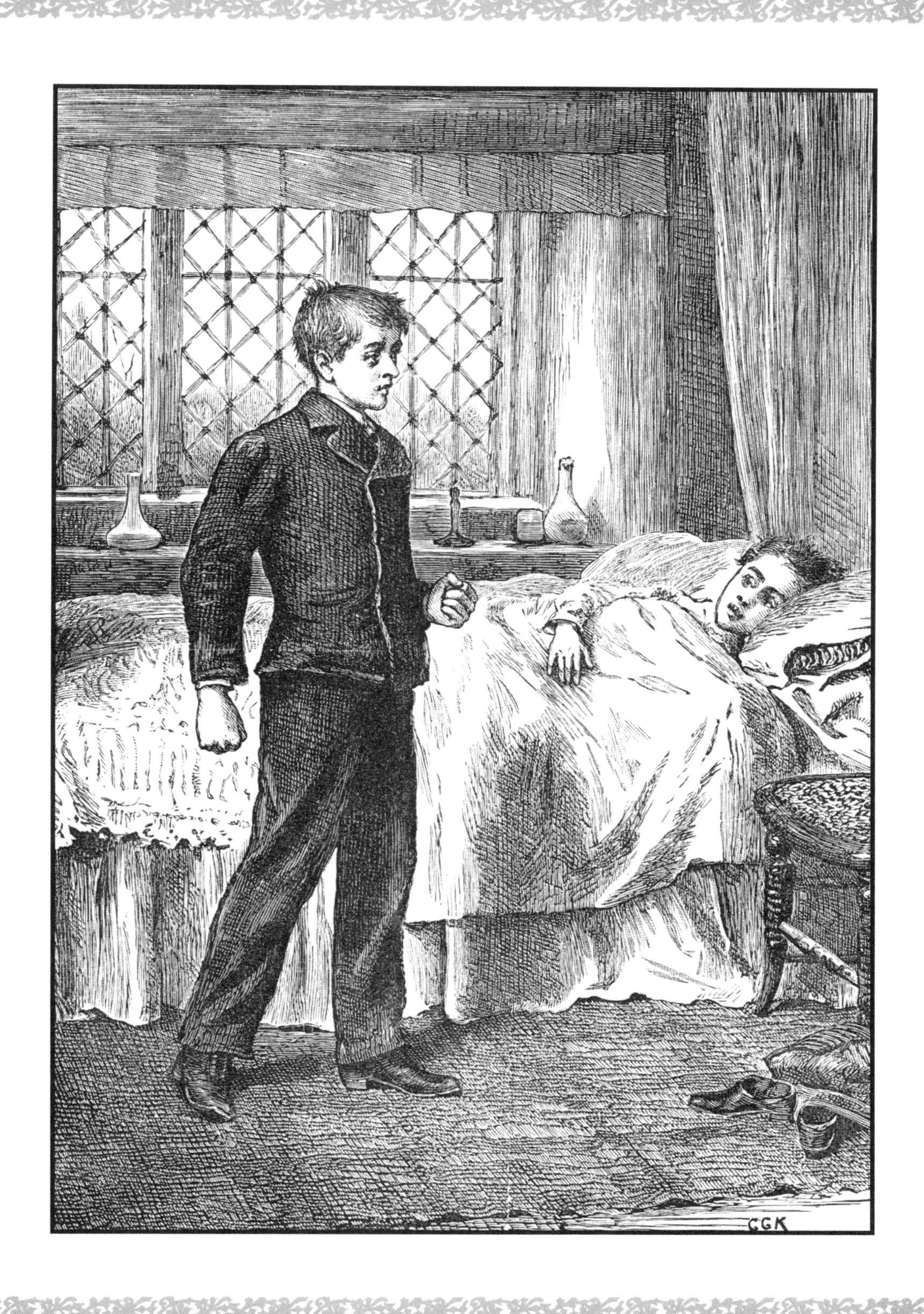
CGK

"I've had it with that bully, Bryan." Sean's hands clenched tightly as he thought about what had happened one week ago. "He's got to be stopped."

"I know what you're thinking," Garrett's sentence was interrupted by a gravelly cough, "but you mustn't. Two wrongs don't make a right."

"Why would it be wrong of me to give Bryan a bit of his own medicine? Don't you believe in self-defense? This bully, who pushed you into the pond, needs to be taught a lesson with a swift punch or two. I saw his laughing face. It disgusted me."

"I've told you already," Garrett continued, coughing again, "I don't believe in getting back at someone by hurting him. Anyway, I don't think Bryan actually meant to push me in the pond. He was just pushing me the way he does now and again, and this time I happened to be standing at the edge of the pond." Garrett finished his defense of the bully with another attack of coughing, which only exasperated Sean all the more.

"Nonsense!" he said, in the middle of Garrett's coughing. "You're ill, Garrett, and you wouldn't *be* so ill if it weren't for him. It's time Bryan paid for what he did. My father has been giving me boxing lessons, and I'm ready to put them to good use!"

Garrett's mother was listening to the boys' conversation through the door. She wasn't a snoopy woman, but the sound of her son's coughing had gotten her attention. It has been her concern that because Garrett is without the influence of a dad, he may be a pushover in every sense of the word. Inspired by the boys' conversation, she gently tapped on Garrett's door, and entered the room.

"Garrett," she said, her eyes twinkling, "what do you say to having a party?"

The two boys look bewildered. "But how will I entertain my guests, Mother, when I'm not at all well?"

"It will be just a get-together, a sort of "get well" party, but we won't call it that. Sean, your father can do some fine sleight-of-hand tricks, can't he?"

"Of course, Mrs. Sullivan."

"Good. That's what I needed to know. Do you think you and he would be willing to provide us with a boxing demonstration as well?"

"I'll ask, him, Ma'am."

"Thank you. I couldn't help overhearing part of your conversation, and I think we can show this bully Bryan that he isn't the only tough one around, and we can do it in such a way that he won't be directly threatened by it."

"You're inviting Bryan to the party?" Garrett asked, stunned. He pulled himself up a little higher upon the pillow.

"Don't you think it's a good idea?"

After a brief pause he said, "It just might work, Mom. You're the greatest."

"I try," she admitted. "Now don't let any of the boys we invite know anything about our secret plan."

Sean was doubtful, but he didn't show it. Walking home after his visit with Garrett, he thought about his own plan again, thinking it was a more satisfying one than Mrs. Sullivan's idea for a party. That very afternoon while walking home from school he had seen Bryan pulling the ear of another schoolmate—an incident he hadn't mentioned to Garrett.

Part of Mrs. Sullivan's plan for the party was to let the bully Bryan see how ill Garrett has been as a result of having been pushed into the pond. She hoped that, accident or no accident, Bryan's conscience

W S Stacey

would be awakened and that he would face the results of his bullying. As soon as she left Garrett's room, she started making plans for the party. She talked to Sean's mother, and told her about her idea with regard to Bryan. Sean's mother, who had heard all about the bully Bryan from Sean, thought it was a wonderful idea and was sure her husband would want to participate. That same evening Mrs. Sullivan wrote her invitations. The next day she hand-delivered them.

When she arrived at the doorstep of Bryan's house, his mother invited Mrs. Sullivan into a cozy parlor. Although the two ladies were only acquaintances they had some tea and a congenial chat. At an opportune moment, Mrs. Sullivan brought up the subject of Bryan's bullying. When Bryan's mother apologized politely for what she called her son's *"idiosyncrasy," Mrs. Sullivan, astonished at her for taking the matter of bullying so lightly, decided *not* to reveal to her the real reason for the party.

As Bryan's mother waved good-bye at the door she added a little nervously, "Thank you for the invitation. I'll have another little talk with Bryan about his way of dealing with his fellow classmates."

Garrett's mother smiled and waved good-bye. As she walked down the front path to the street, she thought, "When some parents love their children, they become blind to the full extent of their faults."

How does the party go?

---

*Bryan's mother used the term "idiosyncrasy" to suggest that her son had a tiny fault in his behavior that needed correction. "Idiosyncrasy" really means behavior that is peculiar and that has no right or wrong attached to it.

## Writing Help

Describe the party; the decorations, the food, the games, and the amazing tricks performed by Sean's dad. What do the boys and Bryan think of the boxing demonstration? Is Bryan invited to participate in the boxing? If so, what happens and what affect does it have on him.

Does Bryan consider why Garrett is sick? Does he feel bad that Garrett is unable to actively join in the fun? Show how he might be affected.

Perhaps you'd like to draw a picture of the scene at the party.

If you are familiar with Dickens' *A Christmas Carol*, you will be familiar with the character Scrooge. Memories, regrets, fear, and new feelings of sympathy soften Scrooge's heart. Will Bryan's heart be softened or humbled? Does he ever stop bullying others? Make the characters of this story feel, act, and speak. What do they do and say because of what is going on around them? You probably can tell that I am leading you to create a happy ending with conflict resolution.

Is asking forgiveness an easy thing to do? Does anyone else in the story have a change of heart by the end of the party? Who? Would you like to put a handshake in your story as part of the reconciliation?

## Additional Challenge

How is humility such a helpful virtue?

# 45

## Making a Call[B]

Mrs. Peppercorn is a shut-in who lives in a handsome house on Front Street. Her son and his family live nextdoor and drop by frequently to look after her. Her house is only a block or two from church and the shops, but walking even that far is too painful to her. Getting in and out of the motorcar is also too painful to her. Yet she rarely complains. Even though she is lonely at times, invitations for "getting out" are always sweetly and politely turned down with the claim that "the weather doesn't agree with my rheumatism."

Samantha and her younger sister Ruth remember old Mrs. Peppercorn, when she did attend church, as being a bit scary. They remember her as a large woman with a powdered face and cheeks painted orange over lots of deep wrinkles, and gray hair that was always tightly pulled back and hidden under a bulky hat. She usually wore an old-fashioned black dress that was rather wide in the skirt. She walked slowly, leaning much of her weight upon a wooden cane, and was noticeably short of breath. Anyone near her detected a slightly sour fragrance of what was supposed to be lavender. She had lovely manners, and she always had a

smile and a greeting for Samantha and Ruth. But the girls had been afraid of her. Their greeting in return was usually less kind and gracious than it should have been.

One morning Samantha was enlightened by a Sunday school lesson. Her teacher was teaching from chapter one of the book of James. She told the children, "As Christians we are to be *doers of the word, and not hearers only*. Hearing comes first," she said, "but the most attentive and the most frequent hearing of the word of God will not avail us, unless we be also doers of it. If we were to hear a sermon every day of the week, and an angel from heaven were the preacher, and yet we rested in mere hearing, it would never bring us closer to God." Samantha was most affected by this exhortation.

At Sunday dinner Samantha shared with her family what she had learned. "You have a wise Sunday school teacher," Samantha's dignified father told her. "Yes, we must practice what we hear. This is why we do good deeds. In doing them we are blessed."

"I want to be blessed," piped in young Ruth.

"And you *shall* be, Ruth. But we are not blessed *for* our good deeds, but *in* them."

"What do you mean, Father?" asked Samantha.

"Remember Psalm One?" Father asked. "You recited it for us last spring. *Blessed is the man who walks* in the righteous way, you explained to us in that recitation. Doing good is the way we shall find blessedness, but it isn't the cause of it. Those who continue in the word of God, are and shall be blessed *in their deed,* blessed *in all their ways,* according to the first Psalm, to which some think James here makes reference. And Jesus said, '*If you know these things, happy are you if you do them.*'"

"Oh, yes," Samantha answered pensively. She had caught the spirit of what her father said, although she didn't quite know the difference between the "fors" and "ins." Then she added, "My teacher also talked about false religion and true religion. She said that true religion is *visiting and providing for the fatherless and the widow*."

Mother joined the conversation and spoke kindly, "It is remarkable that in James the sum of religion is drawn up in these two points. I know some widows I haven't visited in awhile, and I feel quite encouraged to do so now, after listening to your discussion."

Samantha smiled and was quiet for the rest of the meal. The early afternoon sun was shining in bright boldness through the white curtains onto the white dining room tablecloth and Samantha felt a brightening up of her heart, too. She had an idea. Her lesson that morning had given her new courage. Love, with its power to lead us to think more of others and less of ourselves, has a way of setting aside our fears.

"Mother, may I go into the garden to pick some flowers without changing out of my Sunday dress?" Samantha asked.

"May I, too?" Ruth chimed in.

Mother wanted to know what it was all about. Normally she would have said no to such a request. But when Samantha explained her plan, Mother was very pleased and gave her permission with a warm heart.

Look at the picture and explain Samantha's plan. How did the rest of Samantha's Sunday go?

Write what comes to you. Take a peek at Writing Help only if you want more ideas.

## Writing Help

- What did Samantha have the courage to do, based on the power of love? You can see in the picture that the sisters are making a call in their Sunday best. Do you think it might be to Mrs. Peppercorn? What preparations did Samantha and Ruth make before they paid a visit? Did Mother come too? How did the visit go? What took place inside the house?

- How was Mrs. Peppercorn blessed? How were the girls blessed in their good deed? Explain in what ways this visit could have given them a new perspective on their hostess.

# 46

## Marvelous Exertion(B)(I)

A tale was told of a horse of great determination. A clipper ship, the *Horn of Plenty*, was delivering a supply of horses, as part of its cargo. During the voyage, the sky became crowded with thick billows of gray clouds. Gusts of wind hit the mainsails and the yardarm with enough insistence that they were rolled up by order of the captain. Waves rocked the ship fore and aft, up and down. This motion agitated the horses in the hold. One black stallion, a very valuable horse, pulled at his tethers so violently that he broke free and made his way (no one knows how) onto the deck. The deck was soaked by torrents of rain from the sky and by sea spray from cresting waves—water from above and below, a deadly deluge created by the fierce wind. The water stung the stallion's eyes.

Then thunder crackled like a long string of firecrackers from one end of the darkening sky to the other. The stallion did what all horses do when they are terribly frightened. He ran. He ran the length of the deck and made a great leap overboard into the sea. There was nothing the crew could do. The ship had a lifeboat, but how would the crew get the horse into it?

This was the second voyage for the limber-jointed young seaman on watch. He was excited. He kept an eye on the horse as it rose and sank with the waves, disappearing under the frothy spray and reappearing again. He named the horse Tear Drop, because its big beautiful brown eyes seemed to be wet with tears as well as seawater. Tear Drop treaded water steadily trying to keep afloat and stay near the ship. In the morning the watchman reported that the stallion had treaded water all night!

The storm wasn't particularly long. By morning light the sea looked so pleasant one would never have guessed it had been in a bad temper the night before. As soon as the crew sat down to breakfast, they caught word of Tear Drop's marvelous exertion. As one, they left their steaming mugs of coffee and went on deck to witness the feat of strength and determination with their own eyes.

"Well, I'll be a monkey's uncle!" said one.

"What will happen to the fellow?" howled another.

"He deserves to live, this brave one. He'd make any owner proud," Cook spoke out. He had left his hot pot and come on deck when he saw his table had been deserted.

"Think. We gotta do somethin'," the watchman said.

The captain called out to his crew. "Hear this, mateys. You have fifteen minutes to get breakfast in your bellies before full sails ahead." There was a perfect breeze and Captain wanted to deliver his cargo in good time.

"What will happen to Tear Drop?" was the private thought that rushed to the young watchman. Only he, who had witnessed an entire night of the horse's exertion, was daring enough to question his captain. The others clambered below.

"Permission to speak, Captain."

"Permission granted."

"What can be done about the horse, Sir?"

"Do you see that ship off the bow? It looks like it could be Captain Pendleton's ship, *Sea Horse*. I reckon he'll have the equipment to hoist that horse out of the water. I'm putting out a distress signal. With this

good wind, she'll be here in less than a quarter-hour." For the ship to be thus named, *Sea Horse* seemed like an incredible boon to the watchman. It made him believe Providence was at work in answering his prayer for Tear Drop.

He wanted to jump and yell "Yahoo!" to the horse and "Good thinking!" to the Captain, but restrained himself on both points out of respect for ship decorum. Instead, in his excitement, he bounced down into the hold to report the hopeful news to the crew.

"You better get some shut-eye," one told him.

The watchman gave his answer groggily as he tried to fight off an impending yawn, "I wouldn't...miss...this." The men laughed and one passed him a mug of coffee minus the milk.

A man on board the *Sea Horse* spotted something peculiar in the water near the *Horn of Plenty*. "Can't make it out, Captain," the seaman said. Then they heard the distress signal.

Tell the rest of the tale.

## Writing Help

I read that over one hundred years ago a horse fell overboard and stayed with the ship, treading water for nearly three days. This report gave me the idea for this story. So you see, Tear Drop's tale is not as incredible as you might think.

Describe the rescue. In what port did they land? Where did Tear Drop end up?

## Additional Challenge

If you are really ambitious, try your hand at writing a short poem about the main action. Perhaps you could make it into the lyrics the sailors would sing below deck about Tear Drop.

# 47

## A Nasty Drawing

Hartley Hall is an impeccable girl's school—well, almost impeccable. The girls love their teachers. And because of the cheerful atmosphere of the classrooms, friendships thrive. There is something different about this school. The subjects are not long and drawn out as in many schools, and the headmistress forbids the typical lackluster lecture. Instead, subjects are given close attention while the teacher reads aloud from the best sorts of books on a variety of subjects. The girls keep a record of what they learn by putting the reading in their own words and keeping their narration in a simple black and white composition book.

Flora likes the subject of nature study best because she enjoys the nature walks led by Miss St. John every Wednesday afternoon. After a brisk and exhilarating walk in the fresh outdoors to find and identify specimens, it is always pleasant to return to a warm classroom. There the girls watercolor their specimen and copy a nature poem into their nature diaries. They are encouraged to compose their own poems for their books, as well.

Each spring Miss Hathaway's English class puts on a Shakespeare play, and Flora's friend Frances eagerly looks forward to participating in the production. Miss Hathaway claims to be a distant relative of Shakespeare. The play is performed outdoors in the manner of the Globe Theater in Shakespeare's day, and many from the community come to hear it. But few girls look forward to Miss Sitterley's math class with much relish. "Sour Sitterley," Frances calls her.

Walking home after school one day with Frances, Flora thought she had better warn her friend.

"Frances, you shouldn't call any teacher a name," she advised.

Angela, who was rather keen on numbers, admonished Frances as well. "You just don't like math, that's all. Everyone knows you're the best artist in the school *and* the best actress. Anyway, haven't you heard that Miss Sitterley's two younger sisters were married in a double wedding last month and poor Miss Sitterley is without even a suitor? I think she greatly admired one of the grooms at one time, which probably made it even harder for her. Can't you be kind, and realize that her behavior doesn't affect you alone?"

"It doesn't give her the excuse to be cross and impatient with my wrong answers," protested Frances.

"I think you exaggerate. I've never seen her cross with you," responded Flora.

"Neither have I," Angela chimed in. "Your work frequently needs correction, that's all. And I don't mean that as an insult."

Frances turned and left in a huff. Her pretty blond hair floated on the breeze behind her.

Both Flora and Angela knew Miss Sitterely was not the most light-hearted of teachers, but they both liked her, nevertheless.

Still thinking of Miss Sitterely, Flora turned to Angela and said somewhat sadly, “My mother always says, ‘If you don’t have anything nice to say about someone, say nothing at all.’”

“Mine, too,” admitted Angela. And with this, the subject was dropped.

The next day Frances proved that she was unmoved and unrepentant. She was determined that she didn’t need to heed the advice of her friends. During Miss Sitterley’s class, when she was supposed to be doing her math problems, she penciled out a smattering of numbers, then took out drawing paper and decided to have a little fun at the expense of Miss Sitterley. Her artistic talent afforded her the ability to draw caricatures of people, to make likenesses of them, exaggerating their facial expressions.

Explain what happens next in this scene. Make the characters speak.

## Writing Help

These questions are only meant to give you some ideas. You needn’t answer them one by one. Give the questions some thought and then let your story flow.

- How does Miss Sitterley realize that something is up?
- What does Frances do when she is found out? Does she ever repent? What is she most embarrassed about?
- Does Miss Sitterley resolve to be more cheerful? What new thoughts might keep her from self-pity?

- What part did the consciences of the characters play in this story? Your conscience is something in your soul that trains you concerning right and wrong. It is best not to ignore it, or there will be negative consequences.
- What positive long-term consequences would there be for those in this story who take on a change of heart? How would it mend their relationships?

# 48

## Ralph of Red Gables

*When I first mentioned to a ten-year-old friend the title "Ralph of Red Gables," she giggled, because she was very familiar with the story,* Anne of Green Gables. *My made-up title sounded silly to her. Her giggle gave me the confidence to move ahead with the story that had been brewing in my head for some time. Have fun with it. It is told from the point of view of the housemaid.*

Dear Sister,

It's been ages since I last heard from you. As housemaid to the Candlewicks, a middle-aged couple here in this small town of Connecticut, I've been quite content. Red Gables is a quiet abode. My cleaning is done in double quick time and I have much of each afternoon to myself.

Changes have transpired at Red Gables. My employers have a houseguest, a nine-year-old orphan boy that the people of our small town call Ralph of Red Gables. As you know, because of the nearby train station, it is convenient to travel to New York City. Mr. Candlewick goes to the city at least once a month to visit his publisher and an old school chum. His old school chum is Ralph's teacher. Until now, apparently Ralph had never been anywhere besides the orphanage and the school. The two old friends must have talked about Ralph, because Mr. Candlewick brought him home on the train with him that very afternoon, to the surprise of Mrs. Candlewick. Poor boy doesn't even know his birthday. I wonder if he has ever even had a birthday cake.

All Ralph brought with him were two sets of clothes, his return ticket, and his red plaid tam o'-shanter, the only thing left to him by his Scottish parents. He keeps the ticket in his breast pocket whenever he is wearing his better suit.

I overheard Mr. Candlewick tell his wife that Ralph was staying with them for the summer holidays. The country air and change of scenery will do him good. But she must guess that her husband is, in all truth, considering Ralph for adoption. They are childless, and I know they both have always wanted children.

I've probably already told you that Mrs. Candlewick has been in weak health for some years. She has taken iron pills, cod liver oil, and herbal remedies, at the insistence of Mr. Candlewick, but her condition has remained the same. What a gloomy life she lives! She always refuses Mr. Candlewick's invitations and urgings to accompany him to town. Rarely does she step outdoors for any reason except to be driven to church.

For Mr. Candlewick, it is work before pleasure at Red Gables. I'm able to get a good view of the farmyard from the second story windows. I've noticed that, with Ralph by his side, Mr. Candlewick's expression seems sunnier and perhaps the morning chores feel lighter as he shows Ralph what to do to help. Ralph seems to be a fast learner. The newness of the experience has to be a thrill for him. I'm glad that he got over his initial fear of the animals after the first few days and enjoys feeding them all and even cleaning out their stalls.

In the afternoon he and Mr. Candlewick change out of their muddy boots and overalls and put on their "gentleman farmer" garb. It's strange that Ralph keeps his return ticket to New York in his inside pocket. Why, I don't know. He meets a new person in town every day, it seems, as they walk around the town square. Tomorrow, Mr. Candlewick said he would take Ralph down to the brook to teach him how to swim. The afternoons are getting hot. Remember how we used to swim in that same brook? I wonder if they will meet up with other swimmers, like we used to. How we giggled over this.

Cook, who has made the same meals so many times she could do it with her eyes closed, has had her mundane routine interrupted. All of a sudden, Mrs. Candlewick has become particular. She has something to say about everything to be served, wanting each dish to be especially pleasing to Ralph. Mr. Candlewick, much amazed, found her one morning at the edge of the meadow picking wildflowers to decorate the breakfast table.

Later that same day she had me go with her to the attic to help her search for six sets of white ruffled curtains she was sure she had in one of the trunks. When found, the curtains needed washing, bleaching in the sun, and ironing (by me of course) before they could replace the heavy drapes in the parlor and dining room. She smiled when her husband commented about how bright and cheerful the house felt. Before Mr. Candlewick and Ralph went to town, she asked her husband to measure Ralph's arms and torso. Then she handed Mr. Candlewick a piece of paper. I guessed it was a list of things she needed him to get her from town.

The next morning I couldn't believe my eyes. She was sitting at her sewing machine. Mr. Candlewick went about his morning chores without disturbing her. In the afternoon she sat at her writing desk in the parlor, addressing a stack of what looked like invitations. These she hid in a drawer the moment she heard Ralph and Mr. Candlewick enter the dining room for supper. Mr. Candlewick has been what I can only call jolly, a side of him we don't often see. I haven't yet heard him compliment his wife on her sudden surge of energy. Of course I don't dare mention it, as it is not my place.

I must go. I will write you more next week to let you know how things are getting on. Please write me soon about your work in Boston. Is it tiring on the legs to work as a maid in such a large house?

Love, Miranda

Have Miranda write another letter to her sister telling her about more "goings on."

What does Ralph think of Red Gables?

## Writing Help

Can you guess what Mrs. Candlewick might be planning for Ralph? I put some clues early in the story. This is called *foreshadowing.* One instance of foreshadowing was, "I wonder if he has ever had a birthday cake?"

- What caused Mrs. Candlewick to allow her life to become somewhat gloomy? What brightened up her life? Since you are finishing my story, you get to be the one who decides if the Candlewicks adopt Ralph.
- Ralph is attempting to do things that are new to him: swimming, perhaps riding a horse, etc. What does he think of it all? (How might the boys at the swimming hole react?) Add some conflict to the story (things that could go wrong, difficulties, etc., that could be corrected or made better.) Things didn't always go so smoothly with Anne of Green Gables either!

In the end, does Ralph want to stay with the Candlewicks at Red Gables?

## Additional Challenge

You might prefer to tell the story from Ralph's point of view rather than that of the housemaid.

### *Point of View*

If you continue with the housemaid as narrator, you are limited in your knowledge of what is felt or done by the characters. You are limited to what she sees and overhears. In other words, you cannot describe a scene at the creek in much detail if Miranda isn't there to observe. She can only report to her sister what is said when Mr. Candlewick and Ralph return, and describe the facial expressions and moods she observes in the members of the household.

# 49

## Goodbye, Mr. Woodhouse

Spring, at last, had arrived. Mr. Woodhouse was heading off as planned. It was time to say goodbye to the Indian tribe.

Mr. Woodhouse's memory took him back to the middle of the winter when he had found himself lying on his back in a snow bank. He had fallen off his horse when it reared at the sound of a wildcat. The snow had cushioned his fall, but a piece of bluntly-pointed rock that jutted up through the snow had knocked the wind out of him and had pained his back to the degree that he had feared to move. He could only rest in the cold, shivering and wondering what to do. His horse had run off after it had reared, but after a time it had returned to the spot where its master lay, pawing at the snow like a hungry deer to find any plant matter underneath to chew. Mr. Woodhouse had fallen asleep in the snow.

When he awoke he was thirsty. Keeping his body still, he had reached over and scooped some snow into his mouth, let it melt and swallowed it. In doing so, he noticed how the cold had slowed the movements of his arm and he had feared that he would die there. Then his

horse snorted. Lifting his chin to see what had disturbed the horse, he had discovered that three silent Indian men were standing near his horse. They had made a stretcher, rolled him in blankets, and brought him back to their camp.

Throughout the rest of the winter he was nursed and cared for by an Indian princess—the chief's eldest daughter. She was the most curious one of the tribe. The Indians knew some English, and Mr. Woodhouse knew a little of their language. They conversed from this common knowledge. Mr. Woodhouse could do little but talk, as his back pained him, and he was ordered to remain immobile so that his wounds would heal safely.

He spoke to the Indians of various things he had learned in his life. Putting his knowledge in the form of stories was a clever way, he thought, to teach them all sorts of things.

He taught them what he knew about the Scriptures and prayed that God would give them understanding and transform their hearts. Some of them were open to the message and wanted to know more. In others his message seemed to foster discontent and quiet hostility. The restless ones wanted him to leave their camp. Mr. Woodhouse sometimes heard them arguing in their tents and wondered if they were arguing about him. He planned to leave as soon as he could.

Now he was healed enough to ride out of camp. Spring was arrayed in its sweet, delicate blooms, protected; it seemed, from the stronger rays of an overjoyed sun by the tender sprouting leaves of the trees. At the moment of departure, Mr. Woodhouse offered the chief his horse as a thanksgiving gift. Walking would take longer, but he was willing. The chief refused.

"But you've saved my life," Mr. Woodhouse insisted adamantly.

"Your stories from Scriptures have saved us," was the chief's reply.

"It is by faith in Christ that you are saved," Mr. Woodhouse humbly reminded him. But the chief still refused the gift of the horse. A few Indians standing back by the trees scowled. They had no use for a white man's God.

"What you gave my people is worth more than your good horse. And you need it more than we do."

It was time for them to part.

Continue the story from here. Use the picture in your telling if you wish.

## Writing Help

This is one of my favorite pictures in *Story Starters*. There are few things that can cross the barriers of cultures. One of them is love—God's love—which is what came to mind when I gazed at this picture. It does not have to depict the end of a story. It can illustrate the beginning of one. What are the Indian princess and Mr. Woodhouse saying to each other in the picture?

Add your own chapter to the story.

To where was Mr. Woodhouse returning? What was he doing or where was he going when he fell off his horse that winter? Was there anyone back at home worried about him? How did the Indian princess feel about his leaving?

Does Mr. Woodhouse promise to return? If so, does he return just in the nick of time? "In the nick of time" is what makes a story more exciting. Can it also help make Mr. Woodhouse more of a hero? Would he bring anyone with him?

## Additional Challenge

There was discord in the camp after some of the Indians accepted Christianity. If the tribe is split over this issue, how will the members be affected? (Luke 12:51) What changes (or, as the Puritans called them, "reforms") are made by the chief as he attempts to lead his people to live more holy lives? What happens when change is enacted?

### *John Eliot*

John Eliot (1604-1690) was a Puritan missionary to the Indians in colonial Massachusetts. The town of Eliot in southern Maine was named after him. A peacekeeper, John Eliot translated the Bible into an Indian dialect, and supervised fourteen villages inhabited by more than one thousand Indian converts. These peace-loving Christians were known as the praying Indians. Sadly, they were scattered by warring Indian tribes during King Philip's War.

Any knowledge you have of Indian tribes can help you with your story.

# 50

## A Friend in Need[B]

My name is Joseph Trenton. I own a dry goods store in a small town in Ohio, where I live with my wife and children. All of our relatives still reside in eastern Pennsylvania, and my children have never met most of them. Recently, my aunt wrote to tell me that she was sending me the childhood diary of my great-grandmother Charlotte, which had been left to me in her will. We were all very excited when the package arrived.

I read portions of the diary to my children so that they could learn more about our family history. I'd like to share with you one of the stories my great-grandmother recorded. If you like horses as much she did, you will find it interesting. I think Charlotte was about thirteen years old at the time of the writing.

Charlotte lived with her family on a farm near Gettysburg, Pennsylvania, the scene of a horrible battle that took place during the American Civil War. She relates that sometime after this battle, her family was visited by a Mr. McGuire, a war correspondent. Her parents were probably being interviewed for an article he was writing for a

newspaper, but she does not mention this. She writes of a story the war correspondent told during his visit.

Apparently, among the many distressing sights indicative of the miseries of war which were to be found at every turn, the newspaperman took notice of a tired-looking horse. My great-grandmother loved horses, so she listened attentively, and later recorded the correspondent's story as follows:

> *A very dirty white horse was standing motionless, with his fore-leg poised in the air. I went up to it. Without moving in the least, the poor beast turned his great blue eyes to me, saying as plainly as looks could do: "For mercy's sake, help me if you can." I examined the leg, and soon found that a bullet had lodged in the crown of the hoof, which was very much swelled and sore, and the flies had been dreadfully busy with it. Of course, to remove the cause of a week's agony was but a few minutes' work, and if you had seen how grateful the old fellow was when he put down his leg, you would never have forgotten it.*

Turning the pages of the diary, I read elsewhere of another mention of a horse:

> *Today Daddy brought home a white horse with blue eyes. He said he bought it cheap. He isn't sure how much it can do, but he's made a good guess that it once was someone's prize possession. I wonder if this could be the same white horse that Mr. McGuire spoke to us about. It must be. It has the nicest disposition. It has taken to Cinders immediately. I asked Daddy if I could name it and he said I could.*

Cinders was apparently the family dog; the name was probably short for Cinderella. Some pages later, she mentions that the horse and Cinders were constant companions. But then she mentions something distressing. She writes,

*Our neighbor, Mr. Harper, came over to the house today to talk to Daddy. He claims that our Cinders stole away five of his chickens in the last two weeks, because he saw Cinders on his property. Dad asked Mr. Harper if there were signs of a struggle—tufts of feathers anywhere, or a partly eaten bird, or paw prints. Mr. Harper said there were none. Daddy told him that he didn't think Cinders had killed any chickens and that he suspected it was a person who has been stealing them, especially as the door to the coop was latched shut.*

*Mr. Harper only got madder at being contradicted. Daddy told me to leave the room, so I didn't hear the rest of the talk, but I do know that more words were spoken because Mr. Harper was loud and I heard the door slam when he left. Daddy tells me that because so much of our food was given to the soldiers, he guesses people around here are more on edge.*

Further along in the diary Charlotte mentions that Cinders has gone missing. She writes:

*She sometimes likes to run off in the fields, chasing a rabbit or something, but she always comes home for her supper. Where can she be? I hope she didn't go traipsing onto Mr. Harper's land. I wouldn't put it past him to shoot Cinders.*

In her next entry she mentions that Cinders did not return at all that night. In the morning when Charlotte was about to set off to look for her, she noticed that Prince Charming (she evidently had named the new horse) was not in the paddock. She writes:

*I saw Prince Charming last night. He was there. Before I went to bed when we were calling and calling for Cinders, he was in his paddock, watching us.*

*When I told Daddy that Prince Charming was missing too, he stopped his chores and walked with me far from the house to look and call for them both. We walked a long way. The sun was getting hot and we were thirsty, so we entered some woods where we knew we would find a stream. I was so happy when we stopped there, because just beyond, in Mr. Harper's field, I spotted Prince Charming and Cinders. They were together, just as Dad had hoped.*

Continue the story, describing the action that takes place. Remember, Charlotte is writing in her diary. Using the evidence in the picture, describe Prince Charming's friendly deed. What is the conflict in the story? How is it resolved?

Give the meaning of this motto: "A friend in need is a friend indeed." How does your story exemplify this motto?

## Writing Help

Do you think Mr. Harper placed a trap on his property to protect his chickens from Cinders or a fox? Was Cinders where he was because he wanted to kill a chicken? If it is a person who is suspected of being the one doing the stealing, is he or she ever caught? Does Mr. Harper ever apologize?

# 51

## A Man-eating Tiger[(I)]

*Note for the teacher: This exercise may not be suitable for the very young or sensitive child.*

*In the Writing Help I have provided some factual information about the tiger problem in British India about one hundred years ago. I was very surprised to learn these facts when I did my research, and I think you might be, too.*

other, they're here!" Sabu cried out excitedly. All morning Sabu had stared at the dusty road that led to his poor village in India, waiting. Upon hearing his cry, villagers leaned out of their windows and crowded into doorways. They were eager to see his father return with the Englishman. It was the moment everyone in the village had anticipated. Sabu's father had left four days ago, taking upon himself the task of finding Mr. Alden Landsbury, an Englishman with the reputation for being an excellent hunter. How wonderful that he had been found and had agreed to come to their aid.

"They're here!" Mother called to her daughters just as excitedly. She had been saving a portion of their meager rations of food for this hoped-for occasion. Now it was time to prepare it carefully. Hunger was well known these last few weeks in the village. Fear came first—the fear of a man-eating tiger. Hunger followed. After witnessing a villager being dragged away in the mouth of a huge tiger, and being powerless to stop it, the people were horrified. Men, who worked in the fields gathering the harvest, or tending their animals, did so in constant fear that the prowling tiger would strike again. Women made their young children stay indoors. They filled their water jars at the well nervously, their big brown eyes darting back and forth from their task at the well to the edge of the jungle where the man-eater lived.

The tiger did strike again! It was horrible. No one went out to the fields after that. The harvest was destined to rot.

Sabu's stomach grumbled and ached. He had had little to eat for weeks. But the burning in his stomach disappeared as soon as he spotted the face of the Englishman and saw the rifle he held over his shoulder.

Sabu's family and the Englishman sat cross-legged on a woven mat on the floor of their little house and ate. No one spoke of tigers. Mr. Landsbury wasn't a talkative man anyway and had already heard the grim stories of the dreaded man-eater from Sabu's father. He was sympathetic to their plight. Reminded of their hunger, he ate as sparingly as he ate quietly. The sun was now high in the sky. It sizzled the roof of the little house, and radiated through the low ceiling onto their heads. Mr. Landsbury wiped the sweat from his brow with a handkerchief that was nearly useless because it was already saturated. "Thank you for the fine meal," he said. "Now if you'll excuse me, I must be off."

"Please. Take these biscuits," insisted Sabu with an outstretched arm. He was giving up tomorrow's breakfast for Mr. Landsbury.

"I'm very grateful," he nodded, accepting what was offered him. Placing his hat firmly on his head, he smiled his farewell. He picked up his gear and marched out of the little house, out of the village, and into the jungle with a stern look of determination on his face. Actually Alden admired the great strength and beauty of the Indian tiger, but on rare occasions it was necessary to kill a man-eater in order to save a village. Armed with only an axe, his favorite single shot rifle, and a flask of tea, Alden followed the tiger's huge paw tracks. He lost the tracks, found them, and then lost them again over and over during his search. "This tiger is set on outsmarting me," he thought to himself.

Weary, he spent the night in a tree. When he opened his eyes from a short but deep sleep he was alarmed at the sight of the tiger. It was sleeping just below him. That is when he realized that it was the tiger that had been hunting *him*! So as not to awaken the great beast, he moved an arm as slowly as a slithering snake to reach for his rifle. Just as slowly he raised the rifle to take aim. But when he looked through his sights there was no tiger. It had vanished soundlessly into the thick brush. "You *are* a clever one," thought Alden.

All that morning he walked through the humid jungle without any tracks to follow, waiting, watching, and listening. Around noon he spotted a paw print in the soft ground near the edge of a murky pond. There he waited in the brush. Two hours went by. The sun was getting hot. To ward off the wave of sleepiness that had come upon him, he sat down on a rock to eat a stale biscuit and drink his tea. Then he knelt at the pond's edge to splash his hot face with cool water.

Where was the tiger? How did the confrontation begin? Explain Mr. Landsbury's predicament. Describe his struggle. How was the tiger eventually captured? I have provided you with a picture that shows a tiger hunt in progress. You may use it, along with the one of Alden Landsbury, for your story if you'd like.

## Writing Help

When Mr. Alden Landsbury returns to the village what story does he have to tell? What does Sabu think of all of this?

## *What Do You Know About Tigers?*

More than one hundred years ago, a great many large tigers inhabited the jungles of India. These huge cats belong to the same "feline" family as lions but are larger. Male tigers weigh from 400 to 500 pounds. Are you familiar with Rudyard Kipling's *The Jungle Book*? If you are, you are familiar with the tiger called Shere Khan. Mr. Kipling gave this tiger a vicious character. The other animals in the story hate Shere Khan because he kills not just for food but for the taste of blood.

Although *The Jungle Book* is a fictional story, it gives us a fairly accurate picture of how people once thought of tigers. If tigers had remained in the jungles, village people would have had a much better opinion of them, but the tigers did not do so. They soon found out that the cattle and goats that villagers kept were just as good to eat as the wild deer and wild pigs that lived in the forests, and were much more easily caught than wild animals. Therefore, as soon as the young tiger was able to eat meat, its mother generally made her home in the jungle conveniently near a village. Thousands of cows and calves were killed every year and carried off to feed the cubs. In fact, Indian tigers ate about thirty-two thousand head of cattle a year.

Tigers also attacked the Indian people who lived in small villages at the edges of the jungles. When a tiger successfully attacked and ate a person, it would come back again and again to the same village. Man-eating tigers were more often the wounded tigers or older tigers whose energy was lacking and whose teeth were worn. These tigers found it easier to kill people than even tame cattle.

This fact is startling. In British India, between four and five thousand people were killed by tigers yearly. Most of the victims were the men who drove the cattle to and from the grazing grounds each morning and evening. A man's entire head can fit inside the mouth of a tiger. To witness such a thing would have been a horrifying experience.

The villagers were terrified, and often would not leave their villages, even to farm their fields, out of fear of prowling tigers. Some men would try to kill the man-eating tigers with traps, pitfalls, and guns, but often without success.

The older and wiser tigers were difficult to kill. Unlike the bold lion that comes out in the open by day, tigers stay in the jungle where tall grass and bushes hide them. They are excellent swimmers, can climb trees but very rarely do, and hunt by night. To try and rid the jungles of the man-eaters, some men would beat the bush in an attempt to drive the tigers out of their hiding places and into the open, where they could be shot. The men who did the shooting were usually mounted on elephants. I think the bush beaters had to be very brave, don't you?

### A Real Life Hero

Jim Corbet, a brave Englishman who lived in India nearly all his life, loved the native villagers and wrote about them in his book, *My India*. If you go to Kumaon, India, today, you can see a monument put up in his memory by the Indian people. The monument is situated in a large park named in his honor. These memorials reflect the gratitude of the Indian people for Mr. Corbet's work of tracking down and killing man-eating tigers. In his book, *Man-eaters of Kumaon,* you can read the thrilling true stories of his experiences.

Remember, Mr. Corbet hunted man-eaters in particular and only in order to protect the native people he loved. Today, hunting and killing tigers for mere sport would not make the hunters heroes. Jim Corbet's books have been read and appreciated in our family and that is why we can recommend them to you (high school and up).

# 52

## Mr. Featherton and the Eagle

Mr. Featherton was a bachelor who worked in the offices of a bank located in a tall building in Chicago. He worked amid a world of numbers. Mr. Featherton liked numbers. He also liked birds. His office on the fifth floor had a large window which enabled him to gaze out between other tall buildings and see a portion of Lake Michigan, where both water and sky met the horizon. At various times throughout the day, he would rest his eyes from focusing on the tiny numbers on his balance sheets to gaze at the sky which was often dotted with soaring birds.

For Mr. Featherton, each workday was similar to the one before it. He awoke to his alarm clock at the same hour, fried one egg, toasted and buttered one slice of bread, and made a sandwich with two more slices. He fit the sandwich and an apple into his lunch box the exact same way every morning, always adding a handful of peanuts for the squirrels he fed at Grant Park, where he ate his lunch. He then locked the door of his apartment and hopped onto the next available trolley, in order to arrive at his quiet office at a punctual half-past-eight. His trip home involved

a similar routine, but in reverse. The highlight of his day was his lunch hour in the park. The little park creatures grew accustomed to Mr. Featherton's mid-day offerings. Onlookers were amazed at the apparent tameness of the birds and squirrels.

One particular week, however, something strange occurred while Mr. Featherton worked in his office. Now and again his concentration was broken by the faint sound of tapping. Each time he heard it, he tilted back in his chair and frowned at the ceiling directly above him with a puzzled expression. He speculated that the faint tapping might be a loose roof tile, or a piece of debris that had gotten caught in a crevice in the rooftop. Perhaps the wind caused the roof tile to flap, or made debris slap against the tiles. Whatever was causing the tapping, it was distracting him from his work.

During one of those moments when he was resting his eyes by gazing out at the clouds, he thought he saw a remarkably large bird in the sky. Since it was flying away from him, he was unable to identify it without binoculars. Another time, when he looked up, the corner of his eye caught a shadow of something passing by the window. But he had not looked up quickly enough to see what it was. He *conjectured that it was probably a flock of pigeons.

What Mr. Featherton *didn't* know was that a great big beautiful bird—a golden eagle, in fact—had begun to build a nest in the section of roof right above his head. The tapping had been made by the eagle's long talons on the tiles as he carefully fitted and refitted the sticks into place as he constructed his grand nest.

Four days of tapping had aroused in Mr. Featherton a curiosity that had to be satisfied. As a result, he did something unusual: he interrupted his daily routine. He did not walk to Grant Park on his lunch hour. Instead, he decided to make his way onto the roof.

Here is where the adventure begins. Finish the story, keeping in mind Mr. Featherton's character.

---

*To "conjecture" is to make a guess.

## Writing Help

I've established the fact that Mr. Featherton is an animal lover. Could he do anything to aid the eagle? Create a situation where this might happen. How does the eagle react? How sharp are its talons? Maneuvering on a roof is not what most people are used to doing and can be quite frightening considering the danger. How does Mr. Featherton manage? How windy is it up there? What precautions could be taken? What emotions is he experiencing? Write what you both see and hear taking place in your part of the story.

Do the other employees of the bank become curious when they notice Mr. Featherton is acting strangely? Does Mr. Featherton get help from them, or from someone else?

## Additional Challenge

I didn't pick Mr. Featherton's name out of a hat by chance. I made it up. It fits the story in a way that I like. Because Mr. Featherton is a man who likes birds, I put feathers in his name. You can do the same kind of thing when you are the author of a story. You can also add characters to any of the stories I have written in *Story Starters* and give them a silly name or any name that carries with it an implication you would like. A name can tell something about the qualities or idiosyncrasies (habits or peculiarities) of a character. William Shakespeare did this, and so did Charles Dickens and C.S. Lewis. You may find it fun.

This question is a big one: Does this incident with the eagle change Mr. Featherton's life? If so, in what ways? What are his conclusions and new aspirations?

# 53

## Lucy Fairchild[I]

Six-year-old Lucy Fairchild lived in a cottage on the grounds of the Hazlehurst estate in southern England. The manor house of Hazlehurst was a grand and Gothic structure. Her father, Mr. Fairchild, worked for Sir Anthony, the lord of the manor. He was the groom for Sir Anthony's large stable of horses.

Lucy loved romping through the meadows and woods around their cottage in the countryside and watching the men who farmed the fields of Hazlehurst. She had started reading lessons that September with her mother at the kitchen table, but these lasted less than an hour. The latter half of the morning was always free for outdoor exploration.

Lucy had no brothers or sisters, but her dad was always available when her mother rang the lunch bell and hurried over from the stables. All during the summer he would grab their bread, cheese, and pickles at the house and set off with Lucy to share a picnic lunch with her in whatever shady or sunny spot she chose.

Mother let them have some time together and then would always manage to find them, carrying with her some freshly baked spice cakes

or fruit tarts. Then mother and father would have some time together on the picnic blanket while Alice went exploring. Nature held such wonders for her: the birds, the cattle on the hillside, the wildflowers all delighted her equally. She liked to pick wildflowers and berries and bring them to her mother. She was amazed that her mother knew the name of nearly every plant she found over the summer months, be it poppy, clover, thistle, goldenrod, or Queen Anne's lace.

Today she had returned to her mom and dad at the picnic blanket carrying some large ripened nuts.

"Horse chestnuts, these are called," her mother told her.

"Then we shall give them to Daddy's horses," Lucy replied insistently.

"Oh, no," chuckled her father. "I'm afraid these will be too much of a delicacy for Sir Anthony's fine horses."

"Then why are they called horse chestnuts?" Lucy asked, puzzled.

"I don't rightly know," her father admitted.

Only once in a great while was Lucy invited to accompany her parents to the nearby town of Bromley on market day, so today was a very special occasion for her. It was made even more special because her father had been graciously permitted to use an older horse and carriage of Sir Anthony's. The streets were all a-bustle with people. When she and her parents alighted from the carriage, Lucy, who was used to wide open spaces, found it confining to be forced to walk among the crowds on the narrow pavements between the buildings and the dirty street. Had it been otherwise, the accident would never have occurred. Here is how it happened.

Mr. Fairchild was talking with a barber and Mrs. Fairchild had dropped Lucy's hand to tuck a newly purchased bolt of fabric under her arm. Suddenly, she realized that Lucy was gone.

A group of boys down the street had caught Lucy's attention, as they did everybody else's, when they started throwing rocks at Sir Anthony's carriage. Townspeople who didn't know Sir Anthony considered him a haughty, well-to-do landlord, and false rumors had spread about his mistreatment of the servants. The rocks, however, were a bad

way of making a statement against Sir Anthony, because they created a dangerous situation.

"Where's Lucy?" Mrs. Fairchild said with alarm, her wide eyes desperately scanning the crowds. Suddenly she spotted her and called out. Lucy met her gaze directly and began crossing the street. At the same moment, Sir Anthony's horse and empty carriage took off. A rock, meant for the carriage, must have hit the horse. One of the bigger boys among the rock throwers felt a pang of conscience at his terrible wrongdoing. He ran out to try to stop the horse, but he was unsuccessful.

Carry on with the story. What is taking place in the picture? What noises do you hear? Are there any shouts? What emotions do the characters experience, especially Mr. and Mrs. Fairchild and the boy who tried to stop the horse? Now take a look at the second picture I've provided you and continue the story.

## Writing Help

In life there are those who hurt others (sometimes accidentally) and those who help others. Put some helpers in this story. You may create additional characters. Does the lord of the manor, Sir Anthony, enter the story anywhere? Do his further actions prove or disprove what the townspeople say about him? What is the extent of any injuries to the characters in the story and what can be done to help them recover?

Remember that Lucy loves nature. In the part of the story that I wrote, I established that Lucy's father loved her. How sad he is in the second picture! In the part of the story that you write, you can establish the nurse's character by what she says and how she cares for Lucy.

What happened to the mother in the story? Is she in the hospital, too?

Does the boy who tried to stop the horse visit Lucy in the hospital? What is he feeling, and what does he do about it? Do he and Lucy become friends?

## Additional Challenge

I used an impersonal narrator for this story. We don't know who is telling the story. You might want to tell the rest of the story from the father's point of view. As he tells the story describe what he thinks, feels, and sees. Perhaps you would like to tell the story from some other character's point of view.

# 54

## One Big, Happy Family

Mr. and Mrs. Goodliffe lived in Yorkshire, England, in a house that had nineteen rooms and three floors. They loved children and had quite a collection of them. The Goodliffe children were a merry bunch. It was fortunate that their house had a lot of rooms, because the children's extended family of aunts, uncles, and cousins filled many of them when they came to visit. And they came to visit often.

On the top floor was the playroom. How large a room it was! It was long enough to roll a hoop and run races. It was wide enough to play tag or marbles or spin a top and watch it make great swirls across the floor. Better still, this spacious room was so far from the parlor and dining room that these light-hearted, healthy Yorkshire children could make *almost* as much noise as they liked—and at times that could be just short of deafening.

It rains continually in Yorkshire in the winter. Drizzle falls from the gray clouds for hours, but never seems to empty them. The rain and drizzle make the garden muddy and not fit for playing outdoors, especially with cousins in "company clothes." Therefore, when aunts and uncles arrived on winter Saturdays they were served a big dinner and then the cousins all played upstairs in the fabulous playroom. On these days the playroom was never as neat and tidy as it could be. The children blew soap bubbles in it and spilled the soapy water. What was most noticeable was their noise. Running and shouting, turning over tables and chairs as they played tag, blindman's bluff, or cops and robbers, it was a good thing indeed that the furniture in the playroom was very strong. After about three hours of this play the little ones would retreat to the lap of their pretty, good-natured, and patient baby-sitter, Miss Reed. The boys, on the other hand, were riotous by this time. Did their energy know no bounds? Catherine, the oldest of the clan, believed it to be so. When the *frenetic activity began to wear out the girls, she would gather them into a corner and read to them from a picture book. The boys ignored this and played on.

On one Saturday, however, in late February, Catherine didn't feel like reading. She was wondering how long the soggy gloomy winter was going to last. She longed for spring, when the sun shone brightly, the garden and orchard were in bloom, and the damp air was filled with the lovely fresh scent of purple hyacinths and little white lilies. Yes, the playroom was large, but it was still a room with four walls.

"Hey Catherine! How come you're not playing?" her brother Ian asked her.

"I *was* playing, but I'm finished now," was her simple reply.

Ian didn't stand around to argue but fitted himself back into playtime as if he had never been out of it.

Catherine looked around her. What she saw shocked her. Nearly all of the toys were broken. Dolls had lost an eye, an arm, or a leg, and had

---

*The word "frenetic" means to be wildly excited or frenzied.

hair no longer straight and shiny but matted and coarse. There were horses without heads and carts that had to be pushed along the floor because they were without wheels. The rubber balls were flabby and useless, the trumpets were bent, the drums made a dull thud when struck, and the wooden swords had become mere wooden handles.

The next moment Catherine noticed that, as incredible as it seemed, the room was quiet. The little girls were lying on the floor serenely turning the pages of some picture books; a few of the youngest had even fallen asleep on Miss Reed's lap. Huddled around a game of Chinese checkers were the boys. It was the one game that still had all its pieces, only because they had to ask Miss Reed's permission to get it down from the highest shelf.

Duncan and Arnold, two visiting cousins, were not playing Chinese checkers with the others. They were at the far corner of the room curiously looking through the bars of the hamster cage. Five fluffy hamsters were awake. Catherine was relieved at the unusual quiet and breathed a long sigh as she lounged back into an easy chair, still dreaming about spring. What she didn't notice were the smiles Duncan and Arnold were giving each other as they quietly opened the door of the hamster cage.

What happened next? Describe the responses of all the characters in the room to what Duncan and Arnold instigated. Feel free to skip the Writing Help. You may wish to refer it only after you've done some initial writing.

## Writing Help

Do you see the parlor maid and the kitchen maid peeking in at the playroom door?

What do you think they might be thinking and whispering to each other? What drew them to peek into the room? In Victorian days, families like the Goodliffes had maids to do the housework and maids to do the cooking and serving. Are you familiar with the story, *The Secret Garden*, by Frances Hodgson Burnett? It also takes place in a large house in Yorkshire that had servants.

Springtime makes a difference in the lives of the characters in *Secret Garden.* Do you think it would make a difference in our story? Do you live in a place where the winters are long, cold, and wet? If you don't, try to imagine what such a winter might be like. How welcoming are growing things when all has been drab and dead before? You are welcome to create a situation where the children are playing outside in spring. Describe how they would behave in this different setting. How would the sights, sounds, and smells differ from other winters?

## Additional Challenge

Miss Reed would have been called the nanny or nurse. The playroom would have been called the nursery. In our story I call her a babysitter, a word you would better understand. What was Miss Reed like? I don't think she would have been lounging with her eyes closed during the entire playtime, do you? What was it about her that made the children want to please her? How did she keep "controlled chaos" in the playroom?

# 55

## At the Railway Station[B]

Elspeth and her mother were planning to take a railway journey to visit an aunt on the coast of Wales. Elspeth had been looking forward to the journey for many weeks.

At last the day arrived for their departure. All the way to the station Elspeth was so excited she could hardly remember to breathe. They boarded the train, found their seats, and stowed away their luggage. Finally the train started on its journey. Elspeth gave a *cursory glance at the other passengers, and turned to the window. Her attention was soon completely absorbed by the scenes flashing past her as the train hurried along its tracks. She saw flocks of sheep, towns with row houses and smokestacks, country inns, stone churches, forests, parks and ponds, thatched farmhouses and here and there a ruined castle or the great home of some country gentleman.

All at once the train plunged with a shrill whistling into a tunnel, and Elspeth heard a young child cry and howl in panic at the sudden

---

*Elspeth was only *half* paying attention to the inside of the train car. Her "cursory" glance means it was a hasty one. "Cursory" is an adjective.

noise and darkness. Perhaps it had never been on a long train ride before. Returning to the light of day at the other end of the tunnel, a different kind of whistling began. The new sound turned out to be a soft melody merrily played on a tin whistle, an instrument that looks like a small flute. The musician was a poor little hunchback boy in one of the third-class carriages. He seemed to be playing not just for coins but to ease the fears of the child. The grateful passengers put shillings in his cap.

Arriving at a station around midday, Elspeth and her mother got off the train because they had to change to a different train for the next part of their journey. While they stood waiting for that train, Elspeth saw one of the porters kicking a big dog and dragging it along by a chain fastened to its collar. He attached the chain to a post on the platform.

OFFICE
CATTLE

The porter then went about his work, but returned now and then to the dog to kick it some more, speaking harsh words through his teeth. The dog whimpered and trembled.

"If I were a dog," said Elspeth, "I'd bite that man."

"Never mind, Elspeth; here's our train," Mother replied, wishing to redirect her daughter's attention. They walked over to the railway carriage but Elspeth kept her gaze on the poor dog. She wondered how some people could be kind and others cruel and why the grown-ups on the platform had turned their backs on the scene.

At that moment, the stationmaster approached with large strides and a determined expression. Elspeth listened and watched for as long as she could before she had to step into the carriage. In her eyes, the stationmaster was a gentle hero.

What did Elspeth overhear? What did she observe?

## Writing Help

You needn't answer all of the questions here. Choose only the ones that get you thinking.

- Whose dog was it? Was it the porter's dog or was it owned by a passenger? In what way was the stationmaster a good man? What words were spoken? Why would Elspeth think the stationmaster a "gentle hero?" How did the porter react to any correction given to him? What did the porter need to learn? How would the stationmaster show the porter how to best treat a reluctant dog?
- If the dog belonged to a passenger, you might bring the passenger into the story. What became of the dog?

- What else might Elspeth have seen people doing or saying on her journey? Perhaps once she got into her compartment on the train she heard people comment about how the dog had been treated. What might they be saying? What would be Elspeth's views on the matter?
- Did Elspeth leave a dog behind when she left for the journey? What was the dog like? What is the best way to get a dog to behave?

## *A Children's Classic*

If you like trains, you'll like *The Railway Children*, by E. Nesbit. Set in Edwardian England, it is a touching story of a family who must weather difficult circumstances. At first, the family lives well-off in a big house in London, but when the father is sent to prison for a crime he did not commit, finances fizzle out. The mother must let the servants go and resettle the children and herself in the country. The children miss their father "dreadfully." The mother turns to writing to pay the rent and the children turn to trains for entertainment. They meander over the countryside, visit the train station, and befriend the porter and stationmaster. This is when the adventures begin.

## *A Film*

In 2000, Masterpiece Theatre aired *The Railway Children*. Our family liked it so much that we have it on video. This newer film starring Jenny Agutter and Jemima Rooper is a beautiful adaptation of the book.

# 55

## The Cabman's Old Horse

Charles walked daily through the streets of London to attend a boys' school operated by a congenial old man who had room in his house to teach twelve boys. Charles' father had selected it for him because of its small size and its excellent teaching methods. Charles' father was a traveling merchant who had to be away from home for longer periods than he liked. If he returned from a trip in the middle of the week, he would take a cab—which in those Victorian days was a horse and carriage—from the train station straight to the boys' school. If Charles' mother and sister had met Father at the station, they would all go together to pick up Charles. Father expected the teacher to excuse Charles for the rest of the day to visit with his family, no matter what lesson was interrupted.

"This is highly irregular," Mother said the first time Father took Charles out of school at midday. "None of the other children can skip out with their families in the middle of the day."

Father was a man who often got what he wanted. "Don't concern yourself, my sweet. I had a word with the teacher some time ago, and it's all arranged. When I've been away for weeks and the day is a beautiful one, being with my family takes precedence. What shall we do today?" Sometimes a hamper of food was placed in the cab and a picnic was enjoyed along a peaceful stream somewhere outside the city. The cabmen were always happy to wait the hour, as Father paid them generously.

Father and Mother enjoyed watching their children explore. Charles and his sister would wade in the stream, trying to catch slippery pollywogs and delighting in the sparkling blue dragonflies that seemed to race across the water. It was a rare opportunity for the children to experience a bit of country. The cabman would eat his lunch near a chestnut tree. His horse would graze heartily, because the grass was green and luscious near the stream. It was a rare treat for a cabman and a city horse to enjoy a bit of country as well.

One morning on his way to school, Charles stopped to help an old tired horse, one that he had helped before. The horse had worked on this street for as long as he could remember, and he had grown fond of it. As had happened before, the horse had gotten his nose out of the nose-bag of oats and couldn't get it back in. Charles fixed it for him. While he was stroking its ears, Charles couldn't help overhearing the conversation of two cabmen nearby.

"Old *Dreg Legs is no longer up to the long 'ours a cabby's got to put in," said one.

"What are you going to do?" asked the other.

"He's no good as a city horse anymore. What other cabby would buy 'im from me now? And the rich folks with money wouldn't want a slowpoke like this one. There's nothing for it but to sell 'im to Jones."

---

*"Dregs" (the word is usually plural) are the sediment in a liquid, or the residue: "the bottom of the barrel." It is sometimes considered the most undesirable part.

"Not Skull 'n Bones Jones at the slaughter house! But then you'll have to find another horse."

"I've got some money put aside, but if I wait much longer I'll be living off it. I think Dreg Legs keeps customers away. He just isn't peppy anymore."

"What about taking him to the auction in Oxfordshire? You might get a better price for him there."

"That'll mean taking days off work. I'm losing income as it is. No, Skull 'n Bones Jones will give me a good enough sum."

Charles hated to hear the men talking about selling the horse to a man Charles pictured to be of a hideously frightening appearance, who would then slaughter him. Impulsively he ran up to the cabman. "I'll buy him from you, sir!" he exclaimed.

For an instant the cabmen were dumbfounded. When their initial astonishment had worn off, they shared a swift glance, then bust into a hearty laugh. "You?"

"Yes, sir. My father could buy him from you."

"Where's your father, chum?

"He's out of town, but he'll be back any day."

"Well, if he comes back in a couple of days, tell 'im to come over and talk to me. But if I don't 'ear from him soon, I'm going to sell thiz 'orse to someone else."

"Yes, sir!" Charles replied, and ran all the way to school to make up for his dillydallying.

After school he burst into the house and asked his mother when his father would *exactly* be coming home.

"I haven't had word yet, Charles. But you know he's usually gone for more than a week. Why?"

"I have something I need to talk to him about."

"Would I do instead?"

"No thanks; it has to be Father."

Tell what happens over the next few days.

## Writing Help

- When Charles' father returns, what becomes of the horse? Is Charles able to buy it?
- You can make all kinds of things happen in a story when you are the one writing it. You can put surprise circumstances into your

stories. Perhaps Father has some interesting news to share. You can pop in more characters, too. You can develop the ones you already have. What does Charles' sister think of all this? Does Charles share his wish with her?

I've provided you with a third picture that you might like to work into your story.

## Additional Challenge

### *Suspense*

That fact that Charles' father was away, that it wasn't known exactly when he would return, and that the cabman wouldn't wait very long, sets up room for some suspense in this story. Here is a challenge. As you continue this story, try to make your readers wait. Holding them in suspense makes them want more desperately to know what will happen next. Have you heard people say that a certain book was so good that they "couldn't put it down?" It is very likely that what they read kept them in some suspense. We don't know if Charles' father would be willing to buy the horse, either. After all, how practical would it be for Charles' family to own this horse? They probably live in a Georgian square in the city and have no carriage house for it.

### *Foreshadowing*

Keep in mind the clues I've given in the earlier part of the story. What did the family love to do but had only the rare opportunity? Foreshadowing is writing in a clue that gives hints to the reader of possible coming events in the story. It can give the reader hope or dread of things to come. I much prefer hope, don't you?

Also, remember that Charles' father sometimes shows up at the school unexpectedly.

### *A Children's Classic*

If you are fond of horses, you will like the story of *Black Beauty* by Anna Sewell. Anna Sewell wrote her story from Beauty's point of view. Beauty shares his experiences of his life, and what it was like to have both bad and good masters. First published in 1877, during the Victorian era, it is set in the same time period as our story.

You have the option to continue "The Cabman's Old Horse" from the horse's point of view.

### *A Film*

I recommend the faithful movie version of *Black Beauty,* written and directed by Caroline Thompson. Released in 1994 by Warner Brothers, it is a pretty film and a heartfelt delight. The actors Sean Bean and David Thewlis do a fine job. The music by Danny Elfman is just as pretty; in fact, our family thinks it's gorgeous.

# 57

## Hazel Takes a Long Walk

Four-year-old Hazel lived in a log cabin in the Ozark Mountains of Missouri in the 1830s. Her mother and father were settlers; therefore, they were always busy settling in. Hazel watched Dad and her brothers fell trees for logs, clear land of stumps, plant young apple trees, and tend their animals. She watched Ma garden, sew, knit, and make bread, butter and cheese.

Hazel was a happy child until the new baby arrived. She didn't like how much care the baby needed from Ma. She was used to being "the baby" and getting lots of attention. Now she was "the big girl."

One night Dad was woken up by the smell of smoke. Leaping out of bed, he ran to the cabin door and threw it open. Shooting from the barn were bright orange flames. The barn was on fire!

Thankfully, Dad and the boys saved the animals. The barn, however, burned to the ground, even though they worked hard to save it, carrying pail after pail of water from the well until they were all exhausted. "I don't understand it," pondered Dad. Eyeing the destruction brought his spirits

very low. Although the barn was a small one, it had taken months to build. Now it would have to be built all over again.

The next morning Dad looked around at the blackened remains for any signs of what could have caused the barn to catch fire. He didn't see one of his sons quietly push a lantern further into an ash heap with his foot to hide it from view. The wick had been burning low last night, which had made it easy to overlook when the boy's tired body wanted to be done with chores quickly. "Could one of the horses have knocked it off its hook in the night?" he wondered, but kept his wondering to himself. He felt miserable and irresponsible.

At noon, that same day, neighbor Smith stopped by. He was astonished to see the barn burnt. "How'd it happen?" he asked.

"Can't figure it out," replied Dad.

"Could be Injuns," said Smith. "Cooper had his lean-to catch fire two days ago and he couldn't figure it out either. And Peterson's outhouse caught fire last week. Isn't *that* strange?"

"We've been here three years and never had trouble with Indians. They *are* peaceful, I've been told."

"That's what we've been *told*," was Smith's retort. "Keep your eyes open," he snapped, and turned to head home.

The next afternoon, while Ma was rocking the new baby to sleep in the rocking chair, Hazel poked and moped around the house. Ma used to hum and hold *her* in that very same chair. Hazel felt displaced. Ma tried to encourage her by giving her something to do. "Why don't you take that basket and get us some nice blackberries? Do you know where we were collecting them yesterday? I'll make us a nice pie and you can help," Ma told her. "I'll be out to pick blackberries, too, as soon as the baby is asleep," she added for further encouragement.

"Okay," Hazel said brightly. Grabbing the basket, she ran off. The shade of the woods felt cool on this hot afternoon. Hazel liked the woods that surrounded their cabin. She found the big blackberry bushes and began to pick the large juicy berries. After picking only a dozen or so, she sat down to eat them.

At the sound of rustling leaves she looked up from her delicious berries and saw something that touched her heart deeply. Cautiously, from out of the bushes a hungry mother rabbit crept out to feed. Her fuzzy brown bunnies were not as cautious. They were bouncy. Their little hops shot them up in the air and down, and in lively wobbly spurts; they ran back and forth in playful abandon. It was as if they were free to use their little legs for the first time. How enchanting! Hazel dropped her basket and walked over to them. At her approach, the rabbits fled under a bush then ran farther into the woods.

Hazel followed them. She walked and walked, humming to herself and looking for the rabbits, but they had disappeared. Then she realized she was lost and started running. But she was running in the wrong direction. When she called out for her Ma and Dad there was no answer. Suddenly, out from behind a tree appeared an Indian.

What happened to Hazel? Use the pictures, but also let your imagination wander. Write freely, as if you were in the Indian camp watching all that takes place. Build the story with descriptive detail and excitement and then give it a good ending.

## Writing Help

- Describe the scene in which Hazel meets the Indian in the woods. How frightened is Hazel when she is in the arms of the man? Describe her reaction. Why do you think the man picked her up to carry her back to camp? As a reminder to use sensory language, what does Hazel see, hear, smell, and taste at the

Indian camp? How is she treated? Is she curious about the new things she experiences?

- Back at the homestead, how does Hazel's family respond when they discover Hazel is missing?
- How does Dad go about finding Hazel?

## Additional Challenge

Describe the actions and feelings of your characters. What do you think neighbor Smith's opinion of the current crisis would be? Was his, "Could be Injuns," based on evidence or fear? What is Dad's opinion? Does he believe a peaceful tribe would have any reason to kidnap Hazel—as might be suggested to him by his neighbors? Does Mr. Smith decide to take matters into his own hands by *stealth?

Does her brother ever confess to his carelessness? What might compel the boy to confess? Is he connected with the other fires? Your story can show that there are good and unselfish reasons to tell the truth. Forgiveness in a story provides good resolution of conflict.

What can we learn about prejudice and judging by superficial appearances?

How does Hazel eventually reunite with her family? What lesson does she learn?

### *Missouri*

The state of Missouri probably got its name from the name of an Indian tribe believed to mean "those with dugout canoes." What do you know about the history of Native Americans? Any knowledge you already have (or seek to find out) can help you with your story.

---

* "Stealth" is a noun that has to do with stealing, being sneaky or going about things secretly.

# 58

## Vacation at the Seashore[B]

The Richardsons were taking a vacation at the seashore. It wasn't a flashy seashore resort with Ferris wheels and roller coaster rides, hot dog stands, and candy apples. Yes, some of their friends were going to those places. But no, they were vacationing at a much quieter, more remote place—a fishing village. Mr. Richardson had a stressful career in Boston. He liked the challenge of his work, but he also looked forward to visiting the same quiet village with his family each year. The two eldest children of the five, Sinclair and Dora, having heard their friends rave about their action-packed vacations, were secretly not as excited about their old pebbly beach as they once had been. Oh, they still liked collecting shells, watching the sea gulls, and digging for sand crabs. But this year, by the middle of their vacation, they couldn't quite get out of their minds the anticipated thrill of those amusement park rides they had heard so much about. The crowded beaches where their friends were having exciting adventures beckoned to them.

One evening after supper when the sky was soon to turn colors on the horizon, the four oldest children decided to head out once more to

the beach. Before going out the door, they assured their mother they would return before sunset. Betty, the youngest, rather tired from the long day, remained at home with Mother.

Walking down the cobblestone streets between rows of white clapboard cottages, the children's noses met the savory smells of sizzling onions, salty fish, and fried fritters. The villagers were seated at their supper tables and the windows of all the cottages were open wide to the summer breezes. The clink of dishes could be heard. Sinclair, the eldest of the Richardson children, said to his sister, "Mmm, smells good, doesn't it, Dora?"

"Mmm, yes, it does," Dora replied.

Then Sinclair added rather hesitantly, "I probably shouldn't be asking you this, but are you getting bored?"

"I love the sights and smells of the seashore, but I am a bit bored," Dora confessed.

"I'm trying not to think of all the fun Jake and Rob are having at *their* beach," Sinclair admitted.

"*And* the others," Dora added, referring to her girl friends. "I think it's called covetousness."

"You mean, wishing you could have what others have?" asked Sinclair.

"Yes, that's right," said Dora.

After a few thoughtful moments, Sinclair added conscientiously, "Actually, come to think of it, there are plenty of children that would wish for what *we* have."

"You're right, so let's forget the other beach," said Dora soberly but sweetly.

"Hey, come on, you two!" called their younger brothers, Walter and Douglas, who were way ahead of them. The two older siblings ran to catch up with their younger brothers.

The four were together again by the time they reached the shore.

"Look how low the tide is!" cried Douglas. He liked low tide because it revealed the little tide-pool creatures that scurried about and enticed the sandpipers and plovers to poke their long narrow beaks into the sandy pebbles for their supper.

"Yeah, it's good to know about the tides if you go out on 'em," responded a sailor who was sitting behind a section of a wooden boat launch. Startled, because they hadn't known anyone else was nearby, the children turned and stared at him.

The sailor, who knew everyone in the village, recognized that they were tourists. "You like the sea, do you?" he asked.

The children nodded.

"I practically lives on it," he shared in village dialect.

Douglas blurted out, "Then you must have stories."

"About the sea? Oh, sure I does. Hundreds," he boasted.

"Would you tell us one, sir…please?" Sinclair spoke out, remembering his manners.

Once the old sailor opened his mouth his words flowed in torrents. Storytelling was natural to him; in fact, it seemed to be his favorite pastime. Dora thought his stories would fill a book.

"So you never know what the high tide will wash ashore," he said at the conclusion of his last story.

Douglas' curiosity made him ask, "When will it be high tide?"

"Early in the morning, my lad."

The sun was setting making the horizon a hazy purple-pink. It was time to head home, thought Sinclair. "Thank you, sir. We'd best be off."

Sinclair, Dora, Walter, and Douglas ran home, the thrill of the sailor's stories of pirates, whales, sea monsters, and buried treasure still dancing in their imaginations.

Before they reached the cottage, Douglas asked his big brother Sinclair, "Do you want to set out early tomorrow in search of lost treasure? It will be high tide, and you know what that means."

Sinclair agreed with a smile, but only to keep his youngest brother happy. He didn't expect to find anything, of course. Dora, however, had some "what ifs" brewing in her mind and thought it would be fun to explore possibilities.

When they entered the cottage, their father looked up and saw his children's happy faces and felt very good about having taken them on this quiet vacation. He would never have guessed that Sinclair and Dora had had a discussion about boredom earlier in the evening.

"Father, we met a sailor," shared Douglas robustly, "and he told us a heap of stories."

"Did he now? That's capital!" Father said.

"Father, may we set out for the beach *before* breakfast?" Sinclair asked.

"Yes, of course," he responded. "It's beautiful on the beach, isn't it? Why not take some food *with* you?" When Mother came downstairs from settling Betty in bed, she gave them some ideas about what to pack for a picnic breakfast, and said, "It would be nice if you would take Betty, too. You *will* stay away from anything sharp or rusty, won't you? Oh, and not climb on any steep rocks?"

"We will take good care of Betty," Dora promised.

Father said, "Your mother and I will take a walk to the beach sometime after breakfast and try to find you. How's that?"

"Capital!" they all chorused. And very soon the four oldest Richardson children went to bed with the sailor's stories dancing in their dreams.

Using the second picture continue the story. You may wish to skip the Writing Help initially in order to delve into writing whatever is already stirring in your imagination. Afterwards take a peek at what is written below for some ideas for polishing your story.

## Writing Help

- How did the sailor take away any boredom the children may have been experiencing? What ideas did he give them?
- Sinclair was willing to play make-believe with his younger brothers to make them happy. Describe the children's pretending the next

morning up on the beach. What did the children pretend and explore before they came upon a large and mysterious wooden box?

- Who found the box first? How did the children think it got there? What did they say to each other, and how did they feel? What was inside the box, and what did the family do with the contents?
- What took place during the rest of the vacation? Does the sailor re-enter the story? Do Father and Mother play a serious role?

### *Exclamations*

Put some conversation in your story. How about making your characters give some exclamations? Exclamations are short phrases that are said with emotion when one is excited, afraid, or have any strong feeling one wants to express. Use exclamation points for punctuation. Here are some. Wow! Watch out! Hurry! Run! Get down! Look at this! Nonsense! Can you believe it? How wonderful! That's incredible! Fantastic! Let's go! Wait for me!

## Additional Challenge

### *Vivid Verbs*

After you've written your part of our story of the Richardsons, you might want to go back and see where you can use some vivid verbs in place of any weak ones. Choose a vivid verb that will describe the action of your story more precisely—that is, with more accurate meaning.

For instance, instead of "pull" you could use "yank, wrench, drag, heave, haul," etc.

Instead of "fall" you could use "plunge, topple, drop, trip, stumble, crash, smash, collapse, crumble, cave in," etc.

Rather than "run" you could use "sprint, scamper, dart, dash, scurry, hurry, gallop or race."

Rather than "open" you could use some "un" words such as "unlock, unfasten, untie, unbutton, unknot or unravel."

These are just a few ideas. Aren't there a lot of interesting verbs to choose from?

# 59

## Coming to America(I)

I was once told the story of how my Scottish great-grandfather came to America. Ranald, my great-grandfather, had no family that he knew of after his mother and father—who was a tinsmith—died. Angus, who was also an orphan, was his only friend. The two boys lived a hard life on the streets of Glasgow.

One day Ranald and Angus determined to stow away on some large ship bound for America and begin life over again in the country of George Washington. They had heard that in the land of freedom boys had more opportunities in life than they had in Scotland.

They sat in the shadows of the wharf, watching for ships, begging scraps of bread, and eating any raw fish that slid off the baskets that were loaded onto carts to be transported to market. When a very large ship glided out to sea one bright brisk morning in November, she carried two passengers for America, of whom the officers of the vessel were unaware. Down in the dark hold of the ship, huddled close together to keep warm, were the poor stowaways. My great-grandfather Ranald was twelve years old. He had sandy-colored, wispy hair, and was an alert

child with good common sense. Angus was ten. His large dark eyes were usually downcast and his thin body was very small for his age. At the end of the first day, when night had fallen, Angus, frightened and chilled, said to my great-grandfather, "Ranald, do you think we will ever get there? It's awful cold and dark down here."

"Shh, keep quiet, Angus. If the captain should find us, who knows, he might throw us overboard. We'll get safely to land only if we're quiet like ship mice. It'll be some days yet, though." They had with them a little cheese and a few crusts of bread, which Ranald divided up and apportioned with much care, hoping to make the scanty provisions last until they reached America. They found a few other scraps here and there. But days and nights passed, and oh, how long they seemed to the poor little stowaways down in the dark hold of the big ship.

At last Angus grew faint from cold and fright. He frequently moaned and cried himself to sleep. He lost all desire for the scraps of stale and moldy food that Ranald gave to him. It seemed to Ranald that his friend would die unless fresh air, clean water, and a warm sun came to him pretty soon. When Ranald took Angus into his arms, he was even more worried because he could tell that he was feverish. He said a prayer and spoke a few verses of a hymn from memory. How he wished he could remember *all* of the verses. He told Angus to do his best to cheer up, that he was sure they were almost there, and would soon be out in the bright sunshine and fresh, free air of beautiful America. Angus couldn't picture this and gave out a moan.

An officer of the ship happened to be near and heard the curious noise. Ranald was alerted by the sound of the footsteps of the officer approaching and covered Angus with a piece of burlap, then squeezed quickly into a corner, hoping to remain unnoticed. But the officer did see him. Immediately his heart was softened at what he saw. He spoke in muffled but grave tones to Ranald, who was, by this time, shivering with cold and fear.

"The captain will want to know the meaning of this unlawful deed, lad. It would be better for you to tell him than I. Shall we go up on deck together? That would be the only right thing to do." Ranald

agreed, but didn't say anything about Angus who, by this time was deep asleep with fever.

The officer knew his captain well. The captain had a short temper, and could be very loud, but underneath he had a kind heart and believed that taking circumstances into account was a necessary quality of anyone in command of a ship. Still, he wondered how his captain would deal with my great-grandfather—the dirty, smelly stowaway.

Finish telling great-grandfather Ranald's story of how he came to America.

## Writing Help

I've created some characters here for you and put them into a predicament, giving you a problem to solve. If you've already done several story starter exercises, are you beginning to get rather good at solving problems? The rest of the story is up to you. As you describe the events in your portion of the story, be sure to let your readers know something of what the characters are thinking and feeling.

- What's to be done about the stowaways? What would you decide to do with them if you were the captain?
- How close are they to America? What is Ranald's reaction when the seacoast is spotted?
- What happens to Angus, who is very sick?

# 60

## Amos—A Willing Worker

Amos lived in the pleasant and industrious city of Newark, New Jersey. It was pleasant and industrious in the year 1879. Amos' dad was a cabman; that is, he drove a horse and carriage for hire. People liked his dad. He was a friendly man. Amos was an enterprising young lad. He worked odd jobs after school, and all summer he cleaned and shined shoes at a street corner. He, like his dad, was cheerful and hard-working. Amos also helped his dad take care of Samson, the horse who faithfully pulled his father's cab in all kinds of weather.

One winter evening after a day of sweeping snow from many a doorway with his brother Thomas, Amos met his dad in the carriage-house. "Mom says that supper will be ready soon. We're having sausage and biscuits tonight."

"Good," Dad said. "I could eat a horse! Oh, sorry Samson. Not you, of course," he chuckled.

Amos picked up a brush and began helping his father groom Samson's brown coat. "Did you get many sweeping jobs today, Amos?" Dad asked.

"Thomas and I each have a pocketful of nickels."

"Very good, son. You keep saving up your money and soon you'll be able to own your own cab and horse like me. Then you'll *really* be in business!"

Amos smiled, but he was pretty sure he didn't want to be a cabman like his dad. The idea of saving his money for his own horse and cab wasn't as exciting as the idea of going into some other sort of business. What that business would be, he didn't yet know. For now, he was earning and saving until he did know.

"I met up with another Thomas today," Dad announced.

"Do I know him?" Amos asked.

"I know you've *heard* of him. Of all people to ride in my cab! It was Thomas Edison, 'The Wizard of Menlo Park.' "

"Really?" Amos queried, wide-eyed. His curiosity was engaged. News of Edison's invention of the electric incandescent light had recently astounded the world.

"Did you talk to him?" Amos asked excitedly, knowing his dad was a friendly man.

"Yes I did. When he stepped out of the cab to pay me, I asked him a question," his dad said calmly.

"What was that?"

"I told him that my son would embark upon a business in future. Then I asked him if there was a motto he might take to heart in his struggle for promotion and success. After a moment's pause, Edison said, 'Never look at the clock.'"

"Is that all he said?" asked Amos.

"That's all."

"What exactly did he mean by that?"

"He meant that the man who is constantly afraid he is going to work overtime or over hours doesn't stand a chance of competing with the man who completes the task at hand, no matter how long it takes. The carpenter who drops his hammer, uplifted above his head, when the whistle blows, is likely to remain a second-class workman all his life.

The carpenter who occasionally stays fifteen minutes late to finish a job is working toward a shop of his own."

"But I thought you wanted me to be a cabman like you."

"I could help you get you started, that's for certain, but I've never insisted you do what I do."

Amos was much relieved.

Months of menial tasks and saving became somewhat *monotonous, but Amos pressed on. His parents were proud when he graduated from high school. But Amos still didn't know what he wanted to do. That summer he went back to being a shoeshine boy, saving as much money as he could. He could be cheerful and patient with others, yet he found it increasingly difficult to be patient with himself. He was growing discouraged because his goal still seemed very far away. One morning he heard something in a Sunday sermon that gave him hope, which in turn brightened his outlook. The preacher read from the book of Proverbs. Thus Amos learned that patient preparation, hard work, and planning always bear fruit in due season. Those who live by godly principles will be blessed.

That very week, at midday, when the clerks and businessmen were coming out of the office buildings and walking to nearby restaurants or parks for lunch, Amos shined the shoes of a man he remembered seeing before. The man had been observing Amos for some months, and said to him, "I could use a boy like you in my office."

What happens next?

---

* "Monotonous" is an adjective that means tediously repetitious or boring. "Monotony" is the noun.

## Writing Help

- Describe the conversation that follows. What did the man observe about Amos' attitude toward work? If you were Amos, how would you feel and what would you do as soon as your day of work was done?
- What was Edison's motto? Does Amos put this motto to use? What decisions must be made? What does Amos learn in the man's office? Is his employer a good man to work for? Why?
- What does success mean? What is a promotion? Does Amos eventually get to meet Thomas Edison himself? Stretch your imagination and tell what ultimately happens to Amos—what does he become and what happens to his business? What conflict might there be in your story—difficulties or problems to overcome?

## Additional Challenge

One of the characters in my story starter is a real historical person. The story is set in a certain time and place and mentions a person who really lived: Mr. Edison. I looked up Mr. Edison in our encyclopedia in order to come up with the date I needed. I knew Edison had worked in New Jersey because when I was a young girl I lived not far from Menlo Park, and the town of Edison, New Jersey, the town named after this famous inventor. In fact, our neighbor's father had worked for Edison in prior years. If you would like to include Mr. Edison in your part of the story, you will be writing with greater historical context. Feel free to look up Mr. Edison in an encyclopedia, as I did. This will supply you with ideas. A good writer does research so that he can incorporate things into his fictional story that will make it more interesting and believable.

# 61

## Attending to the Wounded[I]

The Civil War was raging in the 1860s. It swept like a thundering storm through towns and villages. Jimmy's father was in the war. But Jimmy didn't know where he was, or in which battles he was fighting. All he knew was that his father was out there somewhere on the battlefield. He and his mother had not gotten a letter from him in a long time.

One day Jimmy could stand it no longer. He ran away from home. He wanted to help the war effort in whatever way he could. Jimmy's mother burst into tears when she read the note he left her the morning he ran away. She opened the front door of her house and stood looking longingly over the rolling hills of the countryside, Jimmy's letter still in her hand. "Jimmy" she called weakly through her tears. A verse she learned as a child then leaped forward in her memory. "I will lift up my eyes to the hills—From whence comes my help? My help comes from the Lord…(Psalm 121). This truth was a comfort to her.

Over the centuries, there have always been brave boys on fields of battle. You've probably heard of drummer boys or water carriers

accompanying the troops to battle. Boys were a support to men in battle, and it had always been against the codes of honor to kill them in battle, because the boys did no actual fighting. Jimmy managed to find a regiment, and was entrusted to the care of the wagon master. Willingly, he did whatever needed doing. He helped with the cooking,

serving, and washing up. In any free time that he had, he made inquiries regarding his father's whereabouts. But no one gave him the answer he wanted to hear.

One day he was away from camp in a nearby forest, gleaning sticks for the cooking fires, when he heard a battle break out in a clearing not far away. Leaving his pile of sticks behind, he set off in the direction of the battle-sounds, intending to help in any way he could. When he arrived at the scene, a few stray bullets were still flying, but it appeared that the forces were moving away. Wounded men lay on the ground before him. He had never seen so much blood before. Although the scene frightened him, with dogged composure and concentration he turned his thoughts away from his queasy stomach and focused on the needs of the wounded men. His father might be on a battlefield like this one, he knew, and he would want someone to help his father if he were wounded.

That same day, miles away, Jimmy's mother was gazing out at the hills, sending a prayer to the God she believed was sovereign in all things. She found it easier to pray this way now. She prayed that Jimmy and his dad would find each other and be safe from harm. There was an eerie quietness over all the countryside, somewhat like the calm before a storm. Then, like the first distant rumbles of far-off thunder, came the sound of cannon fire. Fear made her tremble. It caused her to spring into action. She locked the animals in the barn. Her favorite goat and its two newly born kids she brought into her kitchen.

In the floor of the kitchen was a trap door—the door of the root cellar. Carrying the kids with one hand, she guided the goat down the steep steps into the cellar. She brought in hay and water and then stayed down in the dark cellar to wait. She waited for hours. The gun and cannon fire got louder and made her shudder. At one point it was deafening. She sat motionless. The goat was very uneasy, but finally lay on the hay with its kids. She wished that there was a way to lock the cellar door from the inside, but there wasn't, and she expected it to be flung open at any moment throughout the night. Once she heard footsteps and pots and dishes clinking overhead, but the little cellar door was never opened.

By morning she realized that she hadn't slept all night. How weary she felt! She could still hear firing, but it sounded distant. She opened the cellar door, numb from a night of fright and looked about her kitchen. Someone *had* been there. One peek through the curtains showed her that her farm was in ruins and strewn with debris. Wounded men lay here and there in the farmyard. What should she do? Her husband could be on a battlefield like this one, and she would want someone to help *him.*

"Water," a man called with a gravelly voice, "Water!"

I've supplied you with a picture each of Jimmy and his mother. Continue the story, by describing what happened to Jimmy. Then bring the characters back together.

## Writing Help

Among the wounded men there might be soldiers of both sides. Describe what could happen if Jimmy or his mother had a confrontation with an enemy soldier. Are there any surprise attacks? What kind of conversations would Jimmy or his mother have with the wounded men?

Sometimes the writer of a story will take us back and forth to different scenes to let us know what is happening in the lives of various people in the story who are in different locations. In this story the mother and son are separated, but I describe what is happening to each of them while they are apart. Jimmy is really the main character of the story; therefore, it would be best to continue the story according to what is seen and felt predominantly by Jimmy. Perhaps you will want to bring in other characters.

Does Jimmy find Father? If so, tell how this comes about.

### *A Film*

I recommend the film *Mrs. Miniver*, which is set in England during the Second World War. It was written and produced to help gain American sympathy for the war, and was released before America joined forces with England against the Axis powers. Mrs. Miniver is a lady of poise and courage, a civilian who helps the war effort on the home front. Although this is not a film depicting a *civil* war, it is one that will supply you with ideas. Being one of my favorite films, it came to mind when I was writing this story starter.

# 62

## Charged by a Rhinoceros[B][I]

My name is Winston. Darby is my cousin. Each year Darby meets me in New York City, where I work. We have lunch at an elegant restaurant, during which he always gives me an enthusiastic account of his hunting exploits in Africa. This year he met me for lunch *before* he planned his annual hunting adventure, rather than after.

"What's this all about?" I asked him, bemused.

"Can't you guess?" Darby pressed.

"Oh, no, you're not going to try to persuade me again to go hunting with you. You know I don't take pleasure in shooting, and I couldn't shoot a pigeon with a cannon if I tried."

"This time I'm going for a good purpose. I'll be collecting specimens for the American Museum of Natural History. You told me yourself that you've always wanted to see how these animals lived. Remember, Winston?"

"Yes, I did. But I was thinking how wonderful it would be to sketch or even paint some pictures of African wildlife. As a matter of fact, when I introduced the idea to a publisher here in town—one that publishes children's books—they told me I should go ahead and draw my wildlife pictures. They would pay me for my drawings but they also said that I certainly shouldn't be expecting *them* to pay for a trip to Africa."

"I'll pay for the trip," offered Darby.

"You?"

"Yes, I've been wanting your company for the last several years, but you haven't seemed interested...until now, perhaps?"

"Thank you Darby. That is very generous of you, and I *am* interested. I think it will be rather exciting."

"Marvelous! You can do all the drawing you want. I'll make the arrangements straight away and then get in touch with you."

That's how I got myself into a mess. The next thing I knew I was smack in the heart of Africa. Thank goodness we had men with us to give us aid. We rode on horseback through a grove of lofty, wide-spreading mimosa trees, most of which had been somewhat damaged by the passage through the grove of a troop of elephants about twelve months before, so we were told. Having proceeded about two miles on the grassy plain, we were surrounded by game of all kinds. I stopped to set up my drawing easel. As soon as I did, making sure to attach an umbrella to my easel to shade my work from the glaring sun, Darby let out a great rumble of a laugh at the sight. "You *will* be okay on your own for an hour or two, won't you Winston?" he asked with a smile.

I just nodded and gave him a small gesture of a salute, excited to get on with my work. He instantly threw his head back letting out another large laughing outburst. Then he rode away with his own goals in mind.

How my eyes must have been popping out of my head as I stared at all the creatures before me. Zebras, giraffes, and wildebeests paid little attention to me. Some lions lying in the shade at a distance were

watching the animals drinking at the water hole, just as I was. When I picked up my pencil to draw, I noticed that my hand was trembling in my excitement. So, instead of drawing, I stood for a while studying the animals as they went about walking, drinking, eating, or standing together in a huddle, young ones and old ones together in peaceful contentment. After a time I was calm enough to begin and became so absorbed in my task that the occasional "crack—crack" of the shooting I heard in the far distance didn't disturb me in the least, nor did it distract me from my task. I decided to draw one picture of each kind of animal in view, making it a point to go back afterward and add other drawings of the same animals in different poses.

My collection of pictures was growing and I stopped for a moment to wipe the sweat from my brow and take a drink. When I looked at my watch, I was surprised to find that nearly two hours had passed since the hunters had left me. Picking up my pencil to begin yet another picture, I paused, just as I heard another "crack." This one sounded much closer. To my right a large dark animal caught my attention. A black rhinoceros was running wildly toward the water hole, apparently in a violent disposition. It frightened the other animals around the water hole and then stopped abruptly to grunt and sniff. That's when I saw that it was a crusty old monster of a thing with red blood streaming down its shoulder. I should have remained motionless, but I began packing away my drawings and folding up my easel with great speed, hoping to find a bush I could hide behind before the beast noticed me.

Unfortunately, as a result of my movements, I became the object of his anger. He charged me in the most resolute manner, blowing loudly through his nostrils. I dropped my things and ran toward a withered tree, hoping to take cover, but didn't make it in time. Providence must have been on my side, however, for in my awkwardness I slipped on a rock and rolled like a wheel to one side in some higher grass. I heard a "crack" and, out of uncontrolled curiosity, looked up. The rhinoceros had been hit again. This time, he fell flat on his broad side, but incredibly, regained his feet and resumed his course.

What happened next to Winston, the rhinoceros, and Darby on safari? What happened to Winston's drawings?

## Additional Challenge

What do you know about Africa? Look up some information about climate, vegetation, etc., and try to create a realistic atmosphere for the end of the story. Try to find terms that are distinctly African. Can you find some specific adjectives to describe the heat? How might various animals get into a tussle as predators or over food?

# 63

## The Good Prince and the Pirates(I)

Sometime near the middle of the seventeenth century, a young prince embarked upon a journey through his realm. He had left his usual *entourage at home in the castle, and had taken with him only one attendant—his personal servant and bodyguard.

At the moment Prince Roy was feeling a bit impatient. "I am telling you again, Piers. Do not call me Majesty," the prince admonished his loyal attendant. "Call me simply Master John."

"Yes, Your High—Master John," Piers hastily corrected himself. He had been the prince's attendant for eight years, and his manner of addressing the prince was very hard to change. He was also concerned about the prince's practice of traveling *incognito. He worried about his own ability to protect the prince if he were ever in danger.

---

*His "entourage" would be a group of servants and companions.

*Prince Roy was traveling with his true identity hidden. He was "incognito". "Incognito" is an adjective. Spies or secret agents usually carry out their missions incognito. Wearing a gorilla suit makes it easy to be incognito, too.

Prince Roy liked mingling with the people of the realm and getting to learn their opinions. He ate at the inns and listened to the talk of the shepherds, fishermen, and farmers. He walked the seaports for the purpose of "getting an education," as he called it.

The common people of this seacoast village Prince Roy and Piers were presently visiting believed this young man was the son of a rich duke or lord of a manor perhaps, but they never suspected they were talking to their prince. In the seventeenth century there were no photographs. Therefore, the people really had no way to recognize their rulers unless they had seen them in person. Even then, it was only by the pomp and display of a royal procession that they would recognize that a member of the royal family was passing through. Thus they did not suspect that a prince was in their midst. What would one of such royal and noble blood be doing sitting in a dirty public house?

Prince Roy was a very unusual sort of prince. Back at the castle he had a wise teacher. He had been taught lofty ideals, but was convinced he should not be completely removed from simple living and those who lived simply. He was bored with ceremony and put up with it only because it was his duty. He hoped that someday he would have the opportunity to rule the kingdom according to his own ideas. He loved his country and his people. He also loved his father, the king, but he hoped that he would have the opportunity to rule the kingdom in what he believed would be a better way than that of his father and the rulers who had come before him.

One evening when the prince and Piers were staying in a cottage by the sea, the prince said to his attendant, "If you get us a lamb, I will cook it."

"You, Your Majesty?"

"Yes. I'd like to spend a quiet night in, and I am particularly hungry for mutton. And don't call me 'Your Majesty', even in private. You might be overheard."

"Oh, sorry. Yes, of course. If it please you, Master John."

Piers returned with the sheep and the prince cooked it. They ate in good humor. That night when Piers lay on his bed, he thought his job one of the most important in all the world. He knew Prince Roy would make a good king someday—probably the best their country had ever had.

In the middle of the night the prince awoke to terrible screams. Leaping quickly from his bed, he dashed open the shutters of his bedroom. "Your M—, uh, Master John, I beg you, close the shutters. The men in the street mustn't see you," insisted the attendant. But it was too late. Prince Roy had been spotted. Pirates were pillaging the village. Shops were being broken into and robbed of food and other essentials. Houses were searched and robbed of young men.

With a loud crash, the door of the prince's cottage was broken open.

"What is the meaning of this?" Piers cried indignantly, as several pirates poured into the room. The pirates gave no answer, for they spoke a different language. In an instant they had grabbed the prince roughly and pushed him out the doorway.

"This is kidnapping!" Piers bellowed. Eying his sword, he flew to it as quick as lightening. There was a flash of metal. "Clink, clink" clashed the swords, until two pirates behind him clasped their arms around his neck and pulled his arms back, wrenching the sword from his hand. Piers twisted, but his hands were seized in such a mighty grip that he couldn't free himself. His hands were swiftly tied, and his eyes blindfolded. The pirates shoved him into a corner and left with the captured prince.

Piers was quite bewildered that the pirates had not killed or kidnapped him. He could hear the cries of women in the street and was grieved. He fell on his knees to the hard floor in the dark cottage and muttered a prayer. "I have failed to protect the prince and I will not rest, so help me God, until he is rescued."

The thought came to his mind that if it was truly providential that his life had been spared, it might also be the prince's destiny to survive

and return to rule his people. Thus he had hope, though he knew his mission to rescue the prince was a dangerous one.

"I will do all I can do to find him, as soon I am free of these ropes," was his intently spoken vow.

The pirates, not knowing that the young man they had captured was a prince, brought him to the ship along with the other young men whom they had kidnapped from the village. Prince Roy was chained to the oars. He worked as hard as all the other men. His skin burned from the hot Mediterranean sun and from the lashing of the whip. His longing to survive and someday make his way back to his country preserved his dignity. His patience in his difficult circumstance and his quiet determination to carry his own load set an example for the other men, especially those who were in danger of losing hope of ever being set free from the slavery of the pirates. How long could they carry on?

What happens next to Prince Roy, Piers, the other men aboard the pirate ship, and the pirates?

## Writing Help

- How does the prince escape? Is he recognized? Is there retribution for the pirates? Was a ransom paid? What did the prince learn by being a galley slave that he was trying to learn in his venturing among common folk?
- Pirates are colorful and add suspense. What do you know about the world of pirates? Create some dialogue that includes their lingo. Bring in something about their ships, gear, weapons, etc. that will spice up the story. How about a battle with His Majesty's Royal Forces?
- What becomes of the men of the ship that have become the prince's friends? If the prince is rescued does he give any of these men important positions of state during his reign?

## *Books and Films*

Older boys may wish to try the novels of Rafael Sabatini (1875-1950), three of which have been published by W.W. Norton & Company: *Captain Blood, Scaramouche,* and *Sea-Hawk.* Motion pictures have also been made of *Captain Blood* and *Sea Hawk. Captain Blood*, starring Errol Flynn, Basil Rathbone, and Olivia de Havilland, was produced in 1935, not long after the book was written. *Sea Hawk* also stars Errol Flynn. These films will give you lots of ideas for finishing the story about Prince Roy and Piers.

As extravagant as Mr. Sabatini's plots may seem, they are actually based on his research of the pirates of the seventeenth century. Mr. Sabatini's novels may not have earned him entrance into the halls of "great literature," perhaps because pirate tales are not given much respect among literary critics, but they do spin a good yarn.

# 64

## A Strange Present[B]

One sunny day, down by the winding lane, just inside their own gate, three little girls were standing knee-deep in the high grass, picking daisies. As their mother came down the walk, she smiled at the scene before her. She had always dreamed of having little girls who played happily together, just as hers were doing now. She made sure her girls looked into her eyes as she gave them clear instructions to keep inside the fence and, of course, *not* to go outside the gate. Mother told them that she was on her way to visit the new occupant of the nearby *ramshackle cottage that sat in the middle of a weedy and untended yard.

"You mean old Mr. Green's spooky place?" asked Sophie, the eldest of the three sisters. Mr. Green was the name of the person who had last lived there.

"Who told you it was spooky?" Mom was curious.

---

* "Ramshackle" is an adjective that describes the house as one that is falling apart from poor construction or upkeep, although it is not yet in ruins.

Sophie just shrugged her shoulders.

Mom was already secretly shy about meeting new people, but the mention of "spooky" made her feel even more timid. Nevertheless, she decided to be brave and go. Welcoming a new neighbor was the proper and friendly thing to do. After all, it was a beautiful day; the road was splashed with sunlight, the foliage was brightly green, and flowers were blooming everywhere. As she passed through the gate, she turned and waved at her girls. They returned tiny waves.

"I won't be long," she said, more to comfort herself than them.

The girls went back to picking daisies. They would surprise Mother with a big bouquet when she returned.

"I'm going to bring these to Mom *now*," said Hannah, the youngest, proud of her collection.

Sophie had to correct her. "No, you're not. She told us to not go beyond the gate." But Hannah walked to the gate anyway.

"Don't!" Sophie called out.

"I'm just waiting here," Hannah reassured her nervous big sister. Suddenly Hannah pointed and said, "Look at that cloud of dust!"

The cloud was getting closer and they heard the rumble of feet. Climbing onto the gate, they balanced on the bars and waited. Very soon from out of the cloud they saw a flock of sheep. What seemed like a hundred large balls of white fluff trotted by, here and there a lamb among them. Behind the sheep came a farmer who hurried them on. The girls heard him whistle commands to the sheep dog that ran to and fro, steering the sheep in the right direction. In his arms the man was carrying a lamb.

When he saw the girls, the man stood at the gate and said, "Would you like a present?"

"Yes, please," said Sophie.

"Well," he said, "this lamb is completely exhausted by our journey. If I force her to go on, she's sure to die. She lost her mother, but if you nurse her, she will be as well as ever in a day or two."

"And may we keep it for our very own?" asked Sophie.

"Yes," said the man, "here she is." He lifted the lamb over the gate and put it in Sophie's arms. Then he hurried on after the flock.

Sophie cradled the lamb gingerly in her arms. Its wool was warm and soft. "I will be her mother," she said. Carefully and a little awkwardly she laid it down on the grass in the shade of some trees. The three girls bent over it and Hannah petted it lovingly, but the poor lamb was weak. It had been hours since it had had any milk. Its body quivered as it stretched out its head on the cool grass, but it did not open its eyes.

"She's sick, the poor thing," said Amy, full of pity.

"No, she isn't. Babies do a lot of sleeping. They sleep all the time," replied Sophie, confident in herself and being in the habit of correcting her sisters.

Amy, unconvinced, said, "I'm going next door to get Mom; she'll know what to do for the poor little thing."

"No, Amy. Mom told us to wait here," Sophie said, now trying to restrain the other sister.

What happened next? Describe what the characters see, hear, smell, taste or smell. Explain not only what the characters do, but also how they might be feeling. Include Mother in the second picture as she approaches the old ramshackle cottage.

## Writing Help

- How would you like to be given a present of a baby lamb? What would you do to take care of it? Young lambs need something to eat quite often. What is it? Does Amy walk down the road toward her mother after all? Or what do the girls say to Mom when she returns? Do they keep the lamb? How do they take care of it? Do they ever have to give it away or give it back?
- What do you think their father will say? Could he have a different opinion than the girls and mother?

- What happens to the farmer and his flock? Does he return for any reason?
- Does the lamb cause any disruption? It might eat something it wasn't supposed to, for instance, or get into things it shouldn't. Does it wake up in the middle of the night and cry because it misses its mother? These things I've mentioned bring some conflict that make the story realistic, but you can also add some joy and laughter.
- Who is the new neighbor? Is he or she friendly? Are there any children? You have the option of putting the new neighbor (or new family) into the story.

# 65

## Grandpa's Dog Pepper

Hi. I'm Benjamin. I'm twelve years old. I have blue eyes and sandy brown hair. My skin has turned brown from being out in the summer sun. My dad says the neighbors think I'm from the Mediterranean. "But they know I was born here in Tennessee!" I insist.

He teases and says, "It isn't polite to argue with people." Mom says it becomes me and that "getting some color" is healthy for people.

My grandma and grandpa live just up the road from us. I pay them lots of visits. Grandpa has always had a large garden, and since it is harder now for him to keep it up, I help him with the planting and weeding. When the vegetables and fruits are ripe, Grandma rewards me for my work. The treat might be strawberry rhubarb pie, an oniony omelet, creamy chicken and dumplings with green peas, or a bowl of freshly-made tomato soup. Food never tastes more delicious than when Grandma makes it. Mom, not put out by my compliments to Grandma, tells me that food tastes best to those who have worked hard outdoors.

Grandpa has a dog named Pepper. He is a special dog because he is amazingly helpful. Grandpa says it is all a matter of training.

Pepper helps us in the garden. He likes to fetch things. I pump the water from the well, and Pepper grabs the handle of the bucket between his teeth and walks to the vegetable garden with me. I wonder why

Grandpa needs me when he has Pepper. When I mention this to my mother, she reminds me that there are some things Pepper can't do, such as weed, hoe, and knock off the menacing squash beetles that hide under the leaves. I wish Pepper could pick off those horrifying hornworms on Grandpa's tomato plants. Eeuww! It's my job to collect these fat green caterpillars—avoiding the sharp horn—and feed them to the chickens. I don't relish that activity!

Recently I've noticed that Pepper hasn't been as peppy as usual.

"Grandpa, how old is Pepper?" I asked him one day.

"Almost as old as you," he replied.

"That's old in dog years isn't it?" I commented.

"Yup."

"Is that why he doesn't want to help today?" I asked.

"No, it's not his age. Grandma says he's sulking."

"About what?"

"See 'im over there, Benjamin? He's lying under the fence near the barn door. He's sad that we sold Picadilly."

"Picadilly was a fine horse, Grandpa. Why'd you sell him?"

Grandpa looked sad, too, and didn't reply. He told me that Grandma was calling me in for some of her corn chowder.

When I got home, I told Mom about Picadilly being sold. She said little. I guess she didn't want to talk about it. Then she announced, "You'll be visiting Grandma and Grandpa again tomorrow because I need to see the seamstress in town. Baby Joy will visit, too. You will do whatever needs doing, won't you?"

I agreed.

That morning Grandpa was happy to see me, as always, and he was *very* happy to see Joy. Joy is only one year old. She has a turned-up nose, big blue eyes, and round pink cheeks, so of course everyone finds her

adorable. Grandpa bounced Joy on his knee and gave her things to hold. She finds Grandpa very funny.

I went outside and looked around for Pepper, thinking he'd like to play fetch or something. I couldn't find him anywhere, so I went back into the house to see whether Grandpa knew where he was.

"Grandpa," I said. "Do you know where Pepper is?"

"Maybe he's down by the creek."

I went down to the creek and looked around, but Pepper wasn't there. When I went back inside to report my lack of success, Grandpa said, “Check inside the barn again; he might be moping somewhere in the shadows.”

Moping? Would Pepper really be that sad over the loss of Picadilly? I wondered. When I once more returned from looking, I reported, “He’s not there. He doesn’t seem to be anywhere.”

Grandpa stood up and handed Joy to Grandma. He put two fingers to his mouth and let out a sharp whistle. We waited. He didn’t come.

“Well I’ll be,” he said. “Pepper always comes running lickety-split when he hears his whistle.”

Grandpa started walking. I followed him around the side of the barn, out to the pasture where Picadilly once grazed. We couldn’t believe our eyes. Pepper was running toward us, but not by himself.

Putting your imaginative muscles to work, add to the story. I like the picture of Pepper and Picadilly, running together, don’t you?

## Writing Help

- How did the different characters react to what Pepper was doing?
- What was done about Picadilly? You may wish to explain just how it happened that Pepper and Picadilly were together again. Was Pepper thieving, or did he happen upon Picadilly some other way? How did Picadilly like his new master? What would Picadilly’s new master have to say about Pepper’s possible thievery? Did Pepper know he was thieving? Was the money Grandpa got from the sale of Picadilly already spent?
- Tell us more about Picadilly. Why was everyone so sad that he was gone? Why would he be hard to replace?

## Additional Challenge

### *Artful Adjectives*

I used some adjectives in this story starter to better describe certain things for you. I told you that Grandpa has a *large* garden. It is so large that he needs Benjamin's help. I wrote that Pepper was *special* because he is so *helpful.* Grandma's food tastes *delicious.* The hornworms on the tomato plants were *horrifying* partly because they were *fat* and have a *sharp* horn. (Have you ever seen one?) Something else was *sharp* in the story: Grandpa's whistle.

Go over your first draft and see where you could add some adjectives to describe the things you see in your imagination. Could you use more adjectives to describe Pepper? All I wrote about Picadilly was that he was a *fine* horse. This tells us a little, but what else might be said about Picadilly to describe him? What else can be said to further describe any of the characters in your story?

# 66

## Toby and the Whale

The year was 1851, the month was August, and I, Tobias Farquhar, otherwise known as Toby, was out to sea on the whaling ship *Nantucket.* I was seventeen years old. This was my first journey on the ocean and I was very excited. We were several weeks off the coast of South America when one morning, at about nine o'clock, whales were sighted. "Thar she bl-o-o-ows!" was the eagerly awaited cry from high up in the crow's nest. Instantly the crew scrambled into action. Two harpooning boats were launched from the ship and went after the whales. Captain Gibbs commanded the starboard boat. The first mate commanded the larboard boat. Those of us left on board watched the action through a telescope that was passed frequently from one to another so that we all could see something of the upcoming battle.

Only moments later, faster than any of us expected, the larboard boat harpooned a whale. Several of the harpoons stuck directly behind the whale's head. The wounded whale, perhaps out of fear or anger, started traveling very fast away from the boat, pulling it with

him, as the crew members were holding on to the whale lines (the ropes attached to the harpoons). The crew held on for dear life as the whale took them on what is called a Nantucket Sleigh Ride. Then suddenly the whale stopped, turned around, and headed straight for the boat. Rushing at it with tremendous force, the whale lifted its head above the water, rammed the boat, and crushed it into fragments as small as a common chair. Captain Gibbs immediately commanded the men in his boat to row toward the wreck. Through the telescope we counted the men who hung on the floating debris. Astonishingly, not a man was missing, and we were confident that our captain would succeed in rescuing them all.

The starboard boat would be heavily laden after all the men were picked up and I was ordered to make haste to assist Samuel Smith in boarding another boat to row out to the men. We were armed with harpoons in case the monster from the deep charged at us. I had never been out in a harpoon boat before, and I was glad to be with Mr. Smith, from whom I was "learning the ropes" on board the ship. I was excited to be in the small boat, but at the same time I was frightened of the possible danger.

We rowed with force. The sea around us was not calm, and it seemed to be turning various shades of blue—first dark, then light. Then I gathered that what I must have been seeing was the shadow of a whale passing beneath our boat. Would it gather up speed and thrust itself at the starboard boat?

We were halfway to the starboard boat when Mr. Smith ordered me to stop rowing. I did so, and waited in silence for his next command. Again I studied the water around us. This time I found it to be eerie: it was stained with blood. "What are we doing here?" I almost blurted out to Mr. Smith, but knew it wasn't my place to question his maneuvers, so I resisted the urge to speak.

Suddenly the sea rose up in a mound before us. I thought that at any moment we would be done for.

Continue the action, describing what Toby observed. What came forth from the mound of water? How did Toby react to all that took place before his eyes? Make the characters come alive. Put conversation in your story. Include the scene of the second picture somewhere in your story.

## Writing Help

*Exploring Possibilities*

- Why was Mr. Smith stopping when they were sent to lighten to load of the starboard boat? Could he be making his boat a decoy?
- Was the whale in the picture the same whale that rammed the boat earlier? If so, where are its harpoons and why is it floating on its side? If it is a different whale, where is one that was harpooned?
- When Toby gets up close to the whale, what does he observe is its condition? Perhaps Toby had never seen a whale close up before. Would he find it to be a beautiful animal?
- Are there any new dangers awaiting him?
- Described the mixed emotions of the sailor being rescued in the first picture. How would he describe the experience of a whale staring at him close up? What becomes of the men crowded together in this boat?
- What does Toby think of his adventure? He might find his experience thrilling. On the other hand he might be disgusted and recoil at the work of gutting the dead whale on board the ship.

## Additional Challenge

Toby is inexperienced; therefore much is new to him. Write your part of the story in first person, that is, in Toby's words, as I did in my part. It might help to look up some nautical terms for your own understanding. I found some of the phrases I used, such as "Nantucket Sleigh Ride," in an encyclopedia under the topic of whaling.

### *Vivid Verbs*

After you've written your story, you can go back over it and change any plain verbs for more vivid ones.

As a response to the sailors hearing, "Thar she blows!" I could have written that the men *went* into action. Instead, I said that they *scrambled* into action. Or I could have written that they *sprang* in action. One or more of following verbs may be useful to you in describing the action of the whale, the crew, or the water. Choose any of them, or find your own.

**Vivid Verbs:** awaken, bleed, blink, breathe, break, coil, dive, drip, float, frown, gulp, gasp, gape, haul, hook, howl, holler, leap, lead, labor, toss, measure, mark, net, operate, pray, quake, quiver, roll, rise, ride, sink, slide, splash, tear, thrash, touch, wink, wobble, wheeze.

### *A Film–A Book*

If you enjoy films of action and suspense on the high seas, I recommend *Moby Dick*, starring Gregory Peck. This colorful 1956 film is based on the famous American novel of the same title written by Herman Melville. The film offers you a close-up view of what it was like to hunt whales aboard the great wooden ships of the 1800s. You can almost feel the sea mist on your face as the determined men put their backs to the oars. *Moby Dick* relates the story of a sea captain who is willing to risk his life, his crew, and his ship in a mad quest for revenge against the white whale who took his leg.

The novel is most suitable for more mature readers. It has many dry non-plot related sections that slow down the action. These parts are essays on whaling, etc.

# 67

## Deborah Misses Dad

Deborah's family had just moved into a big house on Ocean Avenue in Portland, Maine. Mother said it needed work, and wished aloud that the painting and wallpapering could have been done *before* they moved in. But Dad was due to make a voyage to Panama and he wanted his family moved in before his departure.

The morning came when the family walked from their new house to the dock to see Father off. "Must you leave, Father?" asked Deborah winsomely. She was very fond of her father.

"Yes; you know I must. And I've already told you that it is important business. However, I hope to be home at first snowfall." The exact date of his return was uncertain.

"Is that a long time away?" she asked.

He wouldn't say yes or no. "I don't like good-byes, either, and I will miss you, too," he said, "but when you are keeping busy with your home education, helping your mother, and playing with your sister, Sonja, the time will go by more quickly than you think."

"Yes, Father," Deborah smiled, following her mother's example of trying to keep the farewell a cheerful one.

Mother said, "Deborah, would you like me to tell you the meaning of the word *goodbye*?"

Deborah nodded a yes and looked puzzled.

"Well, I'll tell you. Hundreds of years ago, when people parted, they bid each other, 'God be with ye.' The expression altered over time into the version we use today. God is, and will be, with your father, and even though your father will be far from *us*, he won't be far from God. Jesus said, 'I am with you always, even to the end of the world.'"

This magnificent truth comforted Deborah, as her mother had intended. After Father boarded his ship, they stood on the pier in the sunshine for quite a long time, watching the ship pull slowly away from the docks and sail away.

"Goodbye, Father," they all finally chorused, giving a last wave before making their way home. Mother, unnoticed, wiped her cheeks dry.

The next morning was Saturday and Mother rallied her children into action. They rolled up their sleeves, put on their aprons, and got to work. Energetically they wetted and scraped off the old paper on Deborah's bedroom walls. What a chore! What a mess! Deborah's brother, Waldo, got into the act most enthusiastically. Mother, in general, found it necessary to correct her seven-year-old son regarding his *slovenly appearance; thus it was only natural that he welcomed an opportunity to get messy. He seemed to love contributing to the crumpled and soggy mounds of wet paper on the floor.

---

*"Slovenly" is an adjective (even thought it ends in an "ly" which is more commonly an adverb ending). I used it to describe Waldo. It means he is habitually untidy.

One wall had finally been scraped free of paper, and the children were preparing to work on the next, when Waldo suddenly exclaimed, "Look! I've found a door!"

Indeed he had. The door had been hidden under the paper. Its presence had been unsuspected because it had no knob and it was half the height of the other doors in the house. It had also been coated with a thin layer of plaster before the wallpaper had been applied.

Mother carefully chipped away the plaster that had been applied to the crack between the door and the frame. "All right," Mother finally said to Waldo, "Go ahead. Open it."

Waldo pushed open the door and, stooping, looked in. Before him was a closet of sorts—empty except for a large object that was covered with a sheet. He stepped into the closet and, reaching the mysterious item, removed the sheet. "Come and see this!" he exclaimed.

Mother peered over the heads of the girls as, one after the other; they stepped gingerly into the closet. Deborah was speechless. Sonja could only breathe, "Oh, Mother!"

The mysterious object, now uncovered, was a large dollhouse. Even through the dust and cobwebs, it was obvious that it was no rough construction, hastily thrown together, but a finely crafted *edifice that had been built with much care and love.

Mother observed that the dollhouse appeared to be a replica of the house they lived in. The rooms were set up exactly the same. Even the wallpaper in one tiny bedroom was similar to the wallpaper they had been scraping, except that the flowers on the "dollhouse wallpaper" were much smaller. "Amazing! " thought Mother, but she said nothing to the children about what she had noticed.

---

*An "edifice" is a building, usually a grand one. In this instance it is a miniature grand one.

Meanwhile, the children had been exploring the contents of the dollhouse. Little Sonja said, "I like the dolls," cradling them tenderly in her little hands.

"The dollhouse will be yours, Deborah, because it was found in your room," Mother proclaimed, trying to be fair.

"May I play with it, too?" Sonja asked. Waldo, who was fascinated with the intricacies of the construction, seconded her query.

"Yes, of course you may both play with the house, but you must be very careful with the pieces of furniture and the little dolls," said Deborah. The pieces were what mother called "antique" and could break easily.

The golden weeks of autumn continued, and everyone in the household was kept busy, just as Father said they would be. There was a lot to do to make the house "livable," according to Mother, and with Mother acting as renovator, school teacher, and cook, her days were full.

"Mother, won't I ever get to play with the dollhouse by myself?" Deborah asked *plaintively one afternoon.

Mother, busy with paintbrush in hand, sought to quickly remedy the situation. "Yes, all right," she said. "As soon I've finished painting this chair, I'll take Waldo and Sonja to the market. I'll buy us a nice haddock for supper. Will you be all right here by yourself for half an hour?"

"Oh, yes, thank you."

Main Street was just two blocks away. Waldo and Sonja liked going on errands with their mother on market day because there was so much to see. While they were gone, Deborah enjoyed having time to herself to play with her dollhouse alone. She hummed quietly as she played. It was a soothing activity.

Perhaps it was that Deborah was less preoccupied with making sure that her siblings didn't damage the furniture. In any case, today, for the first time, she noticed—as her mother had those many months earlier—that the dollhouse was just like the house they lived in. This was a curious thing to her. After awhile, she instinctively removed the father

---

*Deborah asked "plaintively." Her voice was one of woe—a sort of sad complaint.

doll from the household, and put him in a place on the other side of her bedroom, not intending to return him to the rest of the family in the dollhouse until her own father returned. Then all the dolls would celebrate with a grand party, she decided, and she would make a teeny-tiny paper chain to decorate the dining room. Her playful ideas, however, made her miss her father all the more.

As September passed into late October, the air grew increasingly chilly. Knowing how unpredictable the weather could be in Maine, Deborah began looking out of her window every morning to see if it had snowed during the night. She remembered what her father had said, and she had taken him literally. He had *said* that he would be home at first snowfall. "And so he *shall* be," she thought.

Soon the morning she had anticipated arrived. Deborah peered through the curtains and saw snow—October snow! The trees were dusted with white and a few brave birds were still singing. Today she would get everything ready for the doll party. She would go downstairs and tell her mother straightaway about her plans for a party for Father as well.

What happened that day? Do you think Father thought it would snow as early as October? The story can go one of two ways. Either Father doesn't come home that very day, or he does return, rather fantastically. Write freely.

## Writing Help

- How would Mother react to Deborah's insistence on making party preparations?

- How do parents feel about disappointing their children? Does Mother go along with the preparations, even though she is skeptical? Does she warn Deborah that her father's return is uncertain?
- What are all the things Deborah does to make a welcome home party for her father?
- What surprises does her father have for the family?

## Additional Challenge

Why might the closet have been sealed up? Why is the dollhouse an exact replica of the house? The reasons for this would make the story mysterious. Does Deborah's mother ever find out anything from any elderly neighbors, about the people who lived in the house many years before?

After you have written a rough draft, you might wish to go back and incorporate a little suspense into your story. You might also like to include more conflict.

### *Suspense*

Suspense can be created in the story by making the characters wait, by showing anticipation, or by allowing the characters to be more conscious of—and anxious about—the passing of time. Perhaps:

1. Deborah has difficulty concentrating on her math lessons because her thoughts stray onto all she wants to do for the party.
2. Lunch is eaten in haste in order to start making paper decorations. A cake is baked, but it doesn't turn out so well. Another is made. (conflict and delay)

3. A welcome home sign is made, which gets paint on mother's clean table and floor. It must be cleaned up. (conflict and delay)
4. The dining room table is set with the goodies and the front door and central hall is decorated. As they all sit in the parlor, waiting long for Father's arrival, they watch the sun set. Sonja falls asleep.

Suspense and conflict are important components of a good story. I hope the suggestions listed above will give you some ideas for including them in this and other stories.

# Section Three

## Hints for Polishing

# Introduction to Hints for Polishing

If you have written freely, letting your imagination wander, if you've written with gusto, with zest, or more abandon than you are used to, than I am happy, because that means this book wasn't written in vain; that is, you've done the imaginative work I had hoped you would do. Well done. That is the most important aspect of writing, and the main purpose of *Story Starters.*

Now I invite you to go back over your writing to do a little revising and polishing. Proper spelling and punctuation is necessary, but what I am talking about here is giving your story a deeper finish—polishing it until it shines. You want your story to read as vividly and brightly as you see it in your imagination. Therefore, consider using more descriptive words that will deliver particular details about your characters, their setting, and the action.

# Sensory Language

## Using Language of the Five Senses

A writer creates a secondary world for his readers by giving them a sense of "being there." Description makes your writing more interesting. Sensory description makes it more believable. When you write even a short episode, you will enable the reader to "experience" something similar to what you see in your imagination. You do this by not only describing what you *see* in your own imagination, but what you hear, smell, feel, or taste as well.

Below are some examples of sensory language my children and I thought up. Think of some of your own to add to each group. Write them in your notebook or say them aloud to your teacher.

### *Sight*

What you see in your imagination can be colorful, show action, or describe the facial expressions of your characters.

Try to picture in your imagination the following sights.

The main character watched:

- orange flames dancing in the fireplace,
- a black dog shaking his hair dry,
- a red kite bobbing in the bright blue sky,
- a large long yawn with squinted eyes.

Can you picture all of these things in your imagination? You could? Who had the large long yawn? Now provide three of your own sights to behold.

### *Sound*

The main character heard:

- dry leaves crunching underfoot,
- loud piano chords,
- a bee buzzing around his head,
- a door slam,
- two girls whispering and giggling.

Have you heard any these sounds at one time? When you describe sounds in your stories, your readers will hear what you hear, too. Supply three of your own sounds.

### *Smell*

Smells can be nice or not so nice. The main character smelled:

- sweet fresh hay,
- the leather of a new saddle,
- manure.

Can you tell by the odors listed where the character is standing? If you said near a horse barn, you would be correct. If you have been in a barn, you will be able to relate to these smells. Not everyone has been in a barn, but even if the writer includes smells the reader is unfamiliar with, he will be giving the reader a sensory experience.

Mention three fragrances that you think most people have smelled. Then read the odiferous poem below.

**Smells**

*Why is it that the poets tell*
*So little of the sense of smell?*
*These are the odors I love well:*

*The smell of coffee freshly ground;*
*Or rich plum pudding, holly crowned;*
*Or onions fried and deeply browned.*

*The fragrance of a fumy pipe;*
*The smell of apples, newly ripe;*
*And printer's ink on leaden type.*

*Woods by moonlight in September*
*Breathe most sweet; and I remember*
*Many a smoky campfire ember.*

*Camphor, turpentine, and tea,*
*The balsam of a Christmas tree,*
*These are whiffs of gramarye...*
A ship smells best of all to me!
—Christopher Morley

### Taste

The main character puckered his lips at the sour lemonade, swallowed the last bite of his salty Pennsylvania Dutch pretzel and then popped a spicy cinnamon candy into his mouth.

*Take a close look at the picture of the Sunday school picnic. What do the children taste? Use more sensory language to describe the sights, sounds and smells of the picnickers' outdoor surroundings.*

### Touch

The characters in your stories will be active. When people *do* things, they also *feel* things. They may feel what they touch or feel emotions. Some examples of touch are:

The main character felt:

- the cool washcloth on her fevered brow,
- the smooth polished tabletop,
- the wind whipping her hair out of place,
- the kitten's soft ears.

What else might she touch? List three things you've touched.

W. H.
W. H. J

### *Feelings*

Some of the story starters in this book are action-packed and call on you to continue the action. What your characters are feeling can be overlooked when you are focusing on action. That's okay. You can always go back over your story to add some emotion to match the mood or the events. By including emotions you will be creating sympathetic characters, ones with which your readers will sympathize. What do the characters feel in the situations below?

1. Little Jimmy fussed because he couldn't reach the doorknob.
2. Jenny trembled. What would Dad say about his car's broken headlight?
3. Linda shed a tear for the injured bluebird lying limp in her hand.
4. Annie's giggle turned into a belly laugh as Tommy told another silly joke.

(1. Jimmy felt *frustration*. 2. Jenny felt *fear*. 3.Linda felt *pity*. 4. Annie felt *hilarity*.)

Leigh Hunt said,

*There are two worlds; the world that we can measure with line and rule, and the world that we feel with our hearts and imagination.*

I wonder what your characters will feel.

## You Did It

Congratulations if you added more examples to what my children and I thought up for you. You could only do this by using the powers of your imagination. I will remind you from time to time to add sensory language when you complete the story starters. Most of the time, however, you will be on your own. There is no need to use all five senses in every story. Using even one or two will really liven things up.

# Vivid Verbs

Take a look at your verbs. On your rough draft underline your "verbs of doing" in green. Green means "go" and you'll want your verbs to deliver. Deliver what? Deliver a more precise impression of the action taking place. The sentences on the left use verbs that are weak. The verbs to the right are stronger and tell us more.

He got into the helicopter. ✏ He climbed into the helicopter.

He went to his neighbor's house. ✏ He skateboarded to his neighbor's house.

She ate the crackers and cheese. ✏ She nibbled the crackers and cheese.

He threw the ball. ✏ He hurled the ball. He tossed the ball. He pitched the ball.

She walked home. ✏ She meandered home. She raced home. She skipped home.

A thesaurus is handy for finding verbs that more precisely represent the action you wish to depict.

I looked up the word "take" and found these choices: receive, obtain, acquire, catch, seize, capture, win, procure, grasp, pilfer, rob, appropriate, pocket.

If you have a thesaurus, here is a short exercise for you. Choose three of the verbs below and look them up.

| | | | |
|---|---|---|---|
| eat | fight | laugh | run |
| play | work | talk | rest |
| breath | walk | open | pull |

Verbs have *shades* of meaning. If you find a verb in your thesaurus the exact meaning of which you do not know, look it up in a dictionary before you use it. Writers (and thoughtful readers) take the time to look up the meaning of words, even if they think they already have a basic knowledge of their meaning. Sometimes we will be surprised to find that a word will have a somewhat different meaning than we expected.

When you have added your story to one of the story starters, ask yourself this question. Are there any verbs in my story's first draft that I (on second thought) want to replace with a more vivid one?

*Take a close look at the picture of the ice skaters. Use one or two vivid verbs to describe the action of the scene.*

If you want a lesson on verbs, one can be found on page 7 of my book, *Simply Grammar*.

# Artful Adjectives

Take a look at your nouns. Underline them in red on your rough draft. Can you add any adjectives to modify these nouns? To modify means to *change* or *limit*. An adjective will tell you more specifically about the nature of the noun and create a more descriptive picture. As an artist enhances his painting by adding dabs of paint, perhaps to make the sunshine more or less brighter, or his dark clouds more or less gloomy; so a writer paints with words. We can "touch up" our nouns with artful adjectives.

The cat meowed. ✏ The wet cat meowed.

Cats generally dislike being wet. My sentence with the underlined adjective "wet" invokes more pity. It lets us know why the cat may be meowing. Just one adjective tells so much more about the cat.

The wet cat was hungry and meowed.

Now he meows for yet another reason. I added an adjective, this time, *after* our noun "cat." Do you see how just two simple adjectives provide greater description? I could have also put the adjectives in this order: The hungry wet cat meowed.

*Take a close look at the picture of the woolly rhinoceros. Use one or two adjectives to describe this scene. Of course, you can choose a vivid verb that would best describe any action taking place, too.*

If you want a lesson on adjectives, one can be found on page 13 of my book, *Simply Grammar*.

# Advantageous Adverbs

## Examples from *Black Beauty*

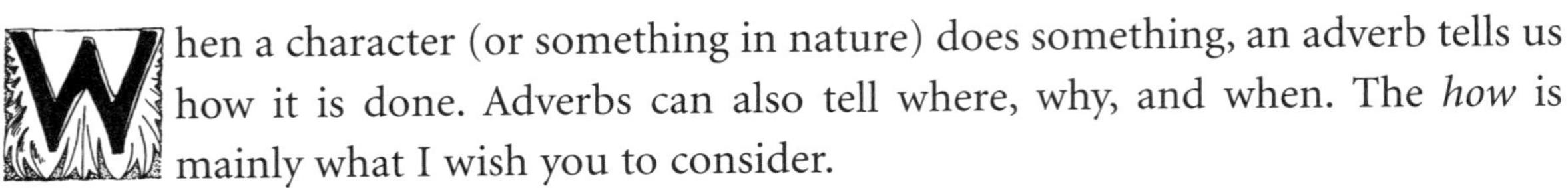

When a character (or something in nature) does something, an adverb tells us how it is done. Adverbs can also tell where, why, and when. The *how* is mainly what I wish you to consider.

Every so often an adverb can be used to describe the action more specifically. An "ad-verb" is "added-to-the-verb," as the word itself implies.

Adverbs will often end in an "ly". Here are some adverbs I have found useful:

Gently, tenderly, instantly, slowly, randomly, happily, sadly, confidently, pitifully, softly, energetically, carefully, frantically, positively, ardently, generously, sorrowfully, effortlessly, painfully, cautiously.

You may wish to use one of these in your story or choose adverbs of your own.

The sentences below have adverbs. Which "ly" words can you find? I picked out these sentences from *Black Beauty*, a favorite book of mine. Point them out to your teacher or make a list of them. Notice how they describe the action.

*(Chapter 1) He gave us food, good lodging, and kind words; he spoke as kindly to us as he did to his little children.*

*(Chap 2) The oldest of the colts raised his head, pricked his ears, and said, "There are the hounds!" and immediately cantered off, followed by the rest of us to the upper part of the field, where we could look over the hedge and see several fields beyond.*

*(Chap 20) There were two horses straining and struggling with all their might to drag the cart out, but they could not move it; the sweat streamed from their*

*legs and flanks, their sides heaved, and every muscle was strained, whilst the men, fiercely pulling at the head of the forehorse [horse in front] swore and lashed most brutally.*

*(Chap 24) I gave a loud shrill neigh for help: again and again I neighed, pawing the ground impatiently, and tossing my head to get the rein loose.*

*(Chap 30) He kept the stable clean and airy, and he groomed me thoroughly; and was never otherwise than gentle.*

If you want a lesson on adverbs, one can be found on page 93 of my book, *Simply Grammar.*

### *For the Advanced Student:*

When a vivid verb is used an adverb isn't always wanted.

He wolfed down his supper.
He ate his supper hungrily.

There is nothing wrong with the second sentence that uses the adverb "hungrily," but the verb "wolfed," tells us a little more than "ate hungrily" because it more vividly implies that the man ate like a wild dog and perhaps not with the best of table manners. A vivid verb often does a better job than a plain verb and an adverb. Therefore adverbs are used in moderation and not too frequently. It is up to you to decide what adverbs you might like to use in your story. Put them where you want.

# Three Kinds of Narrators

Use of first person indicates that the author is writing about himself. He uses the pronouns "I" or "we."

Examples:

*I knelt down to get a closer look at what seemed to be a moose print in the mud.*

*I swallowed a piece of corn chip that I didn't chew well enough and it scratched on the way down.*

*Sitting in the front row, we got a good look at the musicians as well as the singers on stage.*

When using second person, the author is addressing his reader, or "you."
Examples:

*When you are thirsty, the best thing to drink is water.*

*To hike on deep snow, you must first have a pair of snowshoes that fit you well.*

*If you like WWII movies, you are sure to like* Bridge on the River Kwai.

When an author uses third person, he is writing about someone or something else, that is, some person or thing other than himself or you. He uses "he," "she," "it," they."
Examples:

*She and her sister ran to the top of the stairs in answer to their mother's call.*

*They heard a crash when the tree was blown down by the roaring wind.*

*This vacation was one to remember because he had never before been to a foreign country.*

# Description of a Setting

## An Example from Literature

Sir Arthur Conan Doyle describes a setting of a moor in one of his Sherlock Holmes stories, *The Hound of the Baskervilles.* I have never been on a moor. Have you? I can get a good picture of this moor, however, from what Sir Arthur writes, or shall I say, from what he "paints" with words. Notice the adjectives that I underlined:

> *We had come to a point where a narrow grassy path struck off from the road and wound away across the moor. A steep, boulder-sprinkled hill lay upon the right which had in bygone days been cut into a granite quarry. The face, which was turned toward us, formed a dark cliff, with ferns and brambles growing in its niches. From over a distant rise there floated a grey plume of smoke....*
>
> *"It is a wonder place, the moor," said [Stapleton], looking round over the undulating downs, long green rollers, with crests of jagged granite foaming up into fantastic surges. "You never tire of the moor. You cannot think the wonderful secrets which it contains. It is so vast, and so barren, and so mysterious.*

# Character Description—Physical Appearance

## An Example from Literature

Providing a physical description of your characters (painting a picture of them with words) will bring them more clearly into focus. There is only a little physical description of characters in the short stories of this book, because so much emphasis is on the action, but in a longer story, such as Robert Louis Stevenson's *Treasure Island*, whole paragraphs often will describe important characters. The following description is from the first page of *Treasure Island.* How clearly can you picture this character in your mind's eye? After reading it once, go back and read it again, pointing out the adjectives to your teacher or making a list of them. The adjectives are plentiful.

> *I remember him as if it were yesterday, as he came plodding to the inn door, his sea chest following behind him in a hand-barrow; a tall, strong, heavy, nut-brown man; his tarry pig-tail falling over the shoulders of his soiled blue coat; his hands ragged and scarred, with black, broken nails; and the saber cut across one cheek, a dirty, livid white. I remember him looking round the cove and whistling to himself as he did so, and then breaking out in that old sea song he sang so often afterwards:*
>
> *"Fifteen men on the dead man's chest,*
> *Yo-ho-ho and a bottle of rum!"*

If you feel so challenged as to write a whole story yourself from the Just Pictures section, feel free to describe your main character with as much description as Mr. Stevenson gave to his.

# Character Description—Personality

n author paints a picture of what his characters are like in three ways. We learn about a character by

- what he says,
- what he does, and
- what others say about him.

## An Example from Literature

Below is an example of how the reader is introduced to a new character by way of what the other characters say about him. In *The Wind in the Willows*, the author Kenneth Grahame gives us an introductory peek at the character of Toad through the conversation shared between Mole and Ratty. The conversation is carrying a bit of action, too, as they get into a boat to paddle along the river. We do learn much more about Toad by his own conversation and actions as the story progresses.

> *"But what I wanted to ask you was, won't you take me to call on Mr. Toad? I've heard so much about him, and I do so want to make his acquaintance."*
>
> *"Why certainly," said the good-natured Rat, jumping to his feet and dismissing poetry from his mind for the day. "Get the boat out, and we'll paddle up there at once. It's never the wrong time to call on Toad. Early or late he's always sorry when you go!"*
>
> *"He must be a very nice animal," observed the Mole, as he got into the boat and took the sculls, while the Rat settled himself comfortably in the stern.*
>
> *"He is indeed the best of animals," replied Rat. "So simple, so good-natured, and so affectionate. Perhaps he's not clever—we can't all be geniuses; and it*

*may be that he is both boastful and conceited. But he has got some great qualities, has Toady."*

*Rounding a bend in the river, they came in sight of a handsome, dignified old house of mellowed red brick, with well-kept lawns reaching down to the water's edge.*

*"There's Toad Hall," said the Rat; "and that creek on the left, where the notice board says, 'Private. No landing allowed,' is where we'll leave the boat. The stables are over there to the right. That's the banqueting hall you're looking at now—very old, that is. Toad is rather rich, you know, and this is really one of the nicest houses in these parts, though we never admit as much to Toad."*

# A Lesson of Review for Additional Challenge

## An Example from Charles Dickens

During the time I was writing this book, my son was reading the novel *Great Expectations,* by Charles Dickens. At the end of one day I sank into the cushions of our sofa and noticed that *Great Expectations* was lying beside me. Out of curiosity I picked it up and opened it to where it was book-marked. I glanced down the page. "Marvelous," I said.

"What's marvelous?" Nigel asked, coming into the room at that moment.

"This bit here." I read it aloud.

"Oh, yeah," he said with a smile.

It was then that I decided to share the paragraph with you. What do you think of it? This piece of writing works marvelously well at giving us a picture and a "feel" of how the man in the story eats. The descriptive vocabulary **blends** into the background like dabs of paint are blended onto a canvas. Mr. Dickens' brush strokes are so **blended** that they create a picture without calling attention to themselves. Unlike impressionist art, one must get up much closer to examine the strokes. Notice the strokes. I have underlined some of them to give you a sampling of vivid verbs, adjectives, and adverbs. With practice you will be able to identify these in any great piece of writing and consequently to improve your own writing.

> *(Chapter 3) I had often watched a large dog of ours eating his food; and I now noticed a decided similarity between the dog's way of eating, and the man's. The man took strong sharp sudden bites, just like the dog. He swallowed, or rather snapped up, every mouthful, too soon and too fast; and he looked sideways here and there while he ate, as if he thought there was danger in every direction of somebody's coming to take the pie away. He was altogether too unsettled in his mind over it, to appreciate it comfortably, I thought, or to have*

*anybody to dine with him, without making a chop with his jaws at the visitor. In all of which particulars he was very like a dog.*

Noticed: vivid verb—a more specific word than "saw"
Decided, strong, sharp, sudden: adjectives
Snapped up: vivid verb phrase—the narrator himself, on second thought, decides it is a more accurate description than "swallowed"
Sideways: adverb—where he looked
Unsettled: adjective describing the condition of his state of mind
Appreciate: vivid verb
Comfortably: adverb

# Section Four

## Just Pictures

# Introduction to Just Pictures

The work you have put into the story starters has made you a more descriptive writer. Congratulations! The practice you will have with Just Pictures will empower you even more. Do you feel more confident about writing? I hope you do. Your developing skill will carry over to the more formal aspects of writing required in your schoolwork. You and your teacher can be happy about that.

With Just Pictures you make up the whole story yourself. Here is your opportunity to create your own characters and your very own plot. Start by picking a person (or animal) from the pictures—a person that makes you curious to know more about him or her. Then make up whatever you want about your character. It is all up to you.

If you are raring to go, jump in. Be my guest. Dive in headfirst if you like. Make a splash. Write what you like. Later, it will be advantageous to you (now that you have become an experienced story writer) to look at some of the basic elements of a short story. I invite you to take up this additional challenge.

## Additional Challenge

Think for a minute. Which fiction stories are your favorites? Name two. If you were to scrutinize these, you would discover that the authors of your favorite stories always include certain basic elements in their stories. These elements are what help make up a good story. They are the same elements I wish to bring to your notice. It shouldn't be tedious, however. You need not memorize the vocabulary printed in capital letters. No one is testing you on them here. What I hope you *will* understand and remember are the ideas these words represent. Then, you can apply the ideas and make your writing better and better.

# A Lesson on the Basic Elements of a Story

## Characters

The creation and description of your character is called CHARACTERIZATION. The main character is the *protagonist*, of whom your story is about. I have pointed out examples of characterization from literature in Hints for Polishing. Is your character shy or daring, funny or serious? He could be a mixture of all of those things. What impression does he or she make on the other characters of the story? What does he or she like to do?

## Point of View

Who is telling the story? Is it the main character, one of the characters, or is the narrator of the story outside the story looking in? Each story is told from a POINT OF VIEW. In Hints for Polishing you can read about "Three Narrators." POINT OF VIEW can get complicated as it involves how much or how little the narrator knows. You don't need to be concerned with this until you become more involved with story writing.

## Setting

Where is your character? Your description of his whereabouts is the SETTING of your story. Using sensory language in your description will help your reader better "feel" the surroundings. What can be heard, smelled, seen, tasted, touched or felt? You want your reader to imagine the setting you have in *your* imagination. Read over the lesson of sensory language in Hints for Polishing if you'd like to refresh your memory.

## Plot

The PLOT of a story is its sequence of events. What is your main character doing? When the director of a film calls out, "ACTION!" the actors immediately start acting. You can direct your characters to act, too.

The beginning part of a story has what is called RISING ACTION.

## Conflict

The problem of the story has a lot to do with what your main character is doing, or plans to do. Have you noticed that in life things don't always go smoothly? Difficulties or complications arise. CONFLICT is the central problem that causes the action, or propels it forward.

1) The conflict could be between two characters. Some stories have the good guy versus the bad guy.
2) Sometimes the conflict involves the character versus nature or external circumstances: wild animals, sickness, weather conditions, etc.
3) Perhaps your character is struggling with conflict inside himself. He could have stage fright and need to make an effort to steady his nerves before he can play his piece at the piano recital. Some of the characters in the story starters I wrote for you had to muscle up courage they weren't sure they had. Stepping forward (in faith and unselfishness) to do what they thought they ought, made them courageous.

What problems did the characters have in the two favorite stories you mentioned?

## Emotion

A dry, lifeless piece of writing is unfeeling. But where there are life-like characters, there is EMOTION. Even a little emotion helps to bring your character alive and evokes the sympathy of your readers. Is your character happy, frustrated, courageous, longing for something, secretly worried, excited or dazzled by new sights? What is he or she feeling? What does he or she care about? Your readers will know your character better if you show how he or she is feeling. They will care about your character and want to read more.

## Dialogue

Throughout the Writing Help of the story starters, I suggested that you make your characters speak, and that you include conversation in the story. The proper word for this is DIALOGUE. We learn about what a character thinks and feels by what he or she says. Dialogue can help carry the action as well.

## Climax

What is the most exciting, most scary, or most happy part of your story? The story's high point is called its CLIMAX. The rising action leads up to the climax. Perhaps this is also when the plot of the story is at its critical point. Here are some examples:

1) Evening came. It grew dark. The family would not give up their search for their lost puppy, Bingo. Piteous barking was heard coming from a deep pit in the woods. It must be Bingo! Is he okay?
2) In ancient days a dangerous chariot race is in progress. Not all the contestants play fair. Who will win?
3) Such stormy weather brought swelling waves that dragged the little lobster boat out to sea. Rain fell heavily from the darkened sky. Will the fishermen get to shore safely?
4) The party invitations were handmade by the children and mailed a week ago. The cookies and cupcakes were baked two hours ago. All the decorations are up. Now the children wait. Their wide eyes stare out the picture window at all the snow whirling 'round the front yard. Will anyone brave the snowstorm to come to the party?

Not all stories need an exciting climax. A descriptive story that is more calm, and has a less noticeable climax, may still be interesting to read.

## Conflict Resolution

How does your story end? How do things turn out? The way a problem is solved, how your characters deal with life, or the outcome of a particularly happy, scary, or exciting event, is called CONFLICT RESOLUTION. Probably most of what you added to my story starters was that of describing the climax or high point. You may not have realized it then, but if you helped solve any problems in the stories, you were providing conflict resolution, too. I often provided FORESHADOWING (hints and clues in the early part of the story about events that will happen later on) to "set you up." I encouraged you to put a satisfying or happy ending in your stories. I gave you characters that were resilient enough to bounce back and accept difficult circumstances bravely.

## Denouement

With the conflict resolution comes DENOUEMENT. If your story has been exciting here is when your characters (and your reader) can relax and breath easier. The excitement, the worry, the anticipation, the party, is over. Phew! That is not to say that life goes on exactly as it had before. Perhaps the characters learned something by their experiences. Here are some examples of falling action:

1) The huge man-eating tiger was caught and the villagers returned to their everyday tasks without fear.
2) All the merry guests have said good night. It's late. The hosts are tired out, but don't care about the huge mess left behind, because the Christmas party was great fun.
3) The puppy was found, is safe and unharmed, and is sleeping peacefully on its comfortable basket in the laundry room.
4) The bully is repentant and wants to become a true friend with those he has poked and pushed before. He knocks on the front door of the main character's house to sincerely apologize.
5) Tears of joy roll off cheeks when Father returns home from the war with only a broken arm and an enormous appetite for Mother's good 'ol home cooking.

All good stories must come to an end. Some fairy tales end with "And they lived happily ever after."

## Theme

If you are an older student, ask yourself, "What is my story about?" Your story may have a THEME and you don't even realize it until you are in the middle of writing it. As your story unfolds, your theme may show itself. That's okay. You don't really need to start with a theme. But it is helpful to have one. Is your story about working hard for something? Many stories are about good versus evil because that is what life is really all about. More specifically it could be about patience, perseverance, bravery, love, loyalty, hope, or joy. Invisible things like these are behind the motivations and actions of your characters. Why do your characters do what they do? What worldview does your main character have? These are big questions, I know. I made it easy for myself when I wrote my story starters. Most of my characters took on my own worldview without my thinking too much about it. This was most comfortable for me. I have been influenced by Western civilization and so have my characters. I have a conscience trained by the Ten Commandments and the gospel of Jesus Christ and so have they. You may, however, invent characters that have very different worldviews.

## Fun First

If these elements seem a jumble of terms to you, start writing your story anyway. Write freely. Write what comes to you. Storywriters are supposed to have fun first. All writers go back over their work to "clean it up." Making adjustments is not as fun. It can be picky, hard work. Therefore, if you prefer, go back over your story to include (or identify) the basic elements afterward. You'll be less jumbled if you refer to this handy list.

Point of View
Characterization—Emotion—Dialogue
Setting
Plot
Rising Action
Conflict
Climax
Conflict Resolution
Denouement
Theme

GOODS

H
A
O
B
I
D

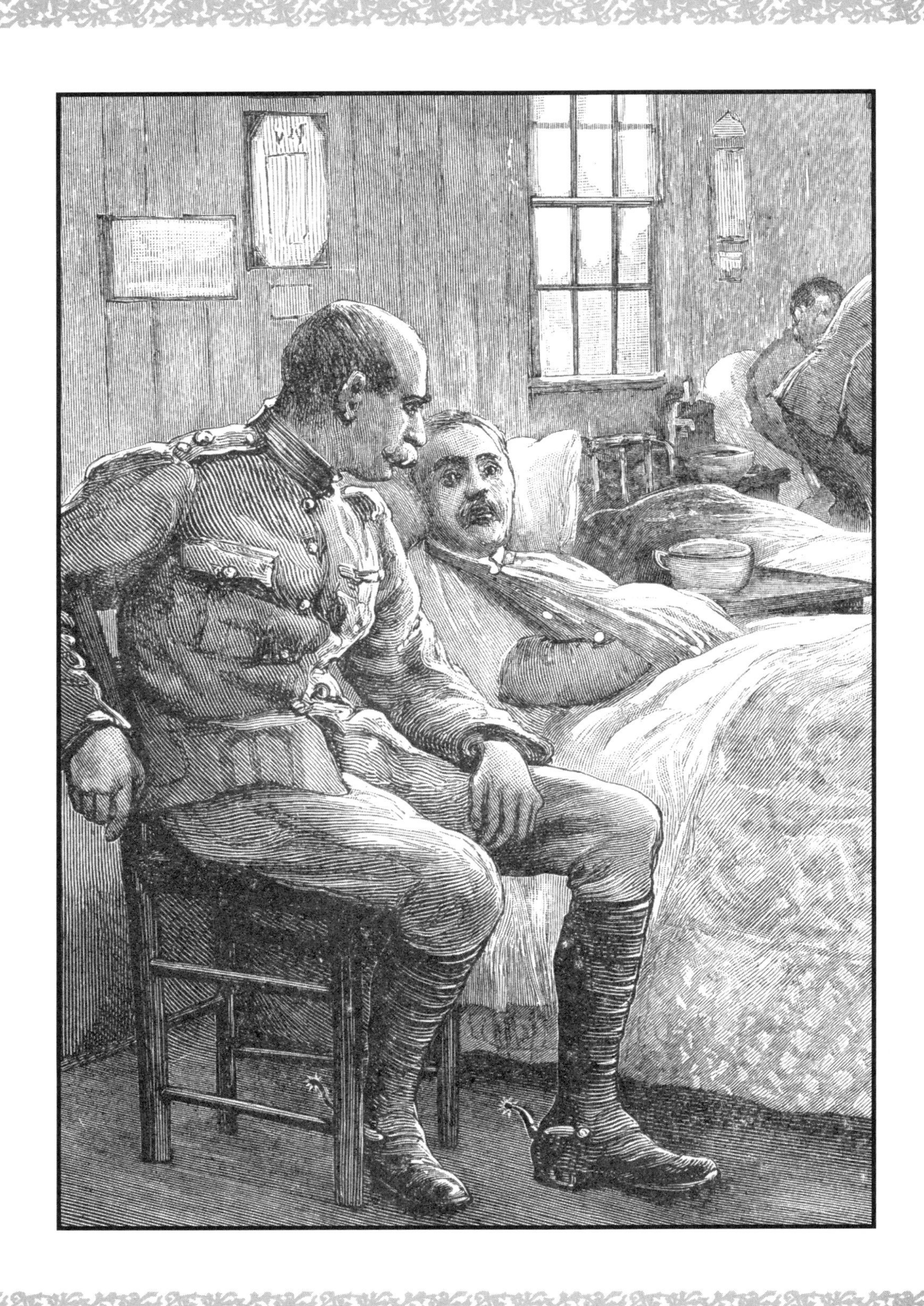

# Section Five

## In Closing

# Narration

## Tapping into the "Talking Resource"

S*tory Starters* takes advantage of the art of narration. What is narration and why is it an important part of a child's education?

Children like to chatter. Have you noticed? When they are young we can't wait for them to walk and talk. We take joy in their first steps and their first words. As soon as they begin school, however, they must sit down and be quiet for long stretches of time. But nineteenth century British educator Charlotte Mason did things differently. She thought it a pity that "this amazing gift with which normal children are born is allowed to lie fallow in their education." Like tapping a sugar maple for its sap, she tapped this talking resource in children. It was a rich commodity. She considered their telling to be the art of narration.

### Putting the Reading in One's Own Words

When a child narrates, he expresses what he has learned by telling it back to you in his own words. It is that simple. Isn't it a pity that the simplest things in life get overlooked? Knowledge is not truly assimilated until it can be adequately reproduced. Miss Mason required children to "tell back" what was read aloud or to write about some part of what they read. "What a child digs for becomes his own possession," she said. This simple, old-fashioned way of learning has been replaced by the convenient use of workbooks and the textbook questionnaire.

### Good Books and Narration Go Hand in Hand

Charlotte Mason discovered that children narrate more readily and enthusiastically from books of literary quality than from the typical schoolbook. One of the first things that impressed me about Miss Mason was her principle of using all sorts of good books for learning. She eschewed the use of the typical schoolbook, with its dry facts, bite-size-pieces of information and excerpts of other books, often watered down.

At a time when there were far fewer children's books Miss Mason was an advocate for using what she called "living" books so called because they were alive with ideas. These kinds of books, she said, "open the door of a child's mind." She experimented. She observed how naturally children take to well-written books, whether fact or fiction. Yet very few books other than textbooks were ever put into the hands of children in school. This, she thought, was a shame, since England is a land so known for its literary genius. Thus, for the children's sake, living books were used in her schools, often taking the place of textbooks. According to Miss Mason "A really good book has the right to be called a schoolbook."

My children were young when I was introduced to this principle. We were already in the habit of visiting the local library. Along with illustrated storybooks, I read aloud from non-fiction picture books. I so enjoyed these cozy read-aloud moments. Therefore it wasn't difficult to carry the principle of using living books into our homeschool during the elementary years when they typically begin to disappear to make room for classroom textbooks.

Over the years we have held fast to the living book principle. Biographies, historical fiction, books with a science theme, and children's classics, are frequently brimming with living ideas. Living books also have a story aspect to them. These kinds of books were not part of my school experience. There were very few stories (or ideas) behind the names, dates, and facts I was supposed to be learning. How about you? Our children's learning experience can be refreshingly different when we trust Charlotte Mason's principles.

## Room for Originality

The sensible simplicity and thoroughness of this method of having a child narrate from living books fascinated me. Over the years I became convinced that Miss Mason was correct in her claim that narration is the best way to acquire knowledge from books. In 1902, Miss E.A. Parish, a PNEU (Parents National Education Union) teacher, said, "Narrating is not the work of a parrot." That is workbook mentality. She continued, "It is the absorbing into oneself the beautiful thought [ideas] from the book, making it one's own and then giving it forth again with just that little touch that comes from one's own mind."

Narration invites children to ponder. Isn't it better to ponder than to parrot? Even today, in PNEU schools, the teacher will read aloud a passage from a well-written book. Children will "tell back" their own version of the passage (or chapter) with surprising fluency, picking up phrases and vocabulary that strike them. We can see how narration invites the child's personality to become part of his learning process.

In Miss Mason's curriculum classic literature was part of each semester's work. In A *Philosophy of Education* she claims,

*...All children show the same surprising power of knowing, [demonstrated] by the one sure test - they are able to 'tell' each work they have read not only with accuracy but with spirit and originality. How is it possible it may be asked, to show originality in 'mere narration'? Let us ask Scott, Shakespeare, Homer, who told what they knew, that is narrated, but with continual [sparks] from their own genius playing upon the written word. Just so in their small degree do the children narrate; they see it all so vividly that when you read or hear their versions the theme is illuminated for you too.*

## The Power of Something so Simple

Let us not undervalue the power of something as simple as the method of narration. Narration is important for the young learner because it challenges and strengthens all the powers of mind. Charlotte Mason categorized some of the mental powers this way: attending, remembering, visualizing, comprehending, synthesizing (seeing the whole from the parts), and articulating. Children may find narration difficult when ideas are not present in what is being read. As ideas are what the mind feeds on, let us aim to give our children at least one idea a day. Living books work best for the use of narration because ideas are required for their sustenance. Children grow and thrive upon ideas for their intellectual life. When you educate with living books, a child's mind does the sorting, rejecting, and classifying for which modern textbook committees think they are responsible.

## Natural and Effective Narration

*Story Starters* is built upon oral and written narration because "telling" is the most natural and effective way to acquire knowledge *and* to develop language skills. Charlotte Mason proclaims in *Home Education*, that

*Narrating is an art, like poetry making or painting, because it is there, in every child's mind, waiting to be discovered, and is not the result of any process of disciplinary education. A creative fiat calls it forth. Let him narrate; and the child narrates, fluently copiously, in ordered sequence, with fit and graphic details, with a just choice of words, without verbosity [...] as soon as he can speak with ease. [...] Bobbie will come home with a heroic narrative of a fight he has seen between Duke and a dog in the street. It is wonderful! He has seen everything, and he tells everything with splendid vigor in the true epic vein; but so ingrained is our contempt for children that we see nothing in this but Bobbie's foolish childish way! Whereas here, if we have eyes to see and grace to build, is the ground-plan of his education.*

## A Listener Rather than a Lecture

With the method of narration, the teacher becomes more of a listener and less of a lecturer. The books themselves (often read aloud) become the teachers. Be available to hear any spontaneous "telling" from your younger-than-six-year-old. Only after the age of six should you begin to require a bit of "telling" from *short* passages read aloud to him. By the age of eight or nine, a child should be able to narrate from an episode, then eventually, half a chapter, and later a whole chapter at a time. Even older children who have had little to no experience can start by narrating from Aesop's fables. These ancient Greek fables (originally written to amuse grown-ups) are short but meaningful. Aesop's symbolism provokes thought. You may also require the older student to narrate from any book that he is particularly interested in.

## Narration Facilitates Writing

Over time a child's ability to narrate orally carries over beautifully to his writing ability. By the age of ten or eleven a student can be required to write his narration. Because narrating is at the heart of good writing it facilitates writing. Workbook activities, true-and-false questions, multiple-choice options, and fill-in-the-blank quizzes do not. These make the student give the expected answer—the only right answer. Narration allows room for a student to form a reasonable opinion or put into words his personal perspective based upon what impresses him most in his reading.

## From a Teacher I Esteem

In my 1992 interview with Eve Anderson, retired headmistress of Eton End PNEU School in Britain, she told of the extensive role narration has played in her school and offered a few hints for classroom use. She relied upon Charlotte Mason's method of narration for the duration of her teaching career. I treasure my memory of meeting her. It was an honor to talk with her. She shared with me that when she was a young student she attended one of Miss Mason's PNEU schools. She loved this school and its teachers and resolved, while she was quite young, to become a teacher in a PNEU school. She states:

*I believe that narration is still of great value, but in fewer subjects than in Charlotte's time, particularly in scientific and geographical subjects, as these are now more factual. Narration can be useful in all literature, Bible study, history, etc. It promotes good concentration. The child who is able to retell a story in his own words can remember the story clearly, as long as a good introduction has been given. The teacher should not get between the text and the child retelling the passage. Avoid too much questioning, summarizing at the end, and if necessary, drawing out a particular point. I think some teachers try to read aloud too long a passage for a narration lesson. This can lead to confusion and a poor narration. Within a narration lesson one can involve most of the class in either giving a recapitulation of the last lesson, a full narration, or filling in after someone else, so there is normally full class involvement.*

## The Marvelous Key

Over the course of sixty years of working with children Charlotte Mason witnessed the results of so straightforward a method. In *A Philosophy of Education* she announced,

*Here on the very surface is the key to that attention, interest, literary style, wide vocabulary, love of books and readiness in speaking, which we all feel should belong to an education that is only begun in school and continued throughout life.*

I am very fond of this quote. Some years ago I purchased a big iron skeleton key after rummaging at an antique store. I use it as a paperweight. I wonder what door it once opened. Was it the door of a Victorian carriage house or the heavy front door of a mansion? When I look at this key, pick it up, and feel its weight, it reminds me of the above quote by Miss Mason and of what I am aiming for with the method of narration.

How can we fit time for narration into the already busy school day? It is difficult keeping up with the many demands of homeschooling. We mothers burn out when we try to serve two masters: both living books with narration *and* a complete set of traditional textbooks and workbooks. Therefore, *in place* of a work sheet or chapter quiz, make occasion to provide what I call "a narration request." This will prompt your student to tell in his own words something he is studying, whether by oral narration or by writing (even if it is just two or three sentences given by the young or new narrator). You will be giving him that marvelous key of which Miss Mason speaks. Keep this key conspicuously handy. Hook it on to a definite place at the door of your curriculum.

Trust in this key. Use it to free yourself from the textbook/workbook grind. A love of knowledge will return. With living books and narration you will experience the kind of educational life you have always wanted for your child.

## Ways of Incorporating Narration with Narration Requests

Here are some examples of how you can prompt children to tell.

**"Tell me all you know about…" (Her favorite request)**

Heidi's visit with Peter's grandmother.
The peculiar habits of a squirrel.
Living creatures in a tide pool.
The Pilgrim voyage of the Mayflower.
The expedition of Lewis and Clark.

**"Explain how…"**

A daffodil is pollinated
Sedimentary rock is formed.
Jesus heals the blind man.
The Declaration of Independence comes to be written.
Elizabeth I becomes queen.
Robinson Crusoe settles on the lonely island.

**"Describe the…"**

Structure of the inner ear.
Landscape of this painting.
Various occupations in a Colonial village.
Winter conditions of Washington's Valley Forge.
Customs of ancient Athens compared with those of Sparta.

**"Describe our…"**

Picnic at the seashore.
Nature walk in the woods.
Visit to the nursing home.
Planetarium experience.
Christmas Day at the grandparents.

**"Tell anything new** you have just learned in this chapter."

**"Tell the story** (passage, episode) back in your own words."

**"What four things** have you learned about—in this chapter?"

**"Ask or write six questions** covering the material of this chapter."

**"Sketch the character and manners of**—from your novel."

**"Draw me a picture,** map or likeness of—"

**"What impressions have you** on the life of (Abraham Lincoln, Oliver Cromwell, Abigail Adams, William Tyndale, Daniel Boone, Sir Isaac Newton, Florence Nightingale, Andrew Carnegie, Julius Caesar, Ebenezer Scrooge, Achilles, Heidi ...) in this chapter?" My examples represent a cross section of characters, factual and fictional, that carry a student into a variety of subjects: history, science, novels, myths. An enormous amount of "inside" information is learned by studying lives.

## *Endnotes:*

Quotations by Charlotte Mason (1842-1923) were taken from her books, *Home Education* (published 1886) and *A Philosophy of Education* (published posthumously). The quote by Miss Parish came from *The Story of Charlotte Mason*, written in 1960 by Essex Cholmondeley.

I go into more detail on the subject of living books on the website: homeschool highlights.com. Click on the article "Living Books for the Mind and Heart."

You will find three chapters on the subject of narration, as well as host of other subjects discussed, in my book, *A Charlotte Mason Companion*.

# Index of Literary Terms and Techniques

In the Writing Help, at the end of most of the story starter exercises, the student is sometimes reminded to use sensory language, employ conversation (dialogue) or is invited to tell the story from the point of view of a different character. The terms below are also presented in the Writing Help. Because the exercises in this book can be used in any order I made an index of them. If there is something in particular that you would like to take a peek at, simply look up the number of the story where it is found. All these terms are relevant to the stories but many can be understood independently.


Artful Adjectives 16, 22, 36, 65

Anthropomorphism 4

Book or film recommendation 37, 55, 56, 61, 63, 66 (*not a term but helpful I think*)

Cause and Effect 2

Conflict 16

Conflict Resolution 17

Exclamations 58

Flashback 5

Foreshadowing 22, 48, 56

Hero—real life hero introduced 49, 51

Hyperbole 10

Moral 2

Onomatopoeia 37

Suspense 2, 56, 67

Sympathy 21

Theme 12

Vivid Verbs (with suggestions) 1, 2, 11, 58, 66

# Writing Resources

### *Elements of a Story*

If *Story Starters* inspires your student to become more serious about creative writing, it might be helpful to keep the elements of a story at your fingertips. J. Weston Walch publishes a resource I like. *Elements of a Story* by Clark Stevens is a set of twenty colorful posters on cardstock. Each poster highlights one element. Its twelve pages of reproducible text, including a quiz, can be kept in a student's notebook.

### *The Write Stuff Adventure*

For tackling a cross-section of creative writing exercises I like *The Write Stuff Adventure,* by Dean Rea. Younger (middle grade) students start by writing letters to Grandmother, their own autobiography, and some creative writing assignments that use sensory language. Later they produce a family newsletter with interviews and are introduced to cartooning. The student's own photographs are used for journalism projects. (Children really get into the photo aspect.) They learn how to write copy for want ads, cover letters, and letters to the editor. Helpful for high school work are lessons on writing a good essay.

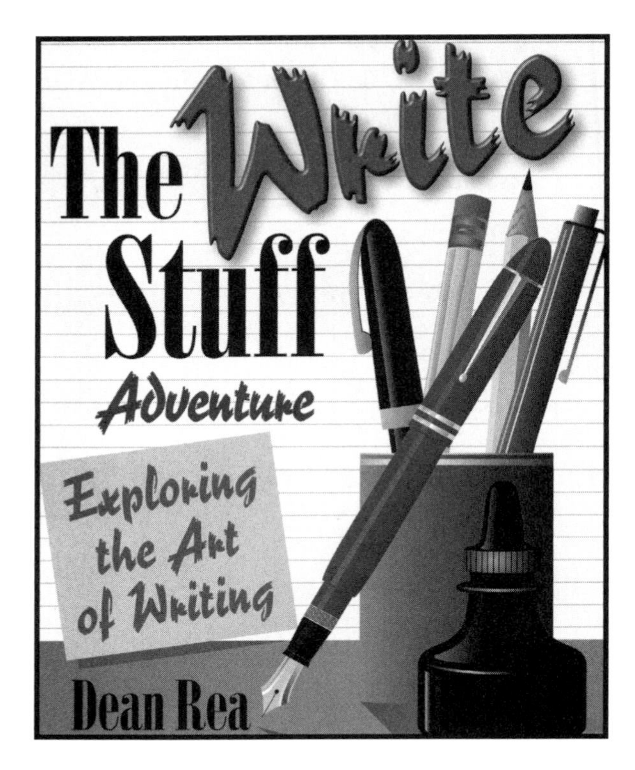


Being a one-book-per-family resource, its range of lessons can be used with children of differing ages and abilities.

Mr. Rea has experience as a university professor and is an award-winning editor of a major newspaper.

## *Learn to Write the Novel Way*

If your student would welcome the challenge of writing a much longer piece of fiction, *Learn to Write the Novel Way,* by Carole Thaxton, is the course for him. It carries a student month-by-month, (novels take much longer to write) step-by-step—all the way to self-publishing the finished project. This consumable worktext is a one-year incremental curriculum for the high school student. Attention to language arts is given throughout the year, during both the planning and writing stages.

**Homeschoolhighlights.com** features book reviews by the whole Andreola family and provides a link to Christian Book Distributors for convenient online purchasing of materials such as the ones listed above.

# About Dean and Karen Andreola

## Beginnings

In 1989, upon returning from overseas missions, Dean and Karen Andreola founded the Charlotte Mason Research & Supply Company and republished the classic six-volume *Original Homeschooling Series,* by the British educator, Miss Charlotte Mason (1842-1923), which had been out of print for nearly eighty years. During slow, careful reading of Miss Mason's books, Karen began to put her study into practice with her children. Both Karen and Dean became quite enthused about Miss Mason's ideas and methods of teaching, and hosted a monthly support group in their home to share what they had been learning.

## Publishing

Borrowing old copies of Miss Mason's magazine, *Parents' Review,* from a British library, Karen would snatch reading time at odd hours to glean ideas from the faded pages of articles. While her young children were occupied with playdough, cut and paste, sandbox, or puddle-pool, she was close by with her face in an old volume of the *Parents' Review,* jotting down notes as things appealed to her. Its articles underscored what she was reading in Miss Mason's books. Excited about her newfound philosophy of education, she published her collection of gleanings and interpretations in her own *Parents' Review*—a magazine for home training and culture. Kept in circulation for six years (1991-1996), this advertisement-free magazine also included a sprinkling of articles from Miss Mason's original magazine, which Karen thought relevant. (All twenty-four issues are still available.) During the years she was editor, Karen was privileged to receive hundreds of letters from grateful readers. Many parents were happily seeing good results of the method in their own homes. Others had questions. After discontinuing *Parents' Review,* she took Dean's advice and collected her writings (and answers to questions) into a chunky and sweetly illustrated book entitled *A Charlotte Mason Companion—Personal Reflections on the Gentle Art of Learning.* Very quickly it became a best-selling title in homeschool circles. She revised Miss Mason's *First Grammar Lessons,* giving it the new title of *Simply Grammar.* She also revised a lovely edition of the classic *Beautiful Girlhood*. In the 1990s Karen was a regular columnist for Mary Pride's *Practical Homeschool Magazine*. Her articles have appeared in other magazines and online as well.

## Speaking

Dean and Karen are sought-after speakers at homeschool conferences nationwide. They share from their pioneering research, making the ideas user-friendly for modern-day parents. "Living book" recommendations and original homespun applications of the CM method provide practical encouragement for living "the educational life." Karen's hallmark term Mother Culture™ is a concept that is also helping mothers find peace and fulfillment in their roles as teachers and homemakers. Dean shares, with down-to-earth humor, the struggles of his public school days and the liberating victories his family has experienced through homeschooling. Dads and teens also find his messages funny and enlightening.

## Another Book and This One

While living in the snowy woods of Maine, Karen was asked to speak each year at the Midcoast Maine Homeschool Winter Retreat. She wished to minister to the needs of her fellow mothers—needs that a great many moms apparently have in common. Desiring to offer further encouragement, she wrote a story for Mother Culture™. The result, *Pocketful of Pinecones* is a sort of teacher's guide to nature study cleverly disguised as a heart-warming story. Designed to be a pick-me-up, each chapter is short enough to minister to a mother who has only snatches of time in which to nourish her soul. Karen strongly urges mothers to take just a little time each day to nourish their souls so that in turn they may be better equipped and refreshed to nourish the souls of their children.

Over the years many moms have shared with Karen their desire to better motivate their children to write. She set out to minister to this need, too. The ideas behind *Story Starters* swam in the back of her mind while she was in the thick of homeschooling. Not until after two of her children had graduated from homeschool did she attempt to write a whole collection of short stories for *Story Starters*.

## Currently

The Andreolas write product reviews for Christian Book Distributor's homeschooling catalog. Dean is a twenty-five-year veteran of the Christian publishing industry. He handles all the necessary paperwork, details, and problems that arise from having one's own business. If you like visiting web sites, you might like to read the free articles posted on homeschoolhighlights.com. The articles are colorfully illustrated and were made "printer friendly" to be read away from the computer. Homeschool Highlights is also a good place to learn what the Andreolas have to say about some of their favorite teaching materials.

## Family

Dean and Karen have homeschooled their three children since the early 1980s.

In 2005 they relocated from Maine to Lancaster County, Pennsylvania, where their neighbors are Amish. Karen keeps baskets of wool around the house and enjoys purloining moments of time for the relaxing hobby of knitting mittens, socks, hats, and vests for her family. Dean is an old-movie buff and enjoys making an oversized bowl of buttery popcorn and showing dramatic films with moral themes to his children.

The Andreolas would be happy to hear from you:

Charlotte Mason R. & S. Co.
PO Box 296
Quarryville, PA 17566

# *Other Books by Charlotte Mason Research and Supply Company*